Rabindranath Tagore's Ideational Challenges

Rabindranath Tagore's Ideational Challenges

Bidyut Chakrabarty

BLOOMSBURY
NEW DELHI • LONDON • OXFORD • NEW YORK • SYDNEY

BLOOMSBURY INDIA
Bloomsbury Publishing India Pvt. Ltd
Second Floor, LSC Building No. 4, DDA Complex, Pocket C – 6 & 7,
Vasant Kunj, New Delhi, 110070

BLOOMSBURY, BLOOMSBURY ACADEMIC INDIA and the Diana logo are trademarks of Bloomsbury Publishing Plc

First published in India 2023
This edition published 2023

Bloomsbury Academic India
An imprint of Bloomsbury Publishing Plc

ISBN: HB: 978-93-56400-12-2; eBook: 978-93-56400-14-6
2 4 6 8 10 9 7 5 3 1

For sale in the Indian subcontinent only

Typeset in Manipal Technologies Limited
Printed and bound in India by Replika Press Pvt. Ltd.

Contents

Contents

Acknowledgements

I heartily express my gratitude to those who contributed to the development and refinement of the arguments made in defence of the principal theme of the book.

Introduction

I

Endowed with extraordinary qualities, Rabindranath Tagore (1861–1941) represented a new stream of thinking. He was born and nurtured in an environment in which colonialism was being challenged ideationally with reference to the indigenous mode of conceptualising human values in particular and humanity in general. Being exposed to various streams of thoughts while being raised in one of the most famous families of colonial Calcutta, Rabindranath articulated his views that were neither totally derivative of Western philosophical discourses nor entirely dependent on the narrowly conceived nationalistic parameters. He realised that the typical language of nationalism, instead of cementing a bond among the Indians, was a source of division given the inherent sociocultural diversities in the country. Implicit in this powerful conceptualisation were two critical ideas which did not appear to be persuasive to those mesmerised by the Western notion of nationalism as a mode of bringing people together; the aforesaid group failed to understand the adverse politico-ideological consequences of such an endeavour. On the one hand, the attempt to seek to homogenise disparate Indians led to the consolidation of the chasm that naturally evolved in one's communal existence presumably because of one's spatial location. Insistence on uniting communities, given their identical religious identities, also laid the foundation for schisms around religious axes. It was to Rabindranath's privilege that he saw the gradual transformation of India's nationalist campaign from being clearly loyalist to being vehemently opposed to British rule once Gandhi appeared on the political scene. During his long life of 80 years, he not only saw the change but also helped generate newer modes of thinking which aided the nationalist assault on the alien governance. The purpose here is not to provide a narrative of how Tagore viewed the metamorphosis in the texture and spirit of nationalism but to show how he conceptualised the change from a uniquely creative mode of thinking. The point being made here is not novel; what is noteworthy is to identify the theoretical roots of his conceptual universe—that was evident in his creative writings. In other words, by saying that Tagore's ideas were organically connected with the prevalent sociocultural reality, what is reiterated here is the famous Platonic dictum that every philosopher is a child of his time. We must add a caveat here since the philosophers who also chart a different course for humanity, despite being rooted in the contemporary sociopolitical and economic contexts, also surpass the historical age in which they are born. Tagore was certainly one of them since the conceptualization, with which he defended his unique mode of thinking, continues to help us understand better contemporary reality irrespective of the fact that he developed his arguments in the late 19th and 20th centuries. Not only are his views transcendental but they also provoke newer thinking with organic relevance to the present century. Crucial here is the claim that Gurudev, as he was christened by the Mahatma, persuasively defended his approach to humanity not only in his novels, plays and other literary tracts but in the innumerable critical essays he wrote in support of what he felt was appropriate for humanity as a whole. What is also unfortunate is the fact that Tagore is generally known for his literary prowess although he also left for posterity many critical writings to firmly establish the alternative politico-ideological discourses that he espoused. Many texts are there to highlight Rabindranath as a great poet of his generation; but there are hardly any attempts to demonstrate that he was an equally creative thinker who addressed contemporary sociocultural and politico-ideological issues. One should also not forget that Tagore's creative writings and critical essays are conceptually compatible and present identical views. In other words, the ideas that Tagore championed in his novel *Ghare Baire* (1916) resonated in his 1904 tract, *Swadeshi Samaj*. What is reinforced here is the view that Gurudev adopted many genres to spread his ideas to a wider set of readers. This is probably one of the reasons why Tagore became a household name during his lifetime; that he continues to remain so is presumably because of the transcendental nature of how he viewed humanity. Furthermore, being a practitioner of what he believed, he also carved an independent space in India's intellectual history. It is therefore not an exaggeration to suggest that Tagore developed that unique prism of history which remained relevant long after he was gone. By being receptive even to those ideas which stood in contradiction to his, he also re-established the argumentative traditions which the ancient thinkers encouraged but lost in British India presumably because the colonisers' sustained endeavour at creating and consolidating intellectual servility was generally zealously complemented by the colonised. Under these circumstances, Rabindranath not only raised an alternative voice but also helped build and strengthen a group of people who thought alike. The task was made a little easier once he was awarded the Nobel Prize in literature in 1913, which instantaneously made him a global icon. With the winning of the

Noble Prize, Rabindranath found many of those Western thinkers who complemented his approach to human emancipation which also helped him evolve a global opinion against British colonialism, deviant from the core values and principles of Enlightenment philosophy. The universal appeal that his argument had was that by being disrespectful to the foundational Enlightenment values, the colonial powers subjected the colonised to ruthless oppression. So, Tagore fought the nationalist battle at two levels: At one level, he challenged British colonialism by evolving a powerful opinion beyond the shores of India through regular dialogues with those who joined hands with him because the British rule in India was hardly true to the fundamental Enlightenment values. On another level, with his sustained campaign for socioreligious amity, Tagore endeavoured hard to create a milieu in which communal division was not allowed to be divisive, presumably because of his firm belief that unless the Hindu–Muslim bond was re-established, the nationalist campaign could hardly be 'nationalist' in the real sense of the term. He realised that one of the major sources of weakness of the nationalist agitation stemmed from animosity, especially between the Hindus and Muslims.

II

Tagore's views were not vitiated by the prevalent conceptual prejudicial template supporting the Hindu–Muslim schism presumably because he was raised in a family that did not seem to have privileged one religious belief over others. It was a cosmopolitan environment which also helped him understand that Indian civilisation emerged out of a confluence of myriad sociocultural traditions and politico-ideological views. While elaborating his genealogical roots, Tagore thus mentioned that

> I was born in what was then the metropolis of British India. Our ancestors came floating to Calcutta upon the earliest tide of the fluctuating fortune of the East India Company. The code of life for our family became composed of three cultures, Hindu, Muslim and British. (Tagore 1962: 89–90)

It was not difficult to understand why, given the environment which evolved out of the cosmopolitan attitude nurtured by his ancestors, the Tagore family represented a creative blend of three cultures. While there was Rabindranath's grandfather Dwarkanath, who brought into the Tagore household those British values which he imbibed by adopting Victorian manners, his father Debendranath rekindled his interests in India's ancient past. It was a unique context in which, as

Rabindranath explained, 'the modern city-bred spirit of progress had just triumphed over the lush green life of our ancient village community' (290). Despite being aware that the Company rule represented a radical sociopolitical metamorphosis of Calcutta as the city was under its exclusive control, the young Rabindranath did not seem appreciative of these new developments which was evident when he expressed his disappointment:

> though the trampling process was almost complete around me, something of the past lingered over the wreckage. In my boyhood days, I often listened to my elder brother dwelling regretfully on a society that had been hospitable, kindly and filled with simple faith and the ceremonial poetry of life. All that was vanishing shadow in the twilight haze of the horizon; the all-pervading fact was a modern city, newly built by a Company of Western traders, and the spirit of the new times striking upon our life, even if it had to face countless anomalies. But it has always been a surprise to me that while this hard crust of a city was my only experience of the world, I was constantly haunted by the nostalgic fancies of an exile. (290)

Implicit here are those fundamental ideas which gradually became integral to Rabindranath's thoughts. First, the boy Rabindranath did not seem to have been mesmerised by the glittering aura of modernity that was associated with the East India Company rule although his grandfather did not seem so critical of the British hegemony; instead, as I have shown elsewhere (Chakrabarty 2022), Dwarkanath proved himself as integrally connected with the British sociocultural ethos—he strongly believed that only by imbibing this ethos was India likely to become intellectually vibrant and economically prosperous. Second, in this persuasive argument he has mentioned above, Rabindranath also had shown his inclination towards the lush green life of the ancient village community because it was *hospitable, kindly and based on simple faith*. Implied here was his sharp critique of the British rule simply because of the gradual decline of the importance of these human values from which the ancient village community was supposed to draw its sustenance. Finally, this long statement is also illustrative of the agony that Rabindranath experienced with the growing hegemony of a mindset in support of the Company-driven modernity; the poet's distress also reflected his critical assessment of the consequences of the British rule in India in which commercial gain was prioritised. Although young, Tagore's poetic mind was also in search of an alternative vision when he longed for an exile from reality. His primary concern was to bring about human emancipation which was not attainable by mere political freedom which was 'meaningless [because] …

perfect freedom lies in the harmony of relationship which we realise not through knowing, but in being' (Tagore 1962: 291). Fundamental here was his concern to build a harmonious relationship which we, argued Tagore, 'attain only through sympathy' (291). This was one of the core aims of his sociopolitical thoughts (Chakrabarty 2020). Not only did he derive this by being nurtured in his cosmopolitan family but he was persuaded to firmly believe so by his own experience as a zamindar in East Bengal—it helped him understand how Hindu–Muslim sociocultural disparities were not only debilitating to the realization of freedom but also a serious impediment towards evolving communal amity in Bengal. The 1916 novel *Ghare Baire* is a graphic illustration of how Tagore felt when mainstream nationalism, instead of bringing people with different religious beliefs together, laid the foundation of a chasm which was responsible, to a great extent, for the dismemberment of India in 1947.

In view of his concern for human liberation, the most contentious issue is why he did not join hands with Gandhi in seeking to fulfil his politico-ideological goals since he also believed that this was possible only by overthrowing the alien yoke. Here, we must add a clarifying point regarding the sense in which Tagore understood the idea of the political. For Tagore, being political meant that one was concerned with safeguarding the communal existence of individuals or more precisely, preserving and promoting exchange and harmony in human society. In this sense,

> political is understood as not being dominated or dominating but as a public construct that guarantees the exercise of freedom of individuals, [which further entails that it] is an ongoing reality, in need of exchange among citizens and mutual re-evaluation and transformation, in view of its essence. (Jahanbegloo 2018: 55–56)

Political thus cements a bond among individuals despite being socioculturally and politico-ideologically disparate. What is emphasised here is the idea that notwithstanding discord and dissent, political is not a means of putting one group against another. Instead, it is directed to build 'solidarity [on the basis of] empathy and a consciousness in the commitments of others to shared purposes [which is also] … the affirmation of the dignity of each person in relation of harmonic exchange' (57). Tagore's approach was then highly political, given the fact that he was not only opposed to the prevalent power relationships segregating one set of individuals from another but also provided a blueprint for a future that was based on harmony, mutual respect and empathy for one another. His letter to Rothenstein confirms the argument that Tagore's idea of political was much wider than it was conceptualised by the mainstream nationalists, including Gandhi. As he elaborated on his point, he wrote that,

> I have nothing to do directly with politics: I am not a Nationalist, moderate or immoderate in my political aspiration. But politics is not a mere abstraction. It has its personality and it does intrude into my life when I am human. It kills and maims individuals, it tells lies, it uses its sacred sword of justice for the purpose of massacre, it spreads misery broadcast over centuries of exploitation and I cannot say to myself, 'Poet you have nothing to do with these facts for they belong to politics.' This politics assumes its fullest diabolical aspect when I find all its hideous acts of injustice and find moral support from a whole nation only because it wants to enjoy in comfort and safety the golden fruits reaped from abject degradation of the human race. (Lego 1972: 277–278)

Nothing can be more eloquent than Tagore's aforementioned conceptualisation. Zealous to weed out the artificial segregation among human beings, the poet expressed most candidly the nature of politics that evolved at the behest of the nationalists in the wake of British rule. Politics is, according to him, a means to dehumanise humanity for it draws its sustenance from the abject exploitation of the disempowered. Written in the late 1920s, this letter is also a comment on the mainstream nationalist endeavour led by the Mahatma. As is well known, the bard was not persuaded by the non-cooperation strategy that Gandhi devised to pursue his political objective. For Rabindranath, the design was hardly protective of the poor—the call for a bonfire of foreign clothes affected the poor since they could not afford home-spun clothes. Similarly, the boycott of schools and colleges was likely to be futile unless there was an alternative to provide what the nationalists thought was appropriate for their cause (Chakrabarty 2006: 93–102). Interestingly, what Rabindranath insisted in the context of the 1905–1908 Swadeshi Movement in Bengal, launched by the Congress to revoke the first Partition, was repeated while challenging the nationalist leadership. Apart from forcefully arguing that nationalist politics was narrowly conceived as it was meant to safeguard the interests of one section against the majority of the people, the bard also provided newer inputs to reconceptualise politics in a fashion that did not seem to have pleased his colleagues in the nationalist campaign. Tagore's idea of politics, therefore, corresponded with what is described earlier as political, which is a mode of generating a sense of belongingness to the community despite sociocultural differences. This he articulated not only in his critical essays but also in creative writings. For instance, the novel *Gora* (1910) portrays how the sociocultural chasm stood as a deterrent towards building togetherness in Bengal's villages. Gora was surprised to notice that due to the well-entrenched sociocultural distance between the Hindus and Muslims and also between the upper and lower castes among the Hindus, the nationalist campaign failed to galvanise the masses even at the peak of the 1905–1908 Swadeshi Movement. What is reinforced here is the point that unless a political act develops and cements a social bond notwithstanding sociocultural separateness, it is reduced to being a mere instrument for partisan aims and objectives. In keeping with this view, Tagore evolved conceptual categories to bring people together amidst various pulls and pressures to the contrary. Hence, for him, the idea of *samaj* was a mode of governance, instead of state or rashtra. By insisting on *samaj* being a determinant for socially mobilising people, Tagore created a new conceptual universe in which the Western category, like the state, no longer remained relevant. In other words, with his preference for the *samaj*-centric governance, the poet discarded the derivative traditions that prevailed in Bengal given the British hegemony. While elaborating on the idea of *samaj*, he justified his preference since it was organic to human existence in rural Bengal. The rules governing the *samaj* were internal to it and a violation was also addressed by stringently applying those rules. What is clear is the point that *samaj* was not merely a collection of people, but also a way of behaviour which derived its sustenance from the belief that it was a time-tested mechanism in India in the sense that it had proved its efficacy by being integrally connected with the evolution and consolidation of human collectivity. Similarly, the idea of mela was unique to Tagore's endeavour at creating togetherness among socioculturally diverse people. Mela was an indigenous public space which was different from meetings, organised to get people together for discussions or deliberations. As per Tagore, attendance in political meetings was solicited and not always spontaneous; a mela immediately attracted people since it was a purely open-ended event. In other words, the participants consciously made their choice by weighing the pros and cons; this was not the case in a mela where people congregated for sheer enjoyment and interaction, not only with their acquaintances but also with those who they had not met in the past. A culturally appropriate space, a mela is a readymade platform to enable the rural folk to deliberate on many issues. As a natural form of associational life for the villagers, the mela, according to Tagore, became integral to the common psyche which was manifested at regular intervals in rural Bengal. Given its obvious importance in rural life, Tagore thus exhorted the swadeshi activists to visit melas, being held in rural Bengal quite regularly, to disseminate political messages.

A careful dissection of Tagore's conceptual universe reveals that his ideas were not only context-driven but also innovative; they were an endeavour to explain in a language and also with the help of imageries which were easily intelligible to those for whom he evolved his conceptual model. It was thus eloquently stated by an analyst who, by characterising Tagore's vision as 'original' thus argued that it was so because the poet

> distanced no less from the colonialist historiography propagated by the Raj and the ideologues of imperialism than from the narrowly sectarian Hindu view of the past that had been influential in nationalist thought since its formulation by Bankim Chandra Chattopadhyay in the 1870s. Tagore overcame his early inclination in favour of the latter to settle eventually on a strong anti-imperialist, secular and liberal-democratic interpretation of Indian history. This was to serve as a basic source of ideas for the freedom movement in its climatic phase between the two world wars. (Guha 2002: 75–76)

While evolving his unique mode of conceptualising humanity as an undivided and also well-knit unit, Tagore did not prioritise the typical way of eulogising the Indian past or completely submitting to the Western mode of thinking or discarding completely what was good in the textual wisdom that developed in ancient India. He evolved a unique mode of thinking by drawing on the libertarian Western discourses and what he believed to be of use from the Vedantic texts, especially the Upanishads. This was probably the reason why he veered neither towards 'radical modernism' nor towards a 'proud and gloomy traditionalism'; his conceptualisation creatively blended the ideas that he derived from both the derivative and indigenous discourses. It was explicitly stated by him when he mentioned that

> the objective of Indian history is not to set up Hinduism or some dominance, but to secure a special kind of fulfilment for humanity, a level of perfection that must be gain for all. In the course of this fulfilment, if Hindus, Muslims and the British have to submerge the aggressive parts of their individuality, it may be hurtful to their national pride but it will not be reckoned as a loss on the scales of truth and human rights. (Tagore 1962: 131–132)

Here is the crux of what constitutes Tagore's conceptual universe: he was not a narrow-minded thinker who was determined to ensure glory and happiness for one group of people at the cost of the other; he was a renaissance man who felt that pursuance of narrow national interests would inevitably jeopardise the growth of humanity, which led him to strongly criticise the proponents of nationalism as a panacea. In his perception, the only way to save humanity from brutality was to develop a mindset free from prejudices on any count. The argument came out very sharply in the analysis of Isiah Berlin who, while commenting on Tagore's unique approach to humanity, thus persuasively argued that,

> Tagore stood fast on the narrow causeway and did not betray his vision of the difficult truth. He condemned romantic overattachment to the past what he called the tying of India to the past 'like a sacrificial goat tethered to a post', and he accused men who displayed it—they seemed to him, reactionary—of not knowing what true political freedom was, pointing out that it from English thinkers and English books that the very notion of political liberty was derived. But against cosmopolitanism, he maintained that the English stood on their feet, and so must Indians. [Later] he once more denounced the danger of 'leaving everything to the unbearable will of the Master', be he brahmin or Englishman. (1960: 265)

Tagore thus redefined the conceptual universe predominant then. By providing a scathing critique of the past sociocultural practices which claimed to have drawn their sustenance from religious texts, the poet evolved new parameters on the basis of his understanding of the so-called holy texts. Condemning the caste-driven social hierarchy, he also put forward his idiom of political liberty which did not just mean liberation from the alien rule but also entailed self-reliance and self-confidence. It was very clearly stated in his novel *Ghare Baire* when Bimala, one of the protagonists of the novel clarified what her husband Nikhilesh believed by saying that 'from the time my husband had been a college student he had been trying to get things required by our people produced in our country' (Tagore 1957: 23) which, she illustrated by drawing attention to his effort in inventing 'an apparatus for extracting the juice from the date tree and boiling it into sugar and treacle' (23). That Nikhilesh was a man with tremendous foresight was reinforced when she further added that he established a bank to ensure safe monetary transactions among the villagers. Not only did he 'teach his countrymen ideas of thrift' (23) he also generated mass interest in keeping money in the bank by assuring high rate of interest which 'made the villagers flock so enthusiastically to put in their money, [that it] ended by swamping the bank altogether' (23). It was an era of swadeshi, which was a political campaign for annulling the first partition of Bengal that was administratively undertaken in 1905. For most of them, it appeared to have been inspirational as it was characterised as the arrival of 'a new epoch [that] came like a flood, breaking down the dykes and sweeping all our prudence and fear before it' (22). It was a new epoch since with the unfolding of the Swadeshi Movement, Bengal witnessed the consolidation of nationalist ideas in forms other than what the Moderates championed. The arrival of the revolutionary nationalists generally with a tilt towards those ideological texts that privileged Hindus against the Muslims brought about radical changes in the texture of the nationalist intervention. The division was formalised in the 1907 Surat Congress when a large contingent of Congressmen formed a radical group, also known as the Extremists, that did not exclude the violent means to politically liberate India.

III

A staunch critic of mechanical civilisation that unfolded with the onset of the industrial revolution, Rabindranath, like Gandhi, wrote scathingly about it. For him, it was a source of gratification as it demonstrated human intelligence; it was equally a source of disenchantment since it debased humanity to a significant extent. Given his commitment to universal humanism, he also felt that mechanisation was likely to be an Achilles' heel for humanity. He thus articulated his views by saying that 'in the modern age, the machine has not only multiplied working capacity, but likewise the scale of profit, and there with the greed gain' (Tagore 2008: 401). As is evident, Rabindranath held views similar to those of the Mahatma who condemned industrialisation as the most debilitating influence on humanity. Similarly, the poet argued that greed led to disharmony among human beings because, in order to satisfy one's greed, one was determined to attain one's goal by hook or crook which means that even at the cost of humanity, one was likely to work selfishly for one's partisan gains. While extending this argument, the bard further noted that the human desire to gain more at others' expenses, also contributed to war to establish the superiority of one section of humanity over another. As a result, the world had become a stage for the strong to flex their muscle over the weak. Tagore succinctly put across the point by affirming that

> it is this greed that has cut at the root of inter-relation of town and village, and the town has become a drain on the village because it has ceased to make it return. The artificial lights of the town are ablaze—lights that have no connection with the sun, moon or star—but the light of the village has gone out. (401)

As far as Tagore was concerned, greed was divisive in two ways: on the one hand, it created a permanent fissure between the haves and have-nots; on the other hand, it also separated the village from the town since the latter brought with itself a new world of human existence which was not even conceivable in the former. The aim here was to generate an artificial separation amongst humanity simply because of the variable access of those living in towns and villages to the benefits of industrialism. Although the industrial revolution might have contributed to the emergence of a glittering world, it did not seem adequate in bringing happiness and peace among human beings presumably because it also contributed to their separation from one another. In poetic language, Rabindranath elaborated this by highlighting that as a consequence of industrialism,

> the dawn no longer comes with its obeisance, the evening with adoration. Not only have the waters of the village run dry, but also its heart. The festivals of life which used to spring up as freely as the meadow flowers, are withered to the dust. (401)

A votary of simple and pristine human life, Tagore was never persuaded to believe that industrial growth was a panacea for humanity; it might have eased the difficulties of day-to-day life, but the cost was high. Simplicity and frugality appeared to have disappeared completely because one's value was assessed with one's capability of amassing wealth. So, industrialism not only introduced a cut-throat competition for further material comforts but also led to enmity among human beings since those who were left behind remained dissatisfied. Furthermore, one of the most devastating consequences of uncontrolled industrial growth was dependence on machines—this meant that human creativity lost its appeal because the growth of wealth generally became machine-dependent. It was most poignantly stated by Tagore when he mentioned that

> so long as life was expansive, it was content to make for itself the simple, beautiful materials of its joy. Now its manufacturers have become its burden, for it has to rely on the machine for their production, and more and more, with such reliance, is paralyzed the creative faculty. (401)

Explicit here was Tagore's stern critique of industrial civilisation which more or less corresponded with that of the Mahatma who, in *Hind Swaraj* (1909), candidly expressed his mental agony for industrialism was not only demonic but also a means to mechanically reorganise human society which was bereft of creativity. As one who always upheld humanity, it was, for the poet, an evil outcome of the mechanical civilisation that unfolded with the unbridled growth of industrialisation. Therefore, what emerges is that by undermining the natural growth of humanity, industrialism was, instead of being an aid, a design to dehumanise humanity. In his play *Muktadhara*, the poet highlighted how unconditional surrender to machines led to a clear debasement of humanity. The play 'raises the more fundamental issue of the free spirit of life set against the more terrible machine of a highly organized and mechanized society which turns me into robots, reducing names to members' (Kripalani 1985: 181). The message that he conveyed was not different from what Gandhi articulated in his many sharp critiques of the ruthless march of industrialism. Not only was it dehumanising but it was also a design to permanently divide humanity into unequal compartments. The play thus expresses a wider concern by highlighting the struggle between the individual and state, between the liberative impulse and the compulsive will, between free intelligence and the cold calculating intellect which 'assumed sinister proportions with the development of the scientific technique' (181). A hardcore rationalist who criticised Gandhi when he attributed earthquakes to 'God's caprice', Tagore was opposed to the widely hyped scientific technique which the dam on the free flow of *Muktadhara* represented; the obstruction of the free flow of the river that provided water for irrigation to other villages was a metaphor he resorted to for articulating evil designs for muzzling the human voice.

An organic intellectual, Tagore also believed that a creative blending of Man with Nature was the best mode of human progress since human civilization had grown 'in its several departments by the conjunction of his own intellect with the gifts of Nature' (Tagore 2008: 404). Emphasised here is the claim that one was futile without the other and vice versa. Hence, he emphatically declared that Nature and human beings 'must work in co-partnership throughout [since] whenever man's intellect, feeling secure by locking up its acquisitions in some strong-room habit, has fallen asleep, his wealth has left him' (404). Besides exhorting the importance of appreciating the dialectical inter-relationship between Man and Nature, the poet also insisted on sustained human contribution to augment wealth for all because if 'the store is not added to [it] goes on dwindling' (404). Instead of living on laurels, he further added that 'we cannot afford to live on the accumulations of a by-gone age for long—in fact, we have already come to the end of our resources' (404). Critical to Tagore's views is the claim that human progress was contingent on symbiotic interactions between Man and Nature. While highlighting this, he also stressed that unless human beings were compassionate towards one another, whatever we had achieved so far would become exclusive to a section of humanity which would, instead of building camaraderie, generate a fissure. With the consolidation of a mindset, supportive of divisive human existence, it was difficult to develop a foundation of bonhomie among human beings located in different sociocultural and economic milieus. This was contrary to the past, as Tagore identified, when 'there was not a wide gulf between rich and poor [because] the

… acknowledged their responsibilities' (402). Here, one notices an imprint of Gandhi's notion of trusteeship. Furthermore, it was possible presumably because

> honour and dishonour did not depend on the command or lack of money; nor was its enjoyment too exclusive, for the riches of one meant the welfare of many. And, so wealth did not then create barriers between man and man, but rather give facilities for varied intercourse. (402)

The story of *Muktadhara* is not simply a battle against the building of a dam to restrict the flow of water; it is also an articulation of an innovative philosophical discourse which also privileged humanity over anything else. In this respect, the play reinforces the core ideational values on which Tagore's approach to humanity rests. One should not also forget that Tagore repeatedly insisted on inclusive development which was not possible by unbridled industrial growth since it was a means to segment humanity between the industrialists and the hapless workers. Being a devout priest of universal humanism, the poet was sure to reject the model. Implicit here was his voice that an attack on the ecosystem in which human lives grew and survived was suicidal for humanity. So, *Muktadhara* contains multiple messages regarding how to empower humanity not by themselves but by being dialectically interactive with Nature.

IV

Interestingly, one of the protagonists of *Muktadhara*, Dhananjay, earlier appeared in *Prayaschitta* (Atonement), a drama published in 1909; representative of humanity, he had raised his voice against oppression by those wielding power. In *Prayaschitta*, Dhananjay, just like his namesake in *Muktadhara,* reiterated the idea by saying that 'as soon as you hold up your head and say, it does not hurt, the roots of violence will be cut. … Nothing can hurt your true manhood, for that is a flame of fire' (Tagore 2003: 260). This was perhaps one of those specific texts where Tagore put forward his politico-ideological preferences in clear terms. One of his biographers, Krishna Kripalani, endorses the claim that Dhananjay of *Prayaschitta* unambiguously captured Tagore's attack on an artificial civilisation that grew in importance with the rise of 'the towering menace of man's diabolical skill' (2008: 343). However, he posits that Dhananjay was a combination of Gandhi's approach to humanity and Tagore's compassion for the oppressors with, of course, a revealing difference because the latter was an opinion-maker while the former expressed his opposition by being involved in attacking the

British for attaining political freedom. We must add a caveat here since Gandhi never undermined Tagore's insistence on human salvation, which was possible, he felt, only after liberation from British rule; this meant that removal of the alien governance was a steppingstone towards reaching the final destiny. Tagore was not persuaded which made him insist that freedom from sociocultural oppression was before anything else.

As argued earlier, Tagore's humanism was an outcome of the wisdom that he derived from multiple philosophical discourses. Besides the study of the Upanishads, Buddhism and Western liberalism, the ideals that the Bengal Bauls propounded through their songs also acted as significant influences on his conceptual mould. In his perception, as regards approach, different religious and politico-ideological discourses had differences among themselves although as far as the goal was concerned, all of them insisted on common well-being. It is evident in the texts. Illustrative here is his 1926 dance drama *Natir Puja* (the dancing girl's worship), which was based on an old Buddhist legend that many of the poets reverberated. The main theme of the narrative was centred around Srimati, the palace dancing girl, who was a devotee of Buddha while the king was a hater of Buddhism. Despite torture which led to her death, Srimati remained steadfastly committed to Buddhism because, for her, Buddha epitomised human salvation. The message was the same: worship of the divine could never be the monopoly of any religious sect. True worship was the unconditional surrender or dedication to the almighty. Social institutions were generated to exalt some and degrade others. In *Natir Puja*, Tagore reaffirmed the view that 'true religion ignores man-made prejudices and restores the basic evaluation by which all human beings must be measured and redeemed' (Kripalani 2008: 376). Furthermore, by her sacrifice, the *nati*, Srimati, 'by her sincerity and devotion redeems the so-called degradation of her calling and vindicates by her death the innate majesty of her spirit' (376). Here, Tagore pitched his argument at two levels: At a rather mundane level, he critically evaluated Buddhism as a faith which allowed human beings to even make the supreme sacrifice for a cause; at a far more perceptive level, he openly challenged orthodox Hinduism that trampled underfoot the claims of the human whose gospel of compassion was violently ignored for satisfying partisan objectives. So, *Natir Puja* was another textual manifestation which reaffirms the views that Tagore so assiduously held as an organic intellectual in the sense that not only did he question the Hindu orthodox beliefs but he also put forward an alternative to reignite human faith in humanity. Despite being born in a family which was earnestly developing a monotheistic religion based on the philosophy of the Upanishads,

> 'it was through an idiosyncrasy of [his] temperament', argued the bard, 'that [he] refused to accept any religious teaching merely because people in [his] surroundings believed it to be true [since, he could not] persuade [himself] to imagine that [he] could not persuade [himself] to imagine that [he] had a religion because everybody whom [he] might trust believed in its value. (Tagore 1996: 120)

A critical Rabindranath was, thus, not persuaded to accept what was transmitted to him for his seniors notwithstanding the fact that he was raised in an environment in which Upanishadic values were privileged. Neither was there any imposition that primarily his father Debendranath allowed his children to grow as per their religio-political inclinations which the bard himself admitted on many occasions (Tagore 2006: 33). Thus, according to the poet, his 'mind was brought up in an atmosphere of freedom—freedom from the dominance of any creed that had its sanction in the definite authority of some scripture, or the teaching of some organised body of worshippers' (Tagore 1996: 120). Nonetheless, as he grew old, he realised that primary to humanism was 'love and cooperation' (122). His insistence on love and cooperation had a clear politico-ideological message in support of universal humanism. Philosophically, he extended his argument by suggesting that only when 'the individual spirit unites with the infinite Divine' do human beings fulfil the purpose of their birth as 'a creation representing the Creator' (126). This was based on his faith in *Ishoponishad*, which also reinforces the idea that once 'our mind and our words come away baffled from the Supreme Truth' (127), the goal remains unfulfilled. How then does one realise the Supreme Truth, asks the poet. In response, he mentions that he too had the experience when his soul 'touched the infinite and [became] … conscious of it through the illumination of joy' (127). This further means that 'he who knows truth through the immediate joy of his own soul is saved from all doubts and fears' (127). The Upanishadic idea reverberated in the core values of Vaishnavism which, by upholding the importance of love and compassion for human beings, reiterates the view that when 'the Vaishnava poet sings of the Lover who has his flute which, with its different stops, gives out the varied notes of beauty and love that are in Nature and Man' (127). It reiterates that only by coming out from the seclusion of a self-centred life into 'the realm of love and truth' (127), can one overcome the hurdle in internalising the Supreme Truth or the Infinite. Hence Tagore concluded that,

> the man whose inner vision is bathed in an illumination of his consciousness at once realizes the spiritual unity reigning supreme

> over all differences. His mind no longer awkwardly stumbles over individual facts of separateness in the human world, accepting them as final. He realizes that peace is in the inner harmony which dwells in truth and not in any outer adjustments. He knows that beauty carries an eternal assurance of our spiritual relationship to reality, which waits for its perfection in the response of our love. (128)

Here Tagore most succinctly elaborated his idea of universal humanism that formed the core of his philosophical discourses. One who never accepted artificial division among human beings, the bard, while pursuing his espoused goal, upheld love, care and compassion for one another. The idea had many roots: the Ishoponishad, the Enlightenment principles of the Western discourses, the Vaishnavite vision of love and concern and also the insistence of the Bengal Bauls on the complete surrender to the supreme soul were the main sources of his philosophical priorities. Throughout his life Tagore endeavoured to restore faith in humanity by creating a sense of bonhomie among people despite their diverse sociocultural locations—he believed that the downfall of humanity was the creation of human beings themselves and that the fundamental values of humanity needed to be developed and protected. With this critique, he established two claims at the same time: On the one hand, by questioning the design to partition humanity, he challenged the colonial project seeking to divide humanity into disproportionate sociocultural compartments; by championing the ideas of indigenous discourses based on his understanding of Vaishnavite thoughts and also the Upanishadic visions, he, on the other hand, forcefully argued that ideationally, the philosophy of Enlightenment was different from the ones that evolved in India.

V

Rabindranath Tagore's idea of nationalism is often misconstrued, if not misunderstood. Conceptually, Rabindranath was not a nationalist if his views are judged by the Western yardstick—he argued that since Indian society had achieved cohesion while preserving its diversity, it must not copy Europe and try to become a nation. Hence, it is argued that 'Indian society would be destroyed if the cultural nationalism [of Europe] was imposed on it' (Chatterjee 2021: 141). While seeking to delineate his conceptual intervention, ordinarily, most analysts draw on his lectures on nationalism, delivered in Japan and the US during the period between late May 1916 and January 1917. Besides theoretical insights, these texts were also a commentary on a period when Europe was passing through a great crisis that emanated from the outbreak of the Great War (1914–1919). Tagore saw the devasting nature of how the nation-states indulged in destroying one another by deploying lethal weapons. It was a vicious attack on humanity a country became victim to the policies that the war-mongering nations undertook without being a party to it. For Tagore, it was not just an attack on humanity, it was also an assault on human civilisation which human beings developed by dint of collective work for generations. In conformity with this argument, E.P. Thompson endorsed the view in his introduction to the three lectures that Tagore delivered. According to him, Tagore's '*Nationalism* is prescient, even prophetic, whose foresight has been confirmed by sufficient evidence —two world wars, the nuclear arms race, environmental disasters, technologies too clever to be controlled' (Thompson 1994: 8). One can thus safely argue that the poet's approach to nationalism was based on his own experience of the impact of the Great War in which nation-states participated to flex their muscles at the cost of humanity. There was no denying that the sufferers were hapless human beings who not only lost their home and hearth but also their lives just for satisfying the ego of a few European nations. Conceptually, the text, *Nationalism*, can be said to be context-driven; besides the devastations that the Great War caused humanity, Tagore was also upset by the way the British colonial state ruled India for partisan goals. Like Gandhi, he also believed that colonialism was a manifestation of the expansionist desires of those nations that thrived on the industrial revolution. So, Tagore's critique needs to be understood as a reaction to what he witnessed as the rising importance of nation-states. This was reiterated by Thompson who, by quoting a letter to him by Prasanta Mahalanobis (8 December 1921), defended the point that Tagore's concern for universal humanism was one of the key factors in his critique of nationalism. To counter what harmed human civilisation, Tagore believed in constructive work which included 'village work, mass education, sanitation and social reform'. Political freedom in India was just an aid to bring people together. Hence, he believed 'Congress Party's work to be useful only in as much as it tends to bring the different people of India into closer contact – that in the socializing effects of politics' (Thompson 1994: 12–13). Instead of segmenting civilisation, what was thus required, believed Tagore, was to contribute to 'social civilization' a conceptual category that was derived from his concern for universal humanism. His political discourse was thus shaped accordingly in the sense that he protested against the rising tide of nationalism in the name of humanity, not in the hope of gaining concessions, 'not as a political weapon, not for creating race feeling, but simply because it is a fundamental moral duty' (14). Thompson rewrote what Tagore expressed in his lecture on nationalism. He equated the belief that mere political freedom was a panacea for India with perhaps the most stupid idea to pursue because the transfer of power was not adequate to eradicate the sociocultural prejudices dividing humanity around the axes of class, caste and ethnicity. Eloquently, the bard put forward his views by saying,

> those of us in India who have come under the delusion that mere political freedom will make us free have accepted their lessons from the West as the gospel truth and lost their faith in humanity. We must remember that whatever weakness we cherish in society will become the source of danger in politics. The same inertia which leads us to our idolatry of dead forms in social institutions will create in our politics prison-houses with immovable walls. The narrowness of sympathy which makes it possible for us to impose upon a considerable portion of humanity the galling yoke of inferiority will assert itself in our politics in creating the tyranny of injustice. (94)

There are two interrelated sub-arguments in Rabindranath's main argument emphasising that salvation of humanity was possible only with the rise of a mindset opposed to the divisive mentality. The first sub-argument is a reiteration of the point that the Western discourses did not seem to be as useful as they appear. The reason needed to be located in the conceptual justification of nationalism leading to the rise and consolidation of nation-states. In other words, the political aim of making India a free nation-state was hardly a solution to the age-old sociocultural issues that India encountered. The second sub-argument was based on his direct attack on the creation and sustenance of artificial social barriers on the basis of the accident of birth. Here, that he was extremely unhappy with the caste segregation was evident, and the aim was to raise a voice against such a division of humanity by those who justified this, as it protected the partisan interests of a few. Being critical of sociocultural divisions, Tagore thus characterised social restrictions as 'tyrannical' drawn on the age-old

> social habit of [the] mind [which] impels us to make the life of our fellow-beings as [sic] burden to them where they differ from us even in such things as their choice of food, is sure to persist in our political organization and result in creating engines of coercion to crush every rational difference which is the sign of life. (95)

Here, Tagore unfolded another dimension of his critique of nationalism by further exposing its limitation; liberation from foreign rule, which meant political freedom, was futile as long as the sociocultural prejudices were allowed to survive. Being a victim of the social habit of the mind, human beings tended to accept the division as inevitable given the social recognition that it received. In other words, that human beings were placed differently in society became axiomatic presumably because (a) it was accepted as a given and (b) there were hardly any challenges to the continuity of such irrational divisions which further legitimised the sustenance of these practices. As a result, the law of life that had emerged in India was just a means to avoid collisions among various social strata by erecting

> boundaries of immovable walls, thus giving to the numerous races the negative benefit of peace and order but not the positive opportunity of expansion and movement; India accepted nature where it produces diversity, but ignored it where it uses that diversity for its world game of infinite permutations and combinations. … Therefore, Life departed from her social system and in its place, she is worshipping with all ceremony and magnificent cage of countless compartments that she has manufactured. (90)

In order to highlight the contradiction of life due to the perpetuation of caste segregation, Tagore candidly expressed that so long as this remained, the idea of freedom made no sense because freedom for one group of humanity meant un-freedom of another group. So long as this distinction was maintained, the liberation of any kind was neither a fulfilment of Tagore's exalted goal of humanity nor did it lead to any visible change in India's social map. In other words, nationalism was futile since it upheld freedom in its most limited sense and was hardly an effective instrument in eradicating the sources of segmentation among human beings. Here, there was no doubt that the poet assessed the idea with reference to his own understanding of India's social reality, which was divided around, religion, class and also space. The argument had two complementary insights: On the one hand, he was not persuaded to accept that nationalism was likely to bring about sociopolitical and economic changes compatible with freedom in its true connotation. On the other hand, he further argued that India's nationalist campaign seeking to wrest power from the British was hardly adequate to eradicate the well-entrenched sociocultural prejudices impeding the country's growth as a well-knit collectivity. Hence, the bard dubbed nationalism as 'a great menace' (87) as it led to the mutilation of humanity. The outbreak of the Great War with nation-states brutally killing and harming humanity provided the poet with the insight that nationalism was, under no circumstances, beneficial for humanity. Keeping this in mind, the poet thus mentioned that

> men, the fairest creations of God came out of the National manufactory in huge numbers as war-making and money-making puppets, ludicrously vain of their pitiful perfection of mechanism. [As a result], ... human society grew more and more into a marionette show of politicians, soldiers, manufacturers and bureaucrats, pulley by wire arrangements of wonderful efficiency. (74)

Nationalism thus evolved a criterion whereby human beings were assessed not as what they were but by their utility in expanding the narrow partisan interests of one section of humanity at the cost of another. Tagore's 1916–1917 lectures are testimony to this. What struck him was that those seeking to fulfil their partisan goals appeared to have ignored that they were under 'the spell of a powerful anesthesia [because] ... under the influence of its fumes, the whole people can carry out its systematic programme of the most virulent self-seeking without being in the least aware of its moral perversion' (73). Nationalism was thus diabolical and had a debilitating influence vis-à-vis humanity. In a nutshell, Tagore's critique of nationalism was founded on his personal experience of how nation-states devastated entire cultures and landmasses for business and territory gains. These lectures thus illustrate the poet's anxiety in circumstances when humanity perhaps received the most severe jolt in human history.

As argued, the poet was critical of nationalism as a conceptual category since it was inimical to humanity in view of the devastations that it had caused to humanity following the growth of powerful nation-states. Does it mean that Tagore was opposed to India's political freedom? A persuasive answer to the question needs to understand the poet's assessment of nationalism not in binary terms, but in a nuanced way which means that his stern criticism of nationalism did not however clearly suggest that he was totally opposed to nationalism as a mode of organising people for liberation from foreign rule in India. In other words, one has to understand Tagore's approach to nationalism at two levels: At the global level, he was unambiguously a baiter of nationalist endeavour since it led to the demeaning of humanity. At the national level, he did not exactly challenge the nationalist campaign against the British presumably because he was under the impression that removal of the British rule could help India decide her own course of action vis-à-vis sociocultural prejudices. This is a conceptual hypothesis that can be tested with r*eference to many* of his literary texts and also the 1904 seminal title *Swadeshi Samaj*. In order to provide a blueprint for future India, the poet evolved a structure of governance which was also a design for attacking the age-old superstitious beliefs justifying many of the archaic and also inhuman practices. He thus argued that whether India was ruled by the British or anybody else, what was required to be done to ensure 'the common well-being was to develop a mindset for sacrificing personal interests for society: instead of wasting time on the useless ideological issues, the country's betterment was possible by sacrifice and service to those who were victims of social torture' (Tagore 1908: 3). His main concern was to cement a bond among the Indians who were divided deliberately by the vested interests for fulfilling partisan ends. There are two levels of argument here: On one level, Tagore was certain that internal division was an impediment to the rise of Indians as a collective unit which means that his criticisms were directed against schisms caused by caste, religion and class. On another level, by insisting on developing unity among the Indians on the basis of sacrifice for and service to the deprivileged, he also endeavoured to generate a specific mindset and a milieu, supportive of the former as a means of deliverance for his countrymen. He also underlined that due to British rule, civilisational distortions led to the rise of a system of exploitation, which gained precedence since Indians themselves, instead of opposing, helped it thrive as it contributed and sustained their hegemony over the rest. In other words, colonialism, by being a system for partisan gains, created an unbridgeable gulf between those who augmented their wealth at the behest of the colonial power and those who were left behind. What can thus be presumed is that in the Indian context, Tagore realised that as long as colonial authority remained, it was difficult, if not impossible, to root out the sources of exploitation which probably explains his keenness for political freedom for India. Did he want India to be a nation? The answer was both yes and no. Tagore wanted India to be free from British hegemony; British rulers no longer respected the values of Enlightenment and they became brutal exploiters ignoring the basic human values of care, concern and compassion. In his 'Crisis in Civilization' (1941), he explained how he was disillusioned with the British Empire which systematised exploitation of the ruled; he admitted that it had been a source of inspiration to him at the outset since Enlightenment values helped build a powerful opposition to the prevalent inhuman sociocultural practices. While elaborating his point, he thus stated that,

> in India the misfortune of being governed by a foreign race is daily brought home to us not only in the callous neglect of such minimum necessities of life as adequate provision for food, clothing, educational and medical facilities for the people, but in an even

> unhappier form in the way the people have been divided among themselves. (Tagore 1996: 725)

So, he supported political freedom because the British rule was reduced to a ruthless machine that unhesitatingly allowed colonised Indians to be exploited as brutally as possible. Political freedom seemed the best alternative also because the colonial government thrived by deploying the principle of divide-and-rule, a strategy that not only generated a fissure between Hindus and Muslims but also contributed to the dismemberment of India in 1947. It is also true that the alienation of the Muslims from their Hindu brethren due to deliberately nurtured sociocultural prejudices helped the British administration to sustain the division and effectively utilise it for its political gain. Being well-conversant with the prevalent socioeconomic and political environment, Tagore thus linked political freedom with the creation of a mindset opposed to constructed value systems as essential for India's salvation, which further confirms that, in his perception, the removal of British rule from India was a definite step towards fulfilling his espousal for universal humanism.

There are three political novels, *Gora* (1910), *Ghare Baire* (1916) and *Char Adhyay* (1934), which are also illustrative of the claim that Tagore endorsed India's political freedom although he differed from the nationalists who undertook the campaign because they also opted for violence for fulfilling their nationalist objectives. Despite having written in different phases of his life, underlying these three novels remain these two interconnected themes: On the one hand, the protagonists were favourably disposed towards political freedom; on the other hand, it was also emphasised that political freedom was vacuous unless it was complemented by freedom from sociocultural shackles. The primary concern of Gora of *Gora*, Sandip and Bimala of *Ghare Baire*, and Atin and Indranath of *Char Adhyay* was to wrest political freedom by means that Tagore did not approve of. Nonetheless, by endorsing that political freedom was a necessity, the poet extended support to the campaigns that evolved at the behest of these protagonists. A hardcore Hindu, Gora felt that his primary aim was to work for India's political freedom which was a necessity for India's inner spiritual soul to unfold without hurdles. Interestingly, being baptised by his adopted father, who also became a hardcore Hindu after retirement, he too upheld the same view in the sense that one of the immediate consequences of British rule was the stifling of India's spiritualism. Gora wanted India to be politically free because it was complementary to the fulfilment of his spiritual goal. Tagore established this point in the novel by involving the protagonists Sucharita, Lolita, Paresh Babu and Binod in a very lively discussion with

Gora. Gora was confronted by the arguments of the rest in favour of the claim that political freedom was not a guarantee for human liberation—a view that articulated Tagore's own vision. However, Gora, by being insistent on political freedom also suggested that the author himself did not completely exclude himself from the idea. As the account shows, the poet was also in a dilemma since he too was swayed by the un-selfish commitment of the youth for freedom against British rule. Here, Tagore can be said to have appreciated the nationalist urge for political freedom. Particularly, despite being critical of nationalism, in this specific context, Rabindranath did not seem to have criticised the nationalist zeal so sternly presumably because he too was persuaded to believe that the British rule was suffocating. For him, the campaign for freedom from the oppressive rule was a clarion call alerting the colonised to their rights and dignity. All in all, *Gora* is a remarkably insightful and nuanced treatment of a nationalist movement that was as multivocal and multifaceted as the subjects on whose behalf it was waged. The novel thus serves as a touchstone for those of us who are persuaded to believe that while Tagore condemned the inherently vicious nature of the nation-state as a political structure, he was nonetheless extremely sensitive to the pressing need for colonised subjects to throw off their shackles.

The same idea reverberated in *Ghare Baire* where the dialogues involving Sandip, Bimala and Nikhilesh direct us to argue that Tagore was not exactly opposed to the nationalist urge for political freedom. Rather, he was cognisant of the many hypocrisies and moral pitfalls characterising many actors in the Swadeshi Movement (1905–1908). The willingness to turn a critical eye upon one's own countrymen was one of the important features of Tagore's profile as a social thinker. Using the character of Nikhilesh as a mouthpiece, Tagore expressed his reservations against how the nationalist movement had been shorn of its social commitments to the underprivileged and called for a moral reckoning of the movement for political freedom. For Sandip and Bimala, the revocation of the first partition of Bengal represented the fulfilment of the nationalist objective. By contrast, Nikhilesh pointed out the defects of the model of nationalism that Sandip championed because, instead of cementing fraternal bonds between Hindus and Muslims, the swadeshi campaign was fissiparous at the base. Tagore's fears were proved correct with the unfolding of the demand for the partition of the country into two nations on the basis of religious differences which culminated in the emergence of two sovereign states, India and Pakistan, in 1947. It is relatively less emphasised that the character of Amulya played a crucial role in driving the plot forward by exposing Sandip's hypocrisy and moral bankruptcy. Realising that her idol had feet of clay, Bimala finally saw

Sandip's grandiloquence for what it was. Mirroring Tagore's qualified espousal of nationalism, she rejected Sandip but continued to believe in the cause. Through these points of tension and resolution, therefore, the bard delineated his richly complex approach towards India's political freedom, in that he was not ready to subordinate one set of concerns to another. *Ghare Baire* is an enshrinement of this insight for within it, we find not the rejection of nationalist impulse, but an argument for a more inclusive version of it.

Written in 1934, *Char Adhyay* is another political novel that also brings out Tagore's qualified approach to nationalism. The plot revolves around a triad of protagonists, Indranath, Atin and Ela, who displayed an unshakable commitment to the nationalist cause, even to the exclusion of natural human desires for love and care. Ela joined Indranath's extremist nationalist group on the condition of celibacy, for it was the group's belief that indulging in the desire for family was detrimental to their goals. The concern for national liberation thus reigned supreme among the members of the group because the British rule was no longer as enlightening as it was in the past. One must note here that Tagore's perception of the British rule was hardly static; he reassessed it in accordance with its changing nature. It was evident in a dialogue between Indranath and another protagonist, Kanai, and highlighted the visible deterioration of the values which adversely affected the rulers in India. Appreciative of the role of the British government in encouraging a new path of life at the outset, Kanai was however disillusioned with the unfolding of a design of governance attacking the very philosophical foundation of the alien administration. Hence, he argued that despite having the power to completely crush out

> 'our manhood, … their better nature did not allow them to do it'. He also did not miss the fact that now 'manhood is deteriorating by the continued exercise of irresponsible power all over their empire, and in such deterioration are being sown the seeds of their own downfall.… [So,] it's not the question whether the British are good or bad. Their rule is one of foreign exploitation, killing our very souls within us. The only option thus left was to try to get rid of this unnatural situation'. (Tagore 2001: 39–40)

Kanai's statement is testimony to Tagore's transformation from being an admirer of the British Empire when it had contributed to the generation of many ideas that helped humanity prosper to a stern critic who supported the campaign for its removal. Later, in his 'Crisis in Civilization' (1941), he elaborated on this point in detail. With his emphatic belief that the Empire was certain to fall because of its deviation from human principles which put the British people ahead of other Europeans, in *Char Adhyay*,

Rabindranath envisioned the success of the nationalist campaign which further means that, in this context, he supported nationalism as an inspiring idea. He however realised that the nationalist path that the Indian revolutionaries had adopted was not the correct one. Hence, another protagonist, Ela, who declined to call her 'a patriot' was not very hopeful of the group's success in wresting political freedom from the British. While explaining the reasons, she thus admitted that 'the patriotism of those who had no faith in humanity … is like a crocodile's back used to ferry to cross the river' (94). What crippled the effort were 'meanness, unfaithfulness, mutual mistrust, secret machination [and] plotting for leadership [which] drag them into the mud at the bottom' (94). Being a votary of universal humanism, the bard was always very caustic in his remarks when attempts were made to undermine human souls. It was thus not surprising when Ela expressed the same sentiment when she emphasised 'that the life of the country can be saved by killing its soul is monstrously false doctrine that nationalists all over the world are bellowing forth stridently' (94). Just like being critical of the Empire for having ruthlessly muzzled human voice, he did not shy away while condemning the methods that the nationalists deployed to pursue their goals. By referring to an act of robbing a hapless widow, Ela resented by saying that it was as bad as the one that the British adopted to harass human beings. The widow had nothing against the nationalists and yet she had to pay a heavy price as she was killed which Ela condemned since, instead of cementing a bond with the colonised, this heinous feat was tantamount to 'murdering our own souls' (113). Critical here are two important claims: On the one hand, the poet supported the activities of those who devoted their lives to India's political freedom, which means that he upheld the conceptual validity of nationalism since it was a source of inspiration for waging a battle for India's freedom. There is, on the other, another significant point which he elaborated by being harshly critical of the effort of the nationalists who hardly restrained themselves from adopting steps contrary to humanity. Ela's criticism of her group for having taken steps to alienate the people of India which she explained as 'killing India's soul' is illustrative here.

An analytical dissection of these three political novels shows that Tagore was 'a nationalist, but not of the wrong type' (Radhakrishnan 2015: 172), according to Radhakrishnan who characterised the poet accordingly while assessing his approach to nationalism. He expanded the point further by stating that

> while he loves his country, he does not hate others. His patriotism is compatible with universal love. While national independence

> is a phase of social evolution to be necessarily passed through, it is ultimately one to be transcended in the conception of a world-whole. As each nation embodies some peculiar elements of value necessary for the full expression of Man, the love of a nation as embodying a part of the essence is not incompatible with the love of mankind as a whole. ... When Rabindranath loves India, it is the love of a soul, of a spiritual principle and not that of land or commerce. (172)

Tagore's nationalist concern was thus nuanced because it evolved out of his dialectical interaction with the reality which he confronted during his life. The 1916 lectures were a scathing criticism of the nation-states that hardly bothered about humanity as the Great War revealed; in India, the British rule was exploitative and brutal which further confirmed that nationalism was hardly supportive of humanism. Hence, he was persuaded to believe that India's political freedom which the nationalists upheld as their final goal was required to be achieved not for her own sake but also for the sake of humanity to prosper without being restrained. Conceptually, it will therefore not be plausible to simply suggest that Tagore was not a nationalist since, as per the aforementioned discussion, his approach to nationalism was dialectically construed, and hence, was nuanced and context-driven. In this respect, the points made earlier, are not only directional but also helpful in reassessing his widely discussed views on nationalism.

VI

Comprising seven chapters, the book proposes to comprehend Tagore's approach to contemporary sociocultural and politico-ideological issues within an innovative conceptual framework. Behind the literary representation of issues of humanity, the poet very clearly articulated his distinct views on many of the issues that impinged on humanity with the consolidation of colonialism in India. Before elaborating the chapters, three comments are required to understand the thematic peculiarity of the proposed book: first, the text is not an attempt to provide a literary critique of the poet's writings; instead, it is an endeavour to conceptualise the ideas that remained critical in the novels that figured in the book. For instance, the book rearticulates Rabindranath's unique understanding of the idea of nationalism. A cursory look at his lectures in 1916 in Japan and US reveals that he was critical of nationalism as a conceptual model of organising people around certain fixed identity markers. There is also the argument that the bard preferred the idea of patriotism as a unifying factor. One finds substance though there are conceptual infirmities in the argument for two reasons: It is beyond question that Rabindranath was opposed to essentialising identities presumably because of his upbringing in an environment in which he was privy to multiple sociocultural influences; it was a natural outcome given India's multicultural texture. On another level, by appreciating Japan as a civilisation which gained strength by drawing on her distinct sociocultural wealth built on her equally rich historical traditions. Being aware of her rich traditions, the Japanese was ready to sacrifice for the 'nation' since it was a service to the country. So, there is a subtle hint that nationalism, to him, does not seem to be always conceptually inappropriate. His critique is based on the effort against the attempt at homogenising human identities. Furthermore, he saw how the British rulers deviated from the Enlightenment principles in order to show their 'nationalist' might which means that nationalism was also a mode of exploiting human beings. So, if nationalism means expansionism, it was to be opposed for the reasons stated earlier; if nationalism means devotion to a collectivity not at the cost of others, which entails respect for oneness with the unit, it appears to have caught the bard's interest. His novel *Ghare Baire* (1916) and *Gora* (1910) are illustrative of this point. The first novel is the poet's sharp critique of nationalism: in order to sustain the unity between the Hindus and Muslims, Nikhilesh, one of the main protagonists in the novel, sacrifices his life. This was perhaps the poet's conceptualization of nationalism being a source of inspiration by emphasising one's love for the people living together for generations. The same idea reverberates in the character Gora in *Gora* who realises the vacuousness of his desire to be a hardcore Hindu by alienation from a large section of the populace simply because they had different religious identities. Rabindranath elaborated his point sharply in *Ghare Baire, Gora, Char Adhyay* and *Chaturanga*, among others. One should however not misunderstand these novels as merely an articulation of the poet's unique conceptualisation of nationalism; they were also sharp critiques of the existent sociocultural prejudices that, according to him, were a serious impediment to the rise and consolidation of togetherness irrespective of sociocultural differences among the communities in India.

Second, while delineating his creative idea of nationalism, the poet dealt extensively with the gender issue which his illustrious predecessors, Rammohun and Vidyasagar, in particular, dwelled on by raising their voices against sociocultural atrocities meted out to the womenfolk which the latter were taught to accept by virtue of their birth. While Rammohun and Vidyasagar focused on the systemic design directed to sustain gender disparity, the poet evolved a powerful voice for gender equality in circumstances when many radical sociocultural views received adequate attention in Bengal. Bimala in *Ghare Baire*, Ela in *Char Adhyay* and Damini in *Chaturanga* were effective challenges against the age-old traditions governing women's behaviour in accordance with those values that had emerged from carefully nurtured patriarchy. It was easier for the bard to understand these powerful voices first, due to his upbringing in a relatively liberal family and second, due to his father's support of these views which ran counter to the prevalent Hindu orthodox understanding of the gender question. Presumably because of this, Sohini of 'Laboratory' did not appear to be a social aberration because she was recognised for her devotion to the mission that he held for herself; furthermore, she was not even questioned because she agreed to raise her daughter who was born out of wedlock. Here, one must add a note of caution. That Rabindranath was also restrained since Sohini was a Punjabi girl, it was perhaps not a social stigma for her to have a child without getting married. The bard apprehended that the situation would create an uproar had she been a Bengali girl, the situation would have been different, and hence, he constructed the character, Sohini accordingly.

Finally, unlike Gandhi, the bard did not oppose British rule openly except perhaps in 1919 when he abdicated knighthood as a mark of dissent due to the brutal killing by the British police of the innocent people gathered in Jallianwala Bagh (in Punjab) for peaceful protest. There was however a great similarity between the Mahatma and the poet since both of them were opposed to the machine civilisation. Gandhi in the 1909 tract, *The Hind Swaraj* and Tagore's 1904 text entitled *Swadeshi Samaj* are exemplary here. Both these texts are illustrative of their specific politico-ideological stance vis-à-vis industrial civilisation. The poet did not stop there; his play *Muktadhara* is an open challenge to the British authority in a figurative way since it was a play against the attempt by the king, Ranjit Singh, to construct a dam to stop the free flow of water from the mountain springs to the neighbouring village Shiv Tarai. The play captures two concerns of the poet: first, the dam was a source of agony for the villagers of Shiv Tarai since the stopping of the water flow caused devastation to their agriculture, the only available source of their livelihood. Second, so long as the dam remained in place, it demonstrated the hegemony of the Uttarakut king over the hapless villagers of Shiv Tarai. By one stroke, he fulfilled his politico-ideological objectives: on the one hand, instead of appreciating the dam as a wonder of science, he questioned its construction as it led to unbearable human suffering. With the demolition of the dam, at the end of the play, he also had shown the collective human might that always prevailed over the torturous rulers despite being endowed with coercive instruments of authority. In *Muktadhara*, Dhananjay Bairagi who also appeared in another play,

Prayaschitta (1909), was a voice of freedom, an urge to break the shackles that human beings evolved to sustain the hegemony of one section of humanity against another. The elaboration of the politico-ideological views was prefaced by a very brief discussion of a short story, 'Balai', which epitomised the human interaction between a young kind and the environment. The bard's purpose was to show that unless there existed a symbiotic relationship between human beings and the environment, the human world was likely to be doomed. The fact that the issues that Gandhi raised in 1909 and the poet articulated in his many creative texts remain pertinent even in the 21st century is the testimony of the foresight that they demonstrated while condemning machine civilisation; it was a civilisation that resulted in colonialism which created circumstances in consolidating the 'inferior other', a perception leading to the consolidation of a group of 'self-proclaimed' guardians among the colonisers.

In view of the absence of a book focusing on Rabindranath's unique sociocultural vision, complemented by equally perceptive politico-ideological inputs, this book shall be useful to unearth the novelty that he had not only evinced as a literary genius but also as, in the broad sense of the term, an innovative ideologue. Besides drawing out the politico-ideological significance of the ideas that the poet upheld, the book is also a conceptual intervention in assessing whether the derivative ideas remain valid. Specifically, by questioning the view that Rabindranath's idea of nationalism meant a total rejection of nationalism as an idea, the book provides new inputs to reconceptualise the bard's unique understanding of one of the most discussed conceptual parameters in the last century. Finally, the book is also an effort to see the bard's creative texts differently by seeking to unearth the politico-ideological and sociocultural contexts in which they evolved. Being a sensitive mind, it was difficult to conceive that the bard remained aloof from the contemporary political processes. By contextualising the texts and also by a critical reading of what he meant to suggest under the circumstances, the book is not merely a rereading of Rabindranath's creative writings, it is also an attempt to unfold a mode of re-assessing some of the acceptable ideas relating to them.

References

Berlin, Isiah. 1960. 'Rabindranath Tagore and the Consciousness of Nationalist'. In *The Sense of Reality: Studies in Ideas and Their History*, ed. Henry Hardy. London: Chatto and Windus.

Berlin, Isiah. 1962. *Towards Universal Man*. Bombay: Asia Publishing House.

Chakrabarty, Bidyut. 2006. *Social and Political Thought of Mahatma Gandhi*. Oxford: Routledge.

———. 2020. *Socio-political Thought of Rabindranath Tagore*. New Delhi: Sage.

———. 2022. *The Three Tagores: Dwarkanath, Debendranath and Rabindranath*. New Delhi: Sage.

Chatterjee, Partha. 2021. *The Truths and Lies of Nationalism: As Narrated by Charvak*. New Delhi: Permanent Black in association with Ashoka University.

Guha, Ranajit. 2002. *History at the Limit of World History*. New York: Columbia University Press.

Jahanbegloo, Ramin. 2018. *The Disobedient Indian: Towards a Gandhian Philosophy of Dissent*. Delhi: Speaking Tiger.

Kripalani, Krishna. 1985. *Tagore: A Life*. New Delhi: National Book Trust.

———. 2008. *Rabindranath Tagore: A Biography*. New Delhi: UBS Publishers' Distributors Pvt. Ltd.

Lego, Mary, ed. 1972 (1920). 'Rabindranath Tagore to William Rothenstein'. In *Imperfect Encounter*. Cambridge: Harvard University Press.

Radhakrishnan, Sarvapalli. 2015 (rpt). *The Philosophy of Rabindranath Tagore*. New Delhi: Niyogi Books.

Tagore, Rabindranath. 1908. *Swadeshi Samaj* (Bangla). Kolkata: Visva-Bharati.

———. 1957 (rpt). *The Home and the World (Ghare Baire)*, trans. Surendranath Tagore and revised by Rabindranath Tagore. London: Macmillan and Co.

———. 1962 (rpt). 'A Poet's School'. In *Towards Universal Man*. Bombay: Asia Publishing House.

———. 1996 (rpt.). 'The Vision', Chapter VI of 'The Religion of Man'. In *The English Writings of Rabindranath Tagore*, ed. Sisir Kumar Das, Vol. 3. New Delhi: Sahitya Akademi.

———. 2001. *Char Adhyay* (Bangla). Kolkata: Visva-Bharati Granthan Bivag.

———. 2003 (1909). 'Prayaschitta'. In *Rabindra Rachanabali* (Collected Works of Rabindranath), Vol. 5. Kolkata: Visva-Bharati.

———. 2006. *My Life in My Words*, selected and ed. with an introduction by Uma Dasgupta. New Delhi: Penguin.

———. 2008 (rpt). 'Sriniketan'. In *The English Writings of Rabindranath Tagore*, ed. Nityapriya Ghosh, Vol. 4. New Delhi: Sahitya Akademi.

Thompson, E.P. 1994 (rpt). 'Introduction'. *Nationalism* by Rabindranath Tagore. New Delhi: Rupa.

Part I

NATIONALISM IN ITS MULTIFACETED FORMS

Comprising two chapters, Part I is an elaboration of how Rabindranath Tagore reconceptualised the notion of nationalism in his two novels *Ghare Baire* (1916) and *Char Adhyay* (1908). There is an established view that the bard rejected nationalism as a conceptual phenomenon. A superficial reading of his widely cited lecture on the nationalism of 1916 is usually referred to while defending the contention, though a deeper probe may lead one to arrive at a different conclusion. Careful study of the lecture confirms that he was not a 'nationalist' in the conventional way: Essentialising human identity, Tagore was certainly a non-nationalist. The governing principles of the idea of nationalism, as it appeared in Western theoretical discourses, justify the point that Tagore was neither a nationalist nor appreciative of the drive to homogenise the sociocultural identity of a collectivity, known as a nation in Western parlance. According to him, nationalism was 'a great menace' (Tagore 1985: 67) since it dehumanised humanity for petty commercial gains of the colonial powers. Here, the poet and Gandhi held similar views; the latter too did not endorse the idea of nationalism as it was not an appropriate mode of bringing socioculturally disparate human beings together for a specific cause. Furthermore, in his well-thought-out argument, nationalism also supported colonialism which was perhaps one of the worst mechanisms of exploitation of one section of humanity by another. It was most poignantly stated by the poet when, while explaining the devastating impact of nationalism on humanity, he stated that nationalism led to a situation in which

> nations fearing each other like the prowling wild beasts of the night-time; shutting their doors of hospitality; combining only for purposes of aggression or defence; hiding in their holes their trade secrets, state secrets, secrets of armaments; making peace-offerings to other others' barking dogs with the meat which does not belong to them; holding down fallen races which struggle to stand upon their feet; with their right hands dispensing religion to weaker peoples while robbing them with their left. (51)

As a priest of human emancipation, it was obvious that the poet was unhappy with the state of affairs that had emerged following the rise of colonialism. Divisive and also exploitative, colonialism thrived by artificially generating a schism among communities in India which were socioculturally separate from one another. The British *divide-et-impera* strategy drew sustenance and also survived on this constructed politico-ideological design. As humanist par excellence, it is conceivable that the poet was aghast at this colonial initiative. His critique of nationalism appeared to have been drawn on this assumption in which attempts were justified to create a feeling of togetherness on the basis of certain distinctive sociocultural characteristics. As a visionary, he might have anticipated the critical importance of M.A. Jinnah's two-nation theory which led to India's dismemberment following British withdrawal in 1947. So, his condemnation of the efforts towards organising a multitude as a nation on the basis of carefully chosen sociocultural features despite being disparate on many counts proved prophetic with the creation of Bangladesh after Pakistan's bifurcation in 1971. In other words, mere religious compatibility cannot sustain a community as a nation unless there exist common sociocultural threads.

There is another point of view that Tagore's idea of battling for political freedom can be captured by the expression 'patriotism': It is a fair illustration though not complete since his argument questioning nationalism was based on how it unfolded in the wake of colonialism and how it developed in the West, comprising more or less homogeneous and also a self-contented group of people. That it was conceptually inappropriate required no elaboration. Now, the fundamental question is whether nationalism is a substitute for patriotism and vice versa. There is hardly a simple answer because nationalism in its conventional characteristics cannot be clubbed with patriotism, which may not be confined to a specific geographical boundary. Nonetheless, it makes sense if one is inclined to understand the anti-British struggle as a manifestation of patriotic Indians.

Now, the fundamental point is made regarding the conceptual impasse on whether, on the basis of scrutiny of his creative texts and also this 1916 lecture on nationalism, he can be said to be a nationalist. The answer does not seem to be an easy one though one can surmise that both the novels, *Ghare Baire* and *Char Adhyay*, represent a very loosely defined version of nationalism which entails love, devotion and sacrifice for the motherland. Two characters, Nikhilesh of *Ghare Baire* and Ela of *Char Adhyay*, epitomise those qualities which Rabindranath identified as characteristic of being a 'nationalistic patriot'. Here nation is equated with the motherland; the clamour for serving the nation is possible once one becomes patriotic. Hence, both Nikhilesh and Ela are nationalistic patriots, given their unflinching commitment to the cause of the nation.

A perusal of the novels also confirms the point that the poet's understanding of nationalism was qualitatively different presumably because of the contextual peculiarities in which he was raised. Being exposed to many kinds of sociocultural influence, he became a renaissance man who was appreciative of many politico-ideological visions that he inherited and later imbibed by interacting with people from various walks of life both in India and abroad. Here, one is tempted to quote from a relatively neglected chapter in the famous 1916 lectures, entitled 'nationalism in Japan. To the bard, Japan held distinct sociocultural values presumably because it succeeded in combining her ancient culture with the new one. This amalgamation helped Japan to carve out a new path for herself that, according to the bard,

> enjoins man to look for his true wealth and power in his inner soul, the culture that gives self-possession in the face of loss and danger, self-sacrifice without counting the cost or hoping for gain, defiance of death, acceptance of countless social obligations that we owe to men as social beings. (31)

What is evident here is the poet's concern for men as social beings which further implies that humanity is always prior to anything else. One is thus expected to discharge one's responsibility as a social being by being sensitive to the concerns that Rabindranath enumerated in clear terms. In view of this categorical statement, it is now plausible to argue that the bard reconceptualised nationalism with reference to those genuine desires of social beings to contribute to humanity and ensure the well-being of mankind as a whole. The idea was unambiguously articulated by the bard in *Ghare Baire* and *Char Adhyay* in which concerns for humanity triumphed notwithstanding the politico-ideological baptisation of the main protagonists in the novels in the narrow nationalist discourses.

Reference

Tagore, Rabindranath. 1985 (rpt). *Nationalism*. Delhi: Macmillan.

1

Ghare Baire: Illustrative of Tagore's Ideational Universe

Rabindranath Tagore represented a voice of challenge to the existing sociocultural prejudices. Being a 'nationalist' of a different order, the poet articulated his opposition to the British rule that gained strength largely due to the social schism at every level of Indian society: it was easy for the foreign ruler to govern a large country like India, divided into caste, class and gender, according to their preferences. Before the advent of the Gandhian non-violent campaign, there was hardly a united platform to organise the people against an unjust system of governance. The bard was always vocal against the prejudicial sociocultural ideas and also the brutal British rule that took full advantage of a divided India. Through his innumerable writings, Rabindranath hit hard his detractors who drew sustenance from these restrictive archaic social rules and mores that were detrimental to the rise of the country as a well-knit unit. For instance, the dance drama *Chandalika* (1938) is a powerful critique of untouchability which, as per the poet, was a serious impediment to the unity that he espoused. By depicting Prakriti, an untouchable herself, as a voice against the artificially created sociocultural division, the poet persuasively argued the point. Similarly, by being ready to accept water from Prakriti, the Buddhist monk Ananda had shown that the practice of untouchability was specific only to a section of Hindus. According to Rabindranath, Buddhism, which emerged out of a rebellion against Hindu orthodoxy, was based on the view that as human beings, the division was hardly justified. In a similar vein, the novel *Gora* (1910), which is perhaps the most elaborate critique of Hindu orthodoxy, narrated a story of how the protagonist realised that prejudicial sociocultural values, being nurtured as integral to Hinduism, created and sustained an unbridgeable gulf among the Indians. It was therefore not just a novel but entailed a powerful sociocultural message against the self-proclaimed moral custodians of Hinduism. One may however argue that being a Brahmo, it did not seem odd for the poet to be fiercely critical of Hinduism. The argument is without substance for two reasons: First, like his father Debendranath Tagore, the poet derived his moral inspiration from the principal Hindu texts, especially the Upanishads. He defended his critique against the well-entrenched prejudicial values against humanism with reference to these texts which never allowed artificial division among human beings on the basis of birth. Critical was the idea that one's knowledge was what differentiated one from another. Second, by uncritically supporting so-called Hindu social festivals and also by drawing on Hindu mythology while articulating his poetic responses, he can be said to have privileged what he deemed appropriate for his sociocultural mission. So, his being a Brahmo was just incidental.

By making a threadbare analysis of the messages that *Ghare Baire* offered, this chapter defends the point that the novel was perhaps the best articulation of arguments that Rabindranath made to firmly establish his distinct politico-ideological beliefs, along with his concern for gender parity. In other words, the novel is a critique of the nature of the mainstream nationalist campaign which, instead of cementing a bond between Hindus and Muslims, made the sociocultural gulf between these communities unbridgeable. Furthermore, the novel provides inputs to comprehend his broader concern for gender equality which was inconceivable given the hegemony of those who remained steadfast in their commitment to nip the campaign with this objective in the bud.

Introducing *Ghare Baire*

Despite being inspirational in appearance, the swadeshi campaign (1905–1908) was, for Tagore, an opportunity to put across his unique politico-ideological views which ran counter to the mainstream nationalist approach. *Ghare Baire* was an articulation of the poet's disenchantment with the mainstream nationalist campaign that evolved in the wake of the Swadeshi Movement. The protagonists in this novel are three: Nikhilesh, the zamindar, who was not persuaded by the means that the nationalists adopted to fulfil their politico-ideological goals; Bimala, his wife, who saw life differently after having met the third protagonist Sandip who, being the leader, took charge of the campaign. At the outset, the bard explained his distinct ideas of human salvation which were possible once the sources of injustice were permanently eradicated. Here, the exchange of views between Nikhilesh and Sandip in *Ghare Baire* epitomises what the author strongly felt. Perhaps, not being aware of the prevalent socioeconomic and political reality, Sandip, while challenging the former, elaborated the conceptual foundation of his belief by underlining that 'successful injustice and genuine cruelty have been the only forces by which an individual or nation has become a millionaire or monarch' (Tagore 1957: 99). Drawing upon the view that 'the great discipline of injustice' was at the root of success, Sandip thus argued that 'deliverance is based in injustice [since] injustice is the fire which must keep on burning something in order to save itself from becoming ashes. Whenever an individual or nation becomes incapable of perpetuating injustice it is swept into the dustbin of the world' (99).

Sandip's argument in defence of injustice was reflective of the political arrogance of the mainstream nationalist leaders presumably because the Swadeshi Movement galvanised one section of the community, especially the Hindus in Bengal, to participate in the campaign for revocation of the vivisection of the province. He seemed to have become overconfident which was evident when he further suggested that

> we, men, with our ideas, strive to give it a particular shape by melting it into a particular mould, into the definiteness of success [because] … all the world-conquerors, from Alexander down to the American millionaires, mould themselves into a sword or a mint, and thus find that distinct image of themselves which is the source of their success. (100)

Based on his comprehension of the prevalent political milieu, Sandip prepared his line of thinking which persuaded him to justify that injustice meted out to the people for success did not seem to be unfair. By referring to the history when physical might or financial strength enabled one to attain success, he also endeavoured to prove that what he was saying was historically defensible. Contrarily, Nikhilesh held the view that success needed to be measured by assessing the fulfilment of the soul-driven desires which was evident when he said that 'winning your kind of success … is gained at the cost of the soul [and] the soul is greater than success' (100). Critical of the mechanical argument of Sandip, Nikhilesh further mentioned that his definition of success was neither linked with life nor was based on concern for humanity. In order to reinforce his point, he drew the analogy of a machine which was, for obvious reasons, devoid of life though it was distinct in its nature and texture. 'In order to gain distinctness,' argued Nikhilesh, and 'if you try … to know life as a machine, then such mere distinctness cannot stand for truth [and, in consequence,] you only lose your soul [in case] you seek it in your success' (101). The fundamental principle here is that human life cannot be conceptualised mechanically since human beings represent a sustained effort to explore the unknown. Furthermore, there is hardly a fixed format in so far as human beings are concerned presumably because they are products of specific socioeconomic and political circumstances.

What Tagore was hinting at was the possibility of multiple moulds in which human beings articulate their responses. So, mere success can never be a yardstick of human satisfaction as it does not entail satisfaction of merely worldly needs but also the fulfilment of those goals that nourish human souls. Illustrative here is the example of Panchu of *Ghare Baire* who offered coconuts to mitigate the sin that he committed (112). This was an eye-opener to Nikhilesh who did not seem perplexed by the revelation of Panchu's humanity in this regard. Despite being poor and unable to even get two square meals a day, Panchu's refusal to accept money from Nikhilesh is testimony to his sense of self-esteem. For the poet, it was reflective of the strength of his character which was manifested when Panchu forcefully stated that 'one time charity may resolve the crisis temporarily, but it cannot destroy the hardship of his lot'. While explaining that temporary help could temporarily solve an individual's problem, he also made one of his most perceptive comments when he said that it was not adequate to address the concerns of many Panchus who suffered equally due to abject poverty: '. . . if the milk in [Mother Bengal's] breast has run dry, that cannot be supplied from outside' (114). Two major arguments uphold the foundational ideas of Tagore's approach to humanity: On the one hand, Panchu's critique of charity formally established the poet's perception that no help was adequate to make a 'nation' self-sufficient—one needed to be receptive to the idea that self-reliance was possible once all countrymen felt the same way; on the other hand, Panchu's statement underlines the point that self-reliance remained an elusive idea unless one undertook those complementary practices to support the objective. Also being a practitioner of what he believed, Tagore had shown how Nikhilesh was a pioneer in this regard because he always 'sharpens his Indian-made pencils with his Indian-made knife, does his writing with red pens, drinks his water out of a bell-metal vessel, and works at night in the light of an old-fashioned castor-oil lamp' (122). The swadeshi way of life that Nikhilesh practised did not however impress his wife who had 'always felt ashamed of the inelegant, unfashionable furniture of his reception-rooms, especially when he had the magistrate or any other European, as his guest' (122). With this powerful and explicit comment, Tagore demonstrated that the swadeshi goals remained distant so long as the votaries fulfilled their responsibilities by merely being slogan-mongers and indulging in bonfires of foreign clothes without realising that this was not, at all, suitable to the poor, regardless of religion.

As argued before, Tagore was not persuaded by the swadeshi activists since their ideological design was divisive and thus lacked substance. He was vehemently opposed to the swadeshi strategy of forcing the poor peasants of his zamindari estate to burn their foreign clothes which they could afford to wear since they were cheaper than home-spun clothes. To him, it was a wrong strategy which alienated them from mainstream nationalism presumably because not only were they tortured if they declined to listen to the swadeshi champions but they were also socially ostracised as they failed in line with them. Here, too, the poet explained his point with reference to the plight of Panchu who, with a financial loan from Nikhilesh, endeavoured to stand on his own. Once Panchu got the loan, he

> began to buy cloth at the market and peddle it about the village. He did not get much cash payment, it is true, but what he could realise in kind, in the way of rice, jute and other filed produce, went towards his account. In two months, he was able to pay back the loan that he received from Nikhilesh. (130)

It was a source of satisfaction because Panchu became self-dependent; this was, however, short-lived since, with the arrival of the students from schools and colleagues to participate in the swadeshi campaign, the scene had undergone a sea-change. Being associated with the firebrand leader, Sandip, they roamed around the market to stop selling foreign goods and Nikhilesh was not spared either when there was a demand that the market that belonged to his estate should have no foreign goods. In response to this demand, Nikhilesh retorted that 'the loss would fall on poor traders and their customers' (131)—a retort that the activists dismissed as negligible for the sake of the country. Here, Nikhilesh came out with a philosophically charged statement by saying that 'the country does not mean the soil, but the men on it; your decision to forcibly stop the selling of foreign goods will contribute nothing, … but to foment your fanaticism' (132). Very curt in his reply, Nikhilesh justified his point saying that the swadeshi campaign unfolded neither a nationalist aim nor was adequate to galvanise the masses. It was based on a design, which instead of bringing people together, helped generate animosity between the organisers and the organised. Given the fact that the former were well-off, it was not possible for them to understand

> the life-and-death struggle for bare living; [they] cannot even imagine the difference a few paise means to them, - so little have [they] in common [because they] have spent [their] whole past in a superior compartment, and now [they] come to use [the poor] as tools for wreaking of [their] wrath [which Nikhilesh characterised as] cowardly. (132)

Nikhilesh spoke in Tagore's politico-ideological idioms, as his critical essays later represent. That he was aghast with the Congress activists who carried forward the campaign was manifested in many ways in the novel. His main point of criticism was based on the argument that the swadeshi campaigners became obstinate while pursuing their political objectives without understanding the adverse consequences of the execution of their plan. According to Nikhilesh, unless the poor associated with the movement, it was unlikely to succeed; this, however, never persuaded the leaders to redesign their mode of operation. This is evident when the poet draws our attention to the inhuman torture and emotional derailment that Panchu underwent when he insisted on selling foreign clothes in the village market. Not only were swadeshi activists resented but the local zamindar, in order to not annoy them, also fined Panchu and threatened to permanently evict him from his ancestral holding. Tagore brought out the agony that Panchu suffered as a result of being a victim of injustice in a very poignant way: When Panchu requested the local zamindar to allow him to sell off his stock, 'bought with borrowed money, promising faithfully never to do it again' (135), the landlord, instead of considering his appeal, 'insisted on burning the foreign stuff there and then, if he wanted to be let off' (135). Panchu refused by saying that he 'can't afford it' and asked the zamindar that 'if you are so keen to burn clothes, you please buy them and burn' (135). Affronted by his gall, the zamindar raged that 'the scoundrel must be taught manners, give him a shoe-beating' (135). This was how swadeshi activism was articulated and which not only upset but also enraged Nikhilesh since it led to indiscriminate torture of the poor. Here, Tagore made a broader point by highlighting the adverse consequences of the politics of force which not only alienated the poor from the nationalist campaign but also created a deep schism between Hindus and Muslims, as the history of Bengal shows. Unfortunately, he hardly had anyone to stand by him presumably because of the overwhelming support that the campaign generated among the educated section of the Bengali middle class, especially the young school- and college-going kids who appeared to have been mesmerised by the revolutionary nationalists' emotional appeal for application of force against the British. These kids were persuaded to accept the swadeshi call that 'in order to attain the goal, one must snatch and zamindars stooped so low that on one occasion, a rent-collector found one of the tenants with nothing which could be sold up to pay his rent, he was made to sell his young wife' (173–174). Under these circumstances, the clamour for swadeshi was futile though Nikhilesh never lost hope because he always nurtured a heart-felt 'desire to plant something greater than Swadeshi' (173) by being respectful to one another despite hierarchical segregation around caste, class and religious axes. The political scene became far more complex by then with the institutionalisation of the Hindu–Muslim division by forming groups, especially in Muslim-preponderant villages. The demand of the swadeshi activists to completely stop the killing of cows further divided the communities which was a source of anxiety to Nikhilesh. His defence for the argument was rebuffed by his Muslim subjects who argued that buffalo sacrifice before a deity in Hindu religious festivals was as devastating to the Muslim psyche as cow killing because both buffaloes and cows were useful for agriculture and the milk that they produced. Hence, 'if the cow is to be held sacred from slaughter, and not the buffalo, then that is bigotry, not religion' (219). This was a tragedy for the country as the nationalists were unable to bring Hindus and Muslims together for a common cause. Tagore characterised this division as 'an epidemic of sin that has been brought into [our country] from foreign lands' (225). Implicit here is the idea of *divide et impera* that the British rulers introduced step by step to cause a permanent fissure between these two major communities in Bengal. Historically speaking, with the consolidation of this chasm between Hindus and Muslims, it was easier for the Muslims to create an institutional platform, the Muslim League in 1906 that took off from Bengal.

Besides being an impressive literary creation, *Ghare Baire* is illustrative of Tagore's philosophical dispositions in an embryonic form. The novel is drawn on some of the foundational ideas that the poet developed in the wake of the nationalist movement in India. An author with tremendous foresight, the bard articulated a voice by taking into account India's complex sociocultural and politico-ideological milieu while evolving his model of a political battle against foreign rule. By drawing attention to the arguments and counter-arguments that the three protagonists, Nikhilesh, Sandip and Bimala, offered, he also evolved a vision which was critical to comprehending the contemporary historical processes at the dawn of India's nationalist movement. The vision was both context-driven and also surpassed the age in which it was articulated. A poet with tremendous foresight, Rabindranath clearly understood that without bringing people together regardless of religion and class, no nationalist venture was likely to succeed in India. *Ghare Baire* is an articulation of the message that he evolved and also nurtured throughout his life since he believed that both Hindu–Muslim amity and compassion for the poor were necessary to create a strong anti-British platform. A humanist to the core, it was easier for him to conceptualise India's complex socioeconomic reality which, he rightly thought, was essential to develop an effective strategy for effectively combating foreign rule and also the well-entrenched sociocultural prejudices against Muslims and indifference to the poor.

Ghare Baire was Tagore's manifesto for the future. In many ways, it was based on the ideas that he developed in his most perceptive tracts entitled *Swadeshi Samaj* (1904). If one reads the novel in juxtaposition with this critical essay, there is no doubt that Nikhilesh spoke in the language in which the poet articulated *Swadeshi Samaj*. Fundamental to Tagore's views were two critical propositions: On the one hand, he always believed that the spirit of swadeshi or indigenous power needed to be inculcated among the Indians to successfully mobilise the masses for political causes. Equally important, on the other hand, was the belief that it would remain heavily constrained so long as the differences between rich and poor or between upper and lower castes existed. What is striking is to note that despite being raised in a family which was not exactly anti-British, he imbibed the 'nationalistic' feelings in an otherwise not-so-favourable milieu. It was not however surprising as the bard himself explained when he stated that

> from an outside point of view, many a foreign custom would appear to have gained entry into our family, but at its heart flames a national pride which has never flickered. The genuine regard which my father had for his country never forsook him through all the revolutionary vicissitudes of his life, and this in his descendants has taken shape as a strong patriotic feeling. Love of country was, however, by no means a characteristic of the times of which I am writing. Our educated men then kept at arms' length both the language and thought of their native land. Nevertheless, my elder brothers had always cultivated Bengali literature. When on one occasion some new connection of marriage wrote my father an English letter it was promptly returned to the writer. (Tagore 2006: 11)

Three significant points need attention here. First, Tagore was nurtured in a family which never indulged in uncritically supporting the foreign rule. As history shows, Dwarkanath, despite being a loyalist, introduced various sociocultural schemes to link the Indians with indigenous intellectual traditions, especially what the Upanishads carried forward. The story is identical to that of his son Debendranath who devoted his energy to institutionalising the search for intellectual roots in ancient texts: He found them to be critical to conceptually defend his arguments for indigenous discourses. Rabindranath, too, followed the footsteps of his father and grandfather as we see articulated in his creative texts. Second, it was realised by the Tagores that without being rooted in one's sociocultural circumstances, the vision for a free India remained an expression with no substance. True to their conscience, they endeavoured to generate ideas supporting the rise and consolidation of a mindset which was not exclusively derivative of the Western discourses. In other words, it was an attempt to sail against the current since the majority of the educated middle class completely surrendered to the British by even not recognising that there existed a rich sociocultural and intellectual tradition in India which was no less appealing than what they accepted as axiomatic. Finally, in order to inculcate the sense of belongingness, what was required, as they strongly felt, was to evolve a milieu in which interests in exploring the indigenous traditions develop organically. It reinforces the argument that India was not merely a 'nation' like its Western counterparts but a unique civilisational text, enriched by a creative amalgamation of multiple ethos and theoretical insights that it confronted while sustaining its credibility and relevance. One of the ways the Tagores maintained this was by being committed to his mother tongue, Bangla. As per the available evidence, in the Tagore household, kids were taught Sanskrit and Bangla by teachers hired specifically for this purpose. Mere learning was not enough; it was required to be utilised to generate a nationalistic consciousness which was evident in Tagores' endeavour for regularly organising Hindu Mela which featured, as Rabindranath mentioned, 'the singing of songs glorifying the motherland, the recitation of poems of the love of country, the exhibition of indigenous arts and crafts and the encouragement of national talent and skill' (11). The aim was to develop concerns for the country and also a counter to the growing importance of intellectual servility to the colonisers. But there was also a caveat which Rabindranath explained when Nikhilesh in *Ghare Baire* exhorted that 'I am willing to serve my country; but the worship I reserve for Right which is far greater than my country [because] to worship my country as a god is to bring curse upon it' (Tagore 1957: 148). This is a meaningful statement highlighting the critical importance of the people to live and reason and in freedom. Along with his qualified support for the nationalist campaign, as the novel shows, he also championed the need for nurturing Bangla as a commonly spoken language. It was therefore not surprising that Rabindranath addressed an annual session of the Bengal Provincial Congress, held in Pabna in 1916, an incident in Bangla which was then unprecedented then. His argument was very simple: given the fact that the participants were Bengalis, Bangla would have automatically become the best mode of communication with them. The contemporary press was very critical of this effort though Tagore held his ground amidst scathing critiques even by the Congress stalwarts.

As the novel dwells on a rather different type of relationship between Sandip and Bimala, the poet was subject to severe criticism since it was not socially acceptable. The novel provoked those supportive of the revolutionary nationalist path for freedom which caught the imagination of many in Bengal. Nonetheless, the bard remained steadfastly committed to the views that he evolved on the basis of his unique understanding of the nationalist campaign. His qualified support for the nationalist agitation and his opposition to the 'unfreedom' of alien rule were based on this. Instead of being confined to the Western conceptualisation of nationalism, the poet appeared to have been persuaded to accept the view that nationalism, as it evolved in the West, was too narrow to become meaningful in a diverse society like India. There is substance in the argument that his idea of nationalism approximates the notion of patriotism which is partly true and partly false: true because patriotism is a concept with a wider canvas and does not need to be nationalistic (in the Western sense) to express one's loyalty to one's country. False, because uncritical faith in patriotism can limit, according to an analyst, 'both the freedom to engage ideas from outside narrow domestic walls and the freedom also to support the cause of people in other countries' (Sen 2005: 98), which means that the conceptualisation of patriotism is also flawed because it is contrary to Tagore's concern for universalism. Furthermore, his steadfast commitment to freedom also underlines his 'firm opposition to unreasoned traditionalism' (98) because it makes one 'a prisoner of the past' (98) which, in the poet's words, was nothing but 'lost in the dreary desert sand of a dead habit' (Tagore 1957: 173). *Ghare Baire* is Tagore's articulation of freedom in a fashion which did not match with that of the mainstream nationalists, whom Sandip represented. It, therefore, did not seem odd when Bimala participated in debates with Nikhilesh since she did not agree with him on the nature of the swadeshi campaign that engulfed the province. With her newly acquired freedom, Bimala freely expressed her views to support Sandip till she discovered that his devotion to the nationalist cause was just a facade to befool his followers. It would not have been possible for her to view Sandip from a proper perspective unless she had had the opportunity to exert herself as an independent agency, immune from being crippled by the prevalent sociocultural prejudices against women.

Bimala in *Ghare Baire*

Set in the context of the campaign to annul the first partition of Bengal (1905–1908), *Ghare Baire* (1916) is a historical novel which primarily deals with the nationalist question in an alternative format of the ideological priorities which Tagore represented. Disenchanted with the way the campaign evolved, the poet gradually dissociated from it since it was contrary to what he thought was conducive to national awakening.

Our purpose here is not to dwell on this issue. What is noteworthy here is the articulation of the bard's concern for gender parity mainly through the character Bimala though he also created the other two principal male characters, Nikhilesh (Bimala's husband) and his friend Sandip, the firebrand nationalist, who led the campaign against Partition.

At the outset, Tagore's Bimala appeared similar to any other woman in Bengal since she nurtured all those feminine qualities which are associated with womanhood. This was evident when Bimala expressed her happiness by being married to Nikhilesh who belonged to an aristocratic family. She was a little disappointed because her husband did not match the picture that she had painted before marriage. Nonetheless, she came to terms with this because of her husband's views on gender equality though she did not always appreciate presumably because of the socialisation processes that instilled in her the idea of the husband always being superior to his wife. Tagore very succinctly put forward his point highlighting the tension between what he felt and what Bimala, being a woman, internalised. In the novel, Bimala thus noted that

> my husband always claimed that men and women have equal rights over one another and hence their love is also on an equal footing. I have argued with him on this [though] … my heart says that devotion doesn't stop people from being equals. It tries to equalise people by elevating them. Hence, the pleasure of becoming equal is ever-present in it and it never turns into a thing of indifference. On the tray of love, devotion is like the light of the lamp in the ritual of worship—it falls the same way upon the worshipper and the worshipped. Today I know for sure that a woman's love is sanctified only through her own veneration —or else it's worth noting. When the lamp of our love glows, the flame rises upwards and only the burnt-up oil remains at the bottom. (671)

The idea is crystal clear. Bimala set out her femininity at two levels: at one level, she conformed to the misogynist trope of marriage necessarily fostering contentment among married women. It was therefore natural that she expressed her devotion to Nikhilesh who deserved to be venerated by virtue of being her husband. Here Tagore seems to have echoed the conventional views on gender. But the statement highlighting Nikhilesh's more feminist stance laid, at the level of conceptualisation, the foundation of his theoretical design for gender equity. The stance was undoubtedly revolutionary though for Tagore it did not seem to be unusual presumably because of the socialisation that he had undergone by being part of a family in which women were hardly discriminated against. As the available sources delineate, the Tagore family, being baptised in Brahmoism, helped create a milieu of sociopolitical equality regardless of gender. Being raised in that environment, Rabindranath Tagore can thus be said to have instinctively embraced these ideas supportive of gender parity.

Bimala became 'a modern woman' since Nikhilesh wanted her to be so; here, Tagore failed to go beyond the conventional ideas making the male the agency of change. She was transformed into a modern woman by Nikhilesh which means that the latter became an agency of change; it further means that Tagore conformed to the core values of patriarchy when the man was considered to be the primary agency for change. Nonetheless, it was worth noting in view of the well-entrenched social prejudices governing woman's life in general. The poet very clearly articulated the ideas when Bimala stated that her husband 'dressed [her] up in contemporary fashions' (673) which made other members of the family, especially her sisters-in-law, jealous. Nonetheless, Nikhilesh was, as Bimala described, unperturbed despite being aware of this. According to her,

> my husband was well aware of all this. But his heart brimmed over with sympathy for women. He would always advise me, don't be upset. I remember, once I had said to him 'women's minds are very crooked, very narrow'. He had replied, 'just like the feet of Chinese woman which are crooked and narrow. The entire society has squashed our women's minds from all sides and made them narrow and crooked. Fate gambles with their lives—their lives depend on the turn of the dice; do they have any powers of their own?' (673)

In a dialogical format, Tagore expressed his preferences very clearly. The views of Bimala were familiar since they corresponded with what was very common to women of the era. As an author, he however put forward contrasting views to firmly argue what he sincerely believed. Here, he was categorical in his choice: This was evident when Nikhilesh condemned the social mores denying rightful places to the widows, including his elder sister-in-law, by saying that 'law or society has not supported my sisters-in-law; it was a great humiliation for them to have to beg for what they once knew to be rightfully theirs, by virtue of their husband's legacy' (673). Not annoyed with his sisters-in-law for being envious of Bimala, he, instead of characterising it as 'unfair', mentioned that 'there is a grain of truth embedded in envy [because] whatever brings happiness should ideally be received by every individual' (674). Bimala seemed to have found an answer and thus asked her husband to get whatever they demanded to attain happiness. Now, Nikhilesh expressed his helplessness because 'it isn't possible to hand them whatever their heart desires' (674), a statement that reinforces the inherent power of the well-entrenched social prejudices which were difficult to neutralise in the then socioeconomic circumstances. So, being angry and envious was natural to them because 'when someone is deprived, this is the only way they know to conquer their deprivation—it is their only consolation' (674), argued Nikhilesh. The point is elaborated further when Bimala's husband made a caustic remark in response to her accusations that the manipulative behaviour of her sisters-in-law created unpleasant situations in the family, affecting her adversely. Nikhilesh condemned his wife for her selfishness since she had 'enough sympathy for [herself] when [her] own feelings were bruised, and [she] had none to spare for those whose lives [had] been ripped to shreds by the cruel arrows of society. Should the loser be made to pay,' he further stated, 'a fine for losing?' (674). The views that the poet had articulated to pursue his concern for gender equality were grounded on his faith in the Enlightenment values supportive of equality, fraternity and togetherness regardless of class, caste and ethnicity. There was also the feeling of being restrained due to the archaic social fabric in which women were denied all worldly comforts as soon as they became widows. The behaviour of women was socially conditioned—a fact which underlines the argument that as women, they were expected to behave in a particular fashion which was axiomatic and thus inescapable. Hence, Nikhilesh expressed uncertainty regarding whether Bimala's love for him 'stem from the deep well of her heart or was it driven by social pressures like the fixed ration of municipal water that one receives daily' (688)? Implicit here was his concern for freedom of choice for women; he was not comfortable if women were forced to love the person to whom she was married; it was love that emerged mechanically which was contrary to how equality was conceptualised in a free society. This was most likely to happen because for choosing a groom for a woman, her views were never taken into account; so, they were denied any role in the entire process; they were told to love whom they had married. This was not acceptable to Nikhilesh. Hence, he was not hesitant to admit that 'it is obvious to me that in [Bimala's] life, I am incidental; the person who [Bimala's] entire being can truly complement, is [the firebrand nationalist leader], Sandip' (2011: 707). A true renaissance man, for Nikhilesh it was neither a source of being annoyed nor upset for Bimala who was not given a choice to select her husband which was clearly stated when he noted that 'no point getting angry; ... instead [Bimala] should be mad at her destiny [because she] didn't pick [him] out in a *swaybar* (an ancient practice which allowed women to pick up her husband among the probable suiters); [she] had to take whatever [she] got with [her] eyes shut' (715). Here too, being very categorical, Tagore put forward another powerful argument to support gender equality in a social context when this was unheard; nevertheless, by raising his views, seeking to ensure the views of the bride while choosing her groom, the poet stated his preferences in unequivocal terms.

Concluding Observations

Ghare Baire is one of Tagore's perceptive novels to understand his politico-ideological preferences with reference to the unfolding of the Swadeshi Movement. Published in 1916, it was easier for the poet to see the events in a rather detached manner since he articulated his views in a sociopolitical context that underwent a sea-change. The apprehension that the bard had due to many strategic mistakes that the swadeshi activists committed came true with the alienation of the Muslims and also a large section of the poor among the Hindus. By rigidly practising social distancing with their Muslim neighbours, the Hindus further consolidated the segregation that gradually became unbridgeable. Since the Swadeshi Movement was largely a Hindu-driven initiative, the Muslims, in general, were hardly active. As a result of the Muslim traders being 'obdurate' (Tagore 1957: 148), Sandip exhorted that the swadeshi campaign for a bonfire of foreign clothes hardly attracted support in predominantly Muslim villages. Besides, their refusal to comply with Sandip's instructions and the Muslim boatmen's decision to carry foreign clothes from one village to another was an open threat to the swadeshi activists which led Sandip to order the sinking of their boats (149). Once this plan was executed, it was easier for the detractors to justify the point that the Swadeshi Movement was an anti-Muslim campaign. The point was persuasive given the age-old social distance between the Hindus and Muslims. The novel is thus a persuasive articulation of how the social gets connected with the political which further confirms Tagore's conceptualisation of freedom being a design which is neither discriminatory nor prejudicial. By so defining freedom, Tagore reinforced his argument for universal humanism which was, according to him, not only indivisible but also a powerful conceptual construct to bring people together.

Ghare Baire is also Tagore's definite ideological response to the ongoing political struggle. The Swadeshi Movement was an occasion when the poet confronted a campaign, which, despite having roused a section of the population, was, as per him, neither nationalistic nor potentially strong enough to initiate a nationalistic campaign. Sandip represented a point of view that Tagore hardly conceded presumably because not only was it divisive but also contrary to the perception that

India was a country of diverse religio-cultural beliefs. Being raised in a family that always privileged social amity regardless of religion, class and ethnicity, Tagore championed sociocultural togetherness which was, to him, a stepping stone towards building a society with no concern, care and empathy for all. *Ghare Baire* epitomised an endeavour which hardly received political support from the mainstream nationalists presumably because they failed to understand the complex historical processes due to the Muslims' estrangement from their Hindu neighbours. The argument appears plausible since the views that Nikhilesh held, besides Sandip's opposition, were not appreciated by his wife Bimala till the last moment when, by paying a heavy price, she realised that without bringing people together, no campaign was likely to succeed. Fundamental to Nikhilesh's conceptual universe was a sustained endeavour to erase the social differences among the people largely due to religion-guided sociocultural differences. According to Tagore, as long as the social distance between Hindus and Muslims remained, it would never bring these communities together. In order to address this, he allowed the Muslims to sit on the seats on the cushions that were denied to them in the past as he believed that it was humiliating to his Muslim subjects (Tagore 2008a: 319). It was a matter of serious concern that the Swadeshi Movement which affected the Hindus was unable to galvanise the Muslims at all; the reason was, as per him, located in 'the misconception of our nationalist leaders to wrongly conceive that India's political freedom was achievable without getting the Muslims in their favour' (318). Implicit here was his belief that he candidly articulated in an essay entitled 'Hindu-Mussalman' by saying that 'it is most unfortunate that religion was always privileged, and not [by] any other means socio-cultural modes, which is neither a manifestation of devotion to religion nor to humanity since the former discards those values which are impediments to the unfolding of the latter without shackles' (Tagore 2008b: 324). What is unique in Tagore's philosophical dispositions was his consistent propagation of means to cement a bond between these two major religious communities. *Ghare Baire* was one of the first persuasive statements in this regard.

The novel is one of the treatises in which Tagore also expressed his conceptually defensible views on poverty-driven social distance. Panchu in *Ghare Baire* exemplifies the concern and also the conceptual parameters to explain how poverty remains an important source of alienation even among Hindus between the rich and the poor. As the novel unequivocally shows, Panchu was subject to inhuman beating by the swadeshi activists with support from the local zamindar which not only upset the poet but also created a zeal to understand the mindset that unhesitatingly endorsed the torture that Panchu suffered. According to the poet, the mindset derived its sustenance from caste division that, by justifying segmentation due to the accident of birth, provided the Hindus with a powerful logic to keep especially the Shudras outside the fold. Given the fact that they mostly engaged in menial jobs, the rich Hindus instinctively nurtured despicable attitudes towards them. It was not thus surprising that the local landlord hardly hesitated to punish Panchu when he decided to refrain from putting the clothes that he bought to sell in the village market. What made Tagore resent that it was a source of joy to Sandip and also his disciples who generally belonged to rich families in Calcutta? They rejoiced at Panchu's cost since they were nurtured to believe that the poor were fated to suffer. For Tagore, it was just a tip of social malice that appeared to have gripped the province. He illustrated his point by referring to an incident that he had witnessed in East Bengal: He found that dipping in the river on an auspicious occasion was preferred to providing care to a seriously ailing individual who was lying on the bank of the river. It did not seem odd to those who came for this holy dip because, for them, service to humanity was never a priority (Tagore 2008c: 395–395).[1] For the poet, it was not only 'disgraceful for him as a human being … but also a serious source of concern as it was a threat to the rise of humanity as a well-knit community' (395). *Ghare Baire* is thus a powerful argument to highlight the point that the Indian nationalist voice remained constricted by (a) Hindu–Muslim schism and (b) the failure of the nationalists to be sensitive to the needs of the poor. By redefining swadeshi also as a mode of making the nation self-reliant, the bard introduced a new dimension to the nationalist discourses that gained momentum especially when Gandhi emerged on the scene though there were differences between them in the modes. Nonetheless, Rabindranath appreciated the Mahatma because he not only created 'a oneness' (Tagore 2007: 23) among the Indians but also instilled among the masses the view that 'the devotion to the country is meaningless unless one takes care of millions of the poor who are reeling in poverty; otherwise, our efforts are doomed to be a failure regardless of our self-less commitment to the nationalist cause' (23–24).

In many ways, *Ghare Baire* stands out not just as a literary creation but also as a visionary document in the sense that it contains some of the distinctive ideas of Indian nationalism that flourished in India in the wake of the later days of the nationalist campaign at the behest of Gandhi. It is a conceptual text articulated in the form of a novel since, in it, Tagore raised those pertinent issues for the future nationalists which helped

1 Rabindranath Tagore elaborated this incident in his essay 'Navayug', reproduced in *Kalantor*.

them understand the futility of conceptualising nationalism in India in the modular format[2] given her sociocultural identity. On the basis of his existential experiences, particularly in East Bengal where Muslims constituted a majority, it was easier for the bard to persuasively explain why the swadeshi campaign failed to develop a strong nationalistic political platform for all irrespective of religion, class and ethnicity. Although it is a matter of surprise that despite having identified the roots of communal schism and the division between the rich and poor, Tagore's warning did not appear to have had any effect on those who led the nationalist campaign in Bengal, as history demonstrates. Nonetheless, not only does the novel *Ghare Baire* provide an alternative nationalistic design for mass mobilisation but is also a powerful creative text to comprehend some of the foundational principles that Tagore upheld while building his conceptual universe.

References

Anderson, Benedict. 1991 (rpt). *Imagined Communities: Reflections on the Origin and Spread of Nationalism*. London: Verso.

Sen, Amartya. 2005. *The Argumentative Indian: Writings on Indian History, Culture and Identity*. New York: Picador.

Tagore, Rabindranath. 1957 (rpt). *The Home and the World (Ghare Baire)*, trans. Surendranath Tagore and revised by Rabindranath Tagore. London: Macmillan and Co.

———. 2006. *My Life in My Words*, selected and edited by Uma Das Gupta. New Delhi: Penguin.

———. 2007. *Mahatma Gandhi*. Kolkata: Visva-Bharati.

———. 2008a (rpt). 'Swami Shardhananda'. In *Kalantor*. Kolkata: Visva-Bharati.

———. 2008b (rpt). 'Hindu-Mussalman'. In *Kalantor*. Kolkata: Visva-Bharati.

———. 2008c (rpt). 'Navayug'. In *Kalantor*. Kolkata: Visva-Bharati.

2 Benedict Anderson, in his *Imagined Communities: Reflections on the Origin and Spread of Nationalism* (Verso, London, 1991 [reprint]), built his model of modular form of nationalism.

2

Rabindranath: A Nationalist in a Non-nationalist Conceptual Mould, *Char Adhyay*

The claim that Rabindranath Tagore was a nationalist does not hold water since he himself questioned the core conceptual principles of nationalism in his widely cited lectures in Japan and the US. There is however the other side of the coin which can be articulated by suggesting that his notion of nationalism needs to be understood differently. It is true that he challenged the idea of nationalism since it tends to homogenise or essentialise human identity—an idea that is inconceivable in India given the kaleidoscopic character of her sociocultural texture. If, however, it is understood as care, concern and empathy for the masses, then one will possibly come closer to the sense in which the poet sought to comprehend the concept. The bard was not persuaded to believe in the one-size-fits-all formula, given his socialisation while being raised in a family which allowed many cultural influences to thrive. So, for Rabindranath, sociocultural unity did not entail the hegemonic presence of one type of sociocultural belief at the cost of the rest. As is well-known, the Tagore family nurtured many sociocultural views despite being pursuant to typical Hindu sociocultural practices. The reason is located in the fact that since Dwarkanath Tagore, Rabindranath's grandfather, the flow of other sociocultural inputs was always encouraged; the trend continued when his father, Debendranath was at the helm of affairs. It is, thus, perfect to accept the view that being nurtured in a multicultural milieu, it was natural for him to imbibe the values questioning the effort towards homogenising India's unique sociocultural existence. Furthermore, during his journey in the Muslim-preponderant East Bengal, the bard also came across those practices which were different from the typical Hindu social and cultural beliefs. Thus, given his exposure to myriad sociocultural inputs and practices, the bard instinctively internalised those ideas.

In the light of the aforesaid explanation, one may tend to equate Rabindranath's articulation of nationalism with patriotism. Of course, that is valid as an argument since patriotism also involves concern, care and empathy for the motherland. Nationalism in its revised sense perhaps captures the bard's idea as well because it also provides a common platform to bring people together for a cause, the success of which is dependent on the consolidation of patriotism. In other words, here, nationalism is not understood in the narrow Western sense, but in its wider connotation by conceptualising the idea as a forum for togetherness, given the appreciation of diversity as integral to those identified as Indians.

There is another aspect that should not escape our notice. Rabindranath's famous critique of nationalism appeared in the public domain during the First World War which saw a nasty appearance of human greed and revenge even by deploying lethal weapons to destroy the so-called enemy. This was a source of his mental agony, which justified his claim that for protecting partisan national interests, human beings ceased to be humane and preferred to be mechanical in their responses to the communities that had different national identities. It was a matter of disgrace to the poet who was humanist par excellence. A witness of human destruction simply because the so-called Other had different socioculturally distinctive traits, the bard developed a distaste for this selfish design prepared by a section of humanity merely to destroy another section. In other words, one of the reasons for the bard's own conceptual model was certainly the war that devastated human existence for fulfilling the narrow objectives of those well-endowed with destructive weapons.

A patriot or nationalist in a very limited sense, Rabindranath was equally appalled when the mainstream nationalist in India, under the aegis of the Indian National Congress, organised a campaign during the Swadeshi Movement (1905–1908) in which the Muslims remained outsiders primarily because of its divisive nature. As his novel *Ghare Baire* (1916) argues very candidly, although the movement succeeded in annulling the first partition of Bengal, it caused a permanent fissure between the Hindus and Muslims. With the formation of the Muslim League in 1906, the division became unbridgeable and culminated in the vivisection of India in 1947. In his creative essay 'Swadeshi Samaj' published in 1904, the poet prepared a blueprint for the future polity in which Muslims were as integral as their Hindu brethren. Fundamental to his argument was the concern for creating bonhomie between the Hindus and Muslims which was only possible by according equal respect by the former to the latter. According to the poet, the created social distance between these communities was the source of alienation, and unless this was effectively addressed, it was difficult to conceive of Hindu–Muslim unity. Being aware that the inherent differences, also nurtured by the forces thriving on account of this schism, the poet always insisted that one was required to pay attention to the root of this chasm; rather than simply treating the illness symptomatically, it would be far more effective if one cared for generating a mindset opposed to segregation because of different religious identities. As Sandip of *Ghare Baire* epitomised, Rabindranath's exhortation did not appear to have changed the perception of those who led the campaign. The poet can be said to have been the victim of the situation: At one level, he was opposed to the partition since he also felt that it was a ploy of the British rulers to politically gain by applying the *divide-et-impera* strategy; he actively participated in mobilising opinion against the British policy in this regard by condemning the effort in so many of his creative texts. At another level, he appeared to be unhappy as he had shown in *Ghare Baire* because the typical Hinduised campaign was a cause of Hindu–Muslim alienation; furthermore, the policy of bonfire of foreign clothes, that adversely affected the poor Muslims since they could not afford to buy expensive homespun khadi, remained a bone of contention between the organisers of the movement and the Muslims in East Bengal. Despite having drawn Sandip's attention to this aspect, Nikhilesh failed to convince him—this, later, helped the aggrieved Muslims to effectively challenge the swadeshi campaigners.

The aforesaid signposting paragraphs situate the principal argument that this chapter seeks to build with reference to Rabindranath Tagore's *Char Adhyay* (Four Chapters), published in 1908. By drawing upon the poet's assessment of the nationalist zeal of the youth along with their humanitarian concerns, the chapter argues that Tagore articulated a new design of the nationalistic urge that was shaped both by humanism and the lack of it. Both these novels dwell on the nature of the Indian nationalist assault on the British in which human sentiments unfolded in a fashion that could hardly be captured in a derivative mould. The chapter is thus an attempt to understand how the ideas developed also out of dialogues, the nature of which differed significantly presumably because of the starkly different politico-ideological priorities shaping them.

Char Adhyay

Char Adhyay (1908) is a novel that revolves around three persons—Indranath, a revolutionary leader; Atindra or Atin, the scion of an impoverished aristocratic family and a young recruit to the revolutionary nationalist campaign; and Ela, an attractive girl who joined Indranath's group on Atin's persuasion and was in love with the latter. The novel has two complementary aspects: On the one hand, the novel was inspired by Brahmamadhav Upadhyay (1861–1907), a Catholic theologian, a Vedantic scholar and a believer in revolutionary nationalist campaigns that drew on violence. In the preface to the novel, Rabindranath mentioned that Upadhyay was hostile and also contemptuous of the poet because he never appreciated the method which was adopted by the revolutionary nationalist (Bose 1979: 6). On the other hand, the novel was a depiction of the love between Atin and Ela, of course, in a context when Bengal rose to prominence as a centre of revolutionary nationalist activities. The love between two individuals constitutes the main thesis of the story though the author took into account the milieu in which their love thrived which he admitted by saying that 'it is influenced also by the impact of their circumstances on them'.[1] What the bard highlighted here was the importance of the context in which they started loving each other, emphasising that it was also a context-driven act since the context critically shaped their unique responses. By drawing an analogy with the flow of a river that changed its texture, Rabindranath thus explained the changing nature of love between Atin and Ela by saying that as

> the river brings down its gushing nature from the mountain top that gives its birth, it however acquires its distinctiveness from the contour of the land through which it flows. The same is the case with love. On the one hand, there is the inner feeling, on the other, the conflict with outward circumstances. It is the combination of these two factors that gives the complete picture its individuality. I have tried in this story to body forth that individuality in the love of Ela and Atindra. I have had to show the capital asset of their transactions as well as to render an account of their transactions with the outside world with which they had to deal with to the last. (vi)

Despite being categorical in his statement that the context was of immense significance, Rabindranath was also aware that there was a possibility, given the circumstances, of pinning him down as a supporter of revolutionary nationalism. According to him, it was his literary creation, pure and simple. His concern was to comprehend the true nature of love between two individuals which was neither motivated nor an offshoot of political exigency but was based on their instinctive care, concern and empathy for each other. Apprehending that emphasis on the context might lead the readers to characterise his views as supportive of specific politico-ideological priorities, the bard thus clarified his position by underlining that

1 Rabindranath Tagore's 'note' in the English version of the novel, *Char Adhyay* or *Four Chapters*, Visva-Bharati, Kolkata, 1950, p. vi.

> there is another bone of contention. In the course of the story the different characters have voiced their views about the revolutionary movement. If these comments on the movement had been entirely absent, the context would have lost all meaning. It must be assumed that the opinions expressed serve only to support and confirm the characterization of the speakers. Should anyone suspect that some of these opinions tally with my own, then I would submit that such speculation is irrelevant and extraneous to the matter in hand.... If the views expressed by a speaker were to be found inconsistent with his character, then only could the author be charged with serious defect in his writing. (viii)

The bard's prefacing remark is crystal clear since it meant to show that under no circumstances, was he either supportive or opposed to revolutionary nationalism; he referred to it solely for drawing the readers' attention to the political context in which their love flourished. The political scenario was needed primarily to add flesh and blood to the characters who evolved in a context when revolutionary nationalism attracted many youths as perhaps the only means of expression of their anti-British sentiments. Descriptions of the revolutionary movement, which just provided 'their love with its dramatic setting' (ix) were, according to Rabindranath, 'of secondary importance [and] what matters is the portrayal of the poignance and pain of their love against the stormy background of the revolution' (ix). An analytical dissection of the bard's explanation reveals that on one level, he was not exactly opposed to the revolutionary movement, given the selfless sacrifice of the Bengali youths, and, on another level, he was reluctant to appreciate the method presumably because of his preference for non-violence which was evident in his 1887 novel, *Rajarshi* and which he reiterated in *Visarjan*, published in 1890. *Char Adhyay*, in contrast, justifies revolutionary nationalism because of the brutal and torturous British rule. Nonetheless, the poet's cautionary note underlines his belief that since violence begot violence, it was harmful to humanity and also detrimental to the universal humanism that he espoused throughout his active professional career as an organic intellectual.

With the above prefacing remarks, let us understand the crux of the novel, which was also Rabindranath's critique of violence, along with his concern for finer human sentiments that appear to have prospered instinctively out of human interactions. On one level, the novel revolves around a mindset that supports violence as a mode of opposing the British—it portrays activists who derived their ideological inspiration from ancient Hindu texts. The characters in *Char Adhyay* were baptised by the revolutionary nationalist vision. On a human level, the novel is also about the coming together of Atindra and Ela since they loved each other; while the former was in a dilemma since he was under the oath that as long as India remained captive, he could not be involved in any relationship which was likely to be a deterrent to the fulfilment of his mission, Ela was different. She believed, in contrast with Atindra, that human relations were not an impediment but complementary to the goal they were jointly working to attain. In fact, Ela was inducted by Indranath to attract youths and Atin, given his intimacy with her, was given the responsibility to bring her to the group.

Char Adhyay provided a narrative in which the poet very persuasively argued how violence was futile not merely because it begot cruelty but also because it generated bitterness among human beings. It was clearly stated by Indranth when he argued that 'in the struggle for power, the cult of cruelty comes first, to be followed at last, … by that of mercy' (Tagore 2009: 6). While castigating Ela for having argued that mercy was a greater virtue, he further added that 'it was nothing unusual for you since you belong to the class of "mothers"' (6). Being kind-hearted was not a quality to be imbibed, warned Indranath. What was needed was for her to display her power because 'your sex is the embodiment of power [which you should transmit] to the men around you' (7). The debate however ended with Ela's straightforward accusation that Indranath 'kept them deluded by his big words' (7). Given her faith in humanism, Ela also raised her voice when he decided to separate Uma from Sukumar since they expressed their love for each other. By challenging that 'punishment for love is nonsense' (10), Ela unhesitatingly supported the views that she held dear. Firm to his own conviction, Indranath laid out the exact nature of the revolutionary nationalists who were 'fire-worshippers but are always ready to sacrifice their personal likes and dislikes for the sake of their noble mission [because] … our conflagration must rage throughout the land and cannot be achieved with those whose fire has gone out or those who cannot control their own flame' (11). Two points require attention here: On the one hand, Indranath, being devoted to the cause of the nation, was opposed to a relationship especially between a man and a woman as he believed that it was a deterrent to the mission that he nurtured; on the other hand, he also held the view that once one was involved in a relationship, it was not possible for him or her to be selflessly devoted to the cause that he espoused. To Ela, it was nothing new because as she remembered during her first meeting with Indranath, he had told her categorically to not get 'entangled in any social relationship [since] you are not for society, but for your country alone' (12). The meaning of the claim is obvious: Involvement in a relationship meant disjunction with the nationalist cause. A determined Indranath hardly wavered even in destroying his enemy as he was oath-bound to do so. Once Ela realised this, she begged for the release of Atin whom she loved; but Indranath confidently replied that regardless of his views, Atin 'shall never leave the group because he remains bound by his own resolve [and, despite] his finer feelings will be hurt at every step, ... his self-respect will keep him with us till the end' (16). In response to Ela's request, he further warned her that 'someday it may become necessary to cause you to disappear without a trace [since] you're making Atin break away from us, and that one break will break something else.' Implicit here is the determination that Indranath had shown; he was a group leader who had succeeded in bringing many youths to his fold because they were persuaded by the cause that he was fighting for. Being confident due to his politico-ideological belief in revolutionary nationalism, it was thus possible for him to declare that

> the power that I have over all of you, because I never came to you as a beggar. I did not ask you to come under delusion, nor lure you to join my forlorn hope, not to show any particular results, but to prove your valour. My temperament is impersonal, so that I can submit cheerfully to the inevitable. And of whom am I to beg and pray that India may be spared its fate while it continues to worship with sandal-paste and vermillion the very germs of its own ruination? Mine is the dispassionate scientific attitude which tells me that if the reasons for decay are left uncured, death must ensue. Yet even in the face of all the signs of impending death, I will not allow dejection to enter my soul. (22–23)

What emerges here are the foundational pillars of Indranath's politico-ideological priorities. He questions the established view that independence was likely to be achieved by providential intervention; that a *karmayogi* like Indranath would dismiss the contention came as no surprise since he was one who was ready to accept death to fulfil his goal. Being a leader, he had his own programme which made him say that his colleagues joined him since they, like him, were inspired by the vision that Indranath put before them. Those who agreed to participate in the political campaign were not lured by any worldly gain but were drawn to him since they also desired to contribute to the struggle to liberate the motherland. At the same time, despite not being favourably disposed towards violence, Rabindranath also admired the youth for their steadfast commitment to the nation's cause. Indranath entailed some of the characteristic features of Brahmamadhav Upadhyay who appeared to have influenced the bard in a significant way in this regard. Although he had stark differences with Upadhyay, he never undermined the mindset that created in him a zeal to serve the country in accordance with his priority. Thus, one is persuaded to argue that it was misconstrued when Indranath was accused of having 'instrumentally used people' (26) for his exclusively individualistic goal. The argument does not seem to be tenable given Indranath's unflinching commitment to even make the ultimate sacrifice for the mission that brought many of his colleagues to him. In his exchange of views with Ela, Indranath made it very clear that if for fulfilling his goal, he was required to sacrifice his life, he was ready to do so.

Nonetheless, Rabindranath simultaneously critiqued the mechanical way in which the revolutionary nationalists undertook the task that was in any case handicapped since it was an exclusive design of inspiration for a few committed individuals. One of the reasons was perhaps the excessive dependence on the leader even if he was at fault. *Ghare Baire* is illustrative here: once Bimala was told by Amulya about the extravagant lifestyle of Sandip, the principal organiser of the swadeshi campaign, she was completely disenchanted because of the incongruence between his made-up concern for the poor and his exact lifestyle. One notices the same emotional setback when Ela evaluated the activities of the group and its leader, Indranath, more or less, in a similar fashion when she said that being 'the Supreme Counsellor (*mantradata*)', Indranath passed orders with the instruction that

> all of you collectively tug at a thick rope [of the chariot of Juggernaut] closing your eyes—this is your only work. Thousands of boys began doing so. Many fell under the wheels; many were maimed for life. Suddenly the instruction changed and everybody was asked to pull the chariot in a reverse direction. The chariot turned the other way. Those whose bones were broken [as a result] were allowed to suffer. The invalids were swept away into the dust heaps on the roadside. The faith in one's own strength was destroyed so fully that everyone proudly agreed to mould oneself after the official ideal of the so-called leader. When in response to the strings pulled by the leader, everyone began to dance the same dance, strangely enough everyone thought it to be a dance of power. The moment the puppeteer loosened his strings, thousands became superfluous. (38–39)

Critical here is Rabindranath's own assessment of revolutionary nationalism as a politico-ideological priority that remained one of the dominant nationalist forms in the anti-British struggle. That the bard was critical of how it manifested in the context of the Swadeshi Movement (1905–1908) was amply illustrated in *Gora* (1910) and later *Ghare Baire* (1916). Despite having been convinced that the youths participated in the campaign for their commitment to the noble cause, he was aghast when the leadership was found to have been guided by their selfish desires. Sandip in *Ghare Baire* and Indranath in *Char Adhyay* are testimonies to this claim. An analytical dissection of the ideas that Rabindranath sought to articulate in the earlier paragraph also needs to be understood with reference to what was unsaid. The poet's caustic remarks that by deciding a specific course of political action in the nationalist context, the leadership alienated many as they were opposed to their mode of action and also the philosophical faith which led to such an action. *Ghare Baire* exemplifies this by showing how the Muslims were estranged from the mainstream as the swadeshi campaign became largely Hinduised; furthermore, the failure of the leadership to gauge that the adverse impact of forcing the poor Muslims who were demographically preponderant in East Bengal accounted for the decline of the campaign. Although the first partition of Bengal was revoked, the consequences of Muslim alienation were disastrous as it led to India's dismemberment in 1947. *Char Adhyay* was a continuity of the ideas that the poet propounded particularly in *Ghare Baire* and *Gora*. Like Sandip and Gora, Indranath was also inspired by the *Gita* which was not wrong by itself, though his disregard for human emotions could never be justified as human beings without emotions ceased to be what they were; his condemnation of Ela for being emotionally involved with Atin is illustrative here. According to Rabindranath, it was detrimental to the growth of human civilisation which means that shunning human emotions was of help, under no circumstances, to build a well-knit collectivity tuned to the achievement of the politico-ideological goal that Indranath sought to attain. There are reasons to believe that Brahmamadhav Upadhyay, the revolutionary nationalist, who was at the back of the poet's mind when he constructed the character of Indranath also realised that their mode of political action was not adequate to accomplish their aspired goal. He, in fact, admitted this when he met Rabindranath by saying that the path that he followed was ineffective because it hardly galvanised the people to adopt the desire for freedom as theirs. Brahmamadhav's confession to the poet that he had 'fallen' also suggests that his decision to join the revolutionary nationalists, instead of helping him realise his goal, killed many of his finer human sentiments making him a machine capable of carrying forward an order but was unable to judge whether it was morally justified or not.

Self versus Self

Char Adhyay is one of the finer expositions of human relations in the context of uncertainty because of the ideological incongruity among the main protagonists in the novel; it is, also illustrative of their internal tension. In view of his steadfast commitment to the national cause, Indranath was ready to sacrifice his interests that corresponded with his firm belief in *Gita*'s dictum *niskam dharma* (expecting nothing in exchange for one's deeds). Atin, who was in love with Ela, was reluctant to express it as it meant deviation from Indranath's teaching; he endorsed Indranath's principle as for him, too, the national cause took precedence over individual liking. Given his unalloyed devotion to the cause, he even undertook to remove Ela since it was likely to put the group in trouble. The trouble was not due to the fact that Ela was not reliable; but, the apprehension that if she persuaded Atin to leave the group, it was likely to adversely affect their foundational unity which was an outcome of continuous hard work put in by the members. A critical assessment of the main characters of the novel reveals that it represents a battle of self versus self which means that one self was in favour of appreciating the basic human values while the other forcibly gagged them as per their goal to attain their politico-ideological objectives.

Of the characters, Ela is perhaps a clearer example to substantiate the fundamental point of how the self was being devalued to pursue goals which were considered prior to primary commitment to the nationalist cause. To understand Ela's preference for human sentiments despite the adverse consequences, the poet referred to her upbringing in a family where her mother rode over the wishes and desires of those who were dependent on the family for their survival. Since she was raised in 'such an unhealthy atmosphere where telling the truth was also misconstrued by her mother, Ela became a rebel in search of freedom'.[2] The rebellious feeling was, as per the bard, 'a reaction to her mother's determined effort to muzzle the voice of opposition' (5). There was another source of her irritation. She never liked the way her father Naresh Dasgupta was regularly abused by her mother for being 'less intelligent than her' (6) though he held a higher degree in Psychology from abroad. Ela also held her father responsible for allowing himself to being continuously abused and harassed. Being terribly hurt, Ela once expressed her resentment by saying that if her mother misconstrued her husband's patience as his weakness, it was unfair. Naresh was not persuaded since he believed that he preferred to not show his 'heroism for it would damage peace in [sic] the domestic front' (7); so, in his perception, it was more of a strategic

2 The 14-page introduction about Ela was articulated by the poet himself only in the Bangla version of *Char Adhyay*, which was published by Visva-Bharati Granthan Bhivag, Kolkata, 2009 (reprint), p. 5.

device to maintain a trouble-free life at home. What was most upsetting to Ela was her mother's ill-treatment of the Muslims. Her young and rebellious mind failed to appreciate her mother discarding a *madur* (a flat sheet made of the locally available leaves of date trees) on the pretext that a Muslim guest had sat on it. She was unable to comprehend why her mother behaved that way because she felt that this was an insult to an individual simply because they belonged to a different religion. While seeking an explanation from her father, she raised a question with wider implications: Why did women nurture such prejudices which were a manifestation of hatred for humanity at the cost of basic human values? In his response, her father referred to the firm grip that age-old socially nourished and carefully maintained prejudices had on women; ironically, this also ensured the continuity of the hegemony of a section of the population by putting another section under bondage. In *Swadeshi Samaj* (1904), the poet, while condemning the social distance between the Hindus and Muslims, worked hard to develop bonhomie between these two religious groups; this was clearly missing as manifest in the recurring communal riots in Bengal. The social distance, argued Rabindranath, was 'a menace which would disappear once for all if the sources of prejudices were permanently eradicated' (Tagore 1908: 25). Women were not the only ones 'responsible for the maintenance of such discrimination, there were many men with women's prejudicial mindset who also helped sustain these harmful beliefs' (Tagore 2009: 8). Realising how Ela was suffering being sandwiched between her own progressive views and her mother's archaic ideas, her father decided to send her to Calcutta for a college education. His decision infuriated his wife who disagreed with the proposal, arguing that the city life was sure to spoil her; led by her traditional mode of thinking, she believed that city-bred individuals found it difficult to adjust to their in-law's home. Ela read her mother's opposition as an endorsement of those archaic ideas which justified the bringing-up of a girl child in a specific mould; it was a mould to prepare her to fit into the life that she had to adjust with. Being one who always maintained independent views on social issues, that Ela sought to question them was natural. She thus argued that what was justified as being socially appropriate was nothing but 'a deliberately-constructed design to take away not only their self-esteem but also the capacity to distinguish between just (or) and unjust (or unfair) values and practices' (9). With the death of her parents in quick succession, Ela was, in a way, fortunate since there was no one left to pressurise her to get married. Except for her uncle Suresh, she had no relatives. After his brother's death, Suresh immediately took over Ela's responsibility and asked her to join him and her aunt in his place of work. Given her impressive behaviour and also her capability of speaking English, she became a great favourite of her uncle and his family. Her happiness was however short-lived since her aunt felt threatened because Ela, with her strong opinion on every social issue, was likely to poison the mind of their daughter Surama; her fear came into the open when she abused Suresh for replacing Adhir, Surama's private tutor, with Ela. Her aunt's apprehension reminded Ela of her illiterate mother when she argued that it was difficult to find a match for the independent-minded Surama; she also felt that since Ela was prettier than Surama, the difficulty would be insurmountable. So, she asked her husband Suresh to find a groom for Ela; the tragedy was that here too, she was used as a pawn by her aunt because most of those who came to see Ela were requested to marry Surama once she outrightly rejected them. Because of her reluctance to get married, she now lost her uncle's support as well which led to an ensuing battle. She thus became a burden to the family which neither had found a way to get rid of her since she expressed her unwillingness to marry nor was able to persuade her to accept their option.

As expected, the poet's elaborate introduction of Ela's early life was directed to situate her in the novel in conjunction with other protagonists. What also emerges are two critical arguments which were revolutionary in so far as the approach to gender was concerned. First, Ela represented a voice of protest against those archaic values and views which justified 'women-in-chains'; Ela's father appreciated her to the extent it was possible within the constraints which also expressed his dilemma: Despite being supportive of Ela, he failed to openly support her; he was aware of the adverse consequences of his wife being angry on the family and did not wish to upset domestic peace. Second, Ela hardly escaped from societal chains even after she shifted from the village to a town where her uncle and aunt invited her to stay with them. The situation did not seem to be qualitatively different as the aforesaid discussion demonstrates. Despite her exposure to a European lifestyle when she accompanied her husband to many get-togethers with Europeans, her aunt also held the same views which were evident when she also planned for her arranged marriage. Ela, thus, had no respite, whether in her parent's house or when she was with her uncle and aunt.

With Indranath's arrival in Ela's life, she saw a silver lining as it allowed her to be independent of her uncle and aunt. In response to her request for a job, Indranath offered her an assignment in the newly started Narayani High School at the behest of the revolutionary to teach the pupils a curriculum that was different from the English one. Appreciating Ela as the harbinger of a new era, Indranath was happy to have found her, something that he mentioned in his exchange of dialogue with her.

Ela was flabbergasted as she was not sure whether she was capable of living up to his expectations. She said that although she might lack the ability to match with what Indranath expected, she would give her best to fulfil the task that she was given to accomplish. There was, however, one condition in the form of a commitment that Indranath put forward before Ela. It was a commitment to remain a celibate since she then belonged to the nation and not to society. Without thinking even for a minute, Ela acquiesced because it corresponded with her priorities, as her continuous opposition to marriage confirms. Given his emotional attachment to his niece, her uncle insisted on her staying on with the family. But, his wife vehemently opposed this since she felt that Ela with her rebellious viewpoints on social values and mores, instead of contributing to the family's well-being, was likely to be a source of bad influence on her daughter. The aunt, however, justified her decision by saying that since Ela was happy being independent of the family, she should not be stopped. By happily accepting her aunt's suggestion, Ela immediately agreed to leave the family,

With his long prefacing remarks, Rabindranath had shown how Ela's two contradictory selves evolved dialectically; the conundrum however appeared to have been resolved with the appearance of Indranath, who by successfully indoctrinating her in his politico-ideological priorities, established that Ela discovered the path that she had been longing for. Her job in the school acted as a cover for her involvement with those political activities which revolutionary nationalists undertook to honour their commitment to the nation. So, Ela became integrally linked with revolutionary nationalism under Indranath's stewardship. Given the ideological compatibility with her colleagues, Ela seems to have had a temporary respite from the contradictions that had bothered her as long as she remained within the familial environment in which sociocultural prejudicial values were predominant. The argument defending the near liquidation of one self and the ascendancy of another, thus, remains justified once Ela came out of the family and joined hands with those who took a vow to work for the nation as per Indranath's directions.

A superficial understanding of Ela's freedom from family life may lead one to conclude that it was a triumph of the self that had been longing to carve a space for itself—a space that had been denied so far largely due to the well-entrenched sociocultural prejudices. Ela was a lone fighter though both her father and uncle Suresh seemed inclined to go along with her. By highlighting the role of Ela's mother and later, her aunt, who reiterated more or less identical views vis-à-vis women, the poet emphasised the importance of an agency which, by supporting specific ideological priorities, played a critical role in sustaining and also consolidating them. Once Ela decided to be part of the revolutionary nationalists, she, probably unknowingly, accepted the importance of an agency in shaping her life; she lost her independence though she believed that by being part of the group, she had the freedom to spend her life according to her priorities. That it was not so was evident when she took an oath to not go for marriage as she belonged to the nation and marriage was meant to bind two individuals within a socially recognised set of rules and regulations. There is a subtle point here: Being an independent-minded person, Ela allowed herself to be controlled by Indranath by eschewing her independence for which she had fought relentlessly during her growing-up years in familial circumstances. In other words, for Ela, the idea of independence remains elusive: While her mother and aunt both sought to control her according to their carefully nurtured views, Indranath too imposed restrictions on her independence.

Self as a Burden

As the novel progresses, it becomes clear that Ela was not entirely free from the conventional ideas of individual freedom which she had committed herself to forego in view of the oath that she took before joining the group. It was her love for Atin or Ontu which made her realise that she continued to nurture those values which were anathema to revolutionary nationalism, given the vow of the members of the group to remain celibate so long as they did not attain their goal. The plot became complicated once Ela refused to marry Atin despite being deeply in love with him since she took a vow not to get married to avoid being diverted from the cause of the nation that she always privileged. Atin, with Indranath's guidance, became ruthless but a committed soldier of the group which, as Ela mentioned, 'dehumanised him' to a significant extent. The relationship between Ela and Atin was thus stressful. Ela's love for Atin and vice versa was not thus shackle-free since neither of them was willing to fulfil their objectives by paying a price. The story took a different turn when Atin was given the task of eliminating Ela because she was considered 'a burden' to the group. She was so much in love with Atin that Ela allowed herself to be killed by her beloved since it meant the fulfilment of her unfulfilled desires due to the peculiar circumstances in which they were placed.

There are two interrelated aspects in the novel vis-à-vis the gender question. First, the leader of the group, Indranath, appreciated Ela's feminine attraction to gather around him a set of dedicated men for the cause. Atin joined the group because it allowed him to be with Ela who,

Atin admitted, was 'a paragon of beauty'. Here, the feminine aspect of Ela was utilised by Indranath to pursue a goal; Indranath justified his action by saying that it contributed to the nationalist cause. While talking about Atin, Indranath also confessed that it was 'Ela's beauty that brought Atin to the group' (Tagore 1418 [Bangabda]: 35). It was true to a great extent since Atin had fallen in love with her and wanted to marry Ela; the latter refused given her apprehension that her marriage would be an impediment to the fulfilment of her nationalist commitment. There was no other reason for her refusal except for her declared commitment to the group devoted to national liberation. Here, Atin was conventional in his thinking while Ela was not. Being impressed by Atin who left no stone unturned to carry out the group's activities meant to liberate the country from chains, Ela was gradually drawn to him and was desperate to be with him—either through nuptial ties or otherwise. However, this time, Atin refused, giving the same reason that Ela had cited while refusing to marry him. The last page of the novel poignantly expresses Ela's love for Atin who was ordered by the group leader Indranath to kill her as she was supposedly responsible for a plot against the group. Here, Ela came out openly to express how deeply she was in love with him. Ela thus exhorted that

> don't have any qualms; am I not yours, wholly yours, even in death. Take me, ... this body belongs to you. ... Ontu [Atin was fondly addressed by her], my Ontu, my king, my god, I have not been able to show you how much I love you. By this love I charge you to kill me. ... Let the last bit of my consciousness be for you. ... Let me die awake in your arms; let our last kiss be eternal. (115–116)

Ela's exhortation does not seem to be striking; rather it seems natural for someone deeply in love. In the first part of the novel, it was Atin who had surrendered to Ela, who at that time, was apprehensive and hence did not respond to his passionate urge. As days passed, Ela began to nurture the same feelings for him which ultimately made her surrender completely to Atin when he was asked to kill her. From the point of view of the storyline, the narrative does not appear to have any particular dimension that shows Tagore in a different light. However, a careful reading of the text reveals the subtility of the message for gender equality that the poet unambiguously articulated. In Chapter 2 of the novel, Atin was vocal in his support of protecting women's rights as being integral to society; so far, it had been dominated by males which was reflective of the usual patriarchal hegemony. By challenging the excessive dominance of males in governing women's lives, Atin, the protagonist of gender equality, thus declared that 'women need to come out of their shell and also challenge whenever attempts are made to put them under chains by reference to the age-old restrictive practices, justified as appropriate by the so-called religious texts' (44–45). On one level, this is a reiteration of the concerns that Tagore had expressed in so many of his creative texts, namely, that women were required to be bold enough to raise their voices against injustice of any kind. On another level, he also made the male counterparts responsible for altering the acceptable social practices which were inhibiting. Besides this, the poet also refers to an instance in which the holy texts were suitably distorted to defend the archaic mores and values seeking to put women under chains.

There is another aspect of concern that Tagore talks about in the novel and which is a reinforcement of the argument that he propounds. He indeed attributes most of the gender-driven restrictive practices and values to patriarchy. Nonetheless, by highlighting the contribution of women in sustaining the system, he does not spare them either. While highlighting the role of women in continuing with the decadent practices, Atin feels the need for strong condemnation of women who were held responsible for this kind of state of affairs. It is very categorically stated when Atin insists that despite being women, mothers-in-law help to continue the system of putting women in chains. Once a person becomes a mother-in-law, she is a different individual, interested 'in expanding her sphere of influence by hook or crook; the first casualty happens to be the daughters-in-law who, by being submissive to the dictates of her mother-in-law (as she was nurtured to behave that way), help create circumstances in which the hegemonic control is allowed and sustained'. Tagore exhorts that this was nothing unusual as it had been the practice which went unchallenged for a long time. While explaining why it continued, he holds responsible the sons who have remained 'captive of [their] mothers' influence [and] neither questioned nor challenged them despite having realised that it was unfair and uncalled-for' (57). Here too, Tagore puts in words the nature of a reality which had emerged due to the failure of those who, notwithstanding having accepted their wives as partners, lost their independent voice by being scared of their mothers presumably because it was a convenient design for protecting their self-interests. Being annoyed with those who abdicated their responsibilities towards their wives, the poet is most caustic in his remarks by saying that 'those who are incapable of supporting and protecting their wives from being unfairly tortured by their mothers should not get married, at all [because] … it is neither humanly-justified nor socially admissible in view of the adverse social consequences that it results' (57). This is one part of the argument; the other part is equally important where Tagore also castigates those henpecked husbands who were also responsible for such a deplorable milieu. Being critical of the role of the mothers-in-law, the so-called obedient sons do not disturb the applecart by being reverent to the prevalent system of social control by their mothers; the husbands, by unconditional surrender to their wives, also helped build an unfair situation in which they preferred to not raise their voice. While delineating the nature of man-woman relations in a Bengali household, the poet is categorical in condemning the restrictive social more vis-à-vis woman. It is through Ela that he expresses what he felt so genuinely for gender parity. Disheartened by the socially nurtured taboos against women, Ela thus argues that 'my punishment is endless; it flogs me all the time. That wonderful good fortune which is beyond all endeavour was before my eyes, yet I could not accept it' (Tagore 2011: 1102). Here, the reader is told that Rabindranath is equally respectful of the humanistic feelings that evolved naturally between Atin and Ela though they are not allowed to ventilate their views openly since they are under the oath of being restrained given their commitment to the nationalist goal. It is unambiguously stated by Ela when she mentions that

> our hearts are united, yet I am like a winder and no woman should undergo my unbearable grief. I was confined within a barrier, but when I saw you [Atin] I became eager to break away. I had never imagined such an upheaval was possible. It would be untrue to say that no one had touched my heart before, but by controlling my feelings, I felt proud of my strength. Now I have no pride in overcoming my emotions, nor do I wish to. Don't go by what you see outwardly, look into my heart, I am defeated. You are my valiant hero, and I am your prisoner. (1102)

A great believer in human emotions being the pillar of human relations, the poet hardly wavers in his expressions; yet, it is not possible for him to bring Atin and Ela together. What is evident here is the fact that he is constrained by prevalent social mores and contextual limitations that do not allow the revolutionary nationalists to be appreciative of feelings of emotions since they concede that, for them, India's liberation is prior to personal happiness. Had it been a one-sided attraction, Ela's emotional connect could have been dismissed easily. But once Atin admits that he too is drawn to her though he has to suppress his feelings, again, due to the oath. It is a no-win situation for both Ela and Atin which the former articulates by saying that 'the haphazard wishes of their restless hearts hit against the walls of their inner dark chambers [which] ... women generally don't like to admit, but [Atin] made [her] to admit it' (1102). Despite being deeply in love with Atin, in view of the oath, Ela is unable to respond to his request to marry him since she was oath-bound not to undertake such an act. In her words, Ela, by being duty-bound to respect the oath, defends her stance by underlining that 'the impediment is not from outside, it is internal' which perhaps means that her commitment to the oath made her stick to the vow that she took while joining the group. Violation of the vow was simply not conceivable because it also amounts to betrayal of her commitment. Her refusal, notwithstanding the emotional suffering, is justified by Ela as a significant contribution to the cause of the group, of which Atin is an integral part. For her, the service to the motherland is prior to anything else. Hence, she does not 'dare to think of binding [Atin] to someone ordinary like [her]'. Her views are elaborated when she further says that

> I would not confine you to the insignificant pursuits of my little world! How can I explain how much I look up to you? Perhaps there are women who would not hesitate to bury even a man like you under the nitty-gritty of life – that is all those women have. I know of the tragic consequences. I have seen how the embrace of the creeper stunts the growth of the tress; these women think that the embrace is enough. (1104)

Ela loves Atin unconditionally and that is evident though her expression is not conventional; she wants Atin to flourish and nuptial binding was likely to impede him from wholeheartedly devoting himself to the cause for which Indranath had selected him. Under no circumstances, does Ela allow Atin to just follow the conventional path of life and she is happily willing to sacrifice her love for him. In other words, as Ela loves him so much, she is not ready to see Atin deviate from the mission that Indranath and his group sought to accomplish. While appreciating men being 'greater than women [since] … they have to prove their worth through endeavour [unlike] the women are equipped with the weapons and spells given nature [that] can be used to win [the] throne cheaply' (1104). She is very critical of those men who treat women as 'an easily available source of enjoyment' (1104); she also says that they were men who, with their valour and steadfast commitment to cause, also proved their 'greatness [though] … in the conventional sense they do not always get noticed' (1104). Inspired by Ela, Atin also speaks his mind. Being critical of the role of mothers-in-law in demeaning the newly-wed wife, he castigates those men who never raise a voice of protest for fear of upsetting their mothers; the sons actually harm their wives which is not, at all, acceptable to Atin.

> A man who cannot protect his wife, argued Atin, from such an abuser is not mature enough to marry. When he is mature enough to protect her, he goes to the other extreme of childlike dependence

> on his wife. When men lack manliness, women are diminished in stature and they bring the men down. As a result, in our countrymen, who have a mission, renounce woman; those cowards are afraid of them. (1105)

The bard minces no words to condemn the prevalent social system in which women were forced to become an appendage to men once they were married. Based on what he saw in most of the Bengali households, he hardly hesitates to sharply argue that married men acted under their mothers' dictations or their wives'; they hardly remained independent although Atin hints at exceptions. What is also brought to light is the widely believed perception that being married was a serious constraint because women tended to pull the men away from any other mission besides taking care of household responsibilities. As a devout believer in gender parity with the strong views that man–woman was an integral creation of nature, Rabindranath also firmly believed that, instead of being an impediment, men–women combinations were a source of tremendous strength. While castigating those men who decided to remain single as women were deterrent to the attainment of their goals, the bard thus argues his point through Atin by emphasising that 'in this country of cowards, you have vowed to remain single just in case a young soul is led astray by your womanly influence! The real man finds fulfilment with the strength of the true women—that is God's ruling, which flows in our bloodstream' (1105). Ela does not seem persuaded because she believes that it is most unfortunate that most men remain almost ignorant of this aspect given the social surroundings in which they are born and raised. There were, of course, men who always held contrarian views despite being hassled at every step. As a woman, she thus justifies the claim by saying that 'I have seen what is good in [men] and their potential for greatness. When I think of the country I think of them, they are my country' (1105). She fails to explain when these men were not welcome at home as they were involved in activities which were likely to cause trouble for other members of the family. That was most selfish of the other members of the family who failed to appreciate their contribution to the nationalist cause, which 'breaks [Ela's] heart [since] they had no place in their homes' (1105). There are three points that merit attention here: First, Ela is mesmerised by Atin's commitment to the nation along with other members of the group who had come together with the same vow. What is emphasised here is the unflinching devotion to the cause of the nation which brought the members of the group together under Indranath's stewardship. Second, the dialogue between Ela and Atin also establishes the argument that gender division was an anathema for amicable social existence of human beings as a well-knit collectivity. Men were as useful as their female counterparts given equal utility in society. Both Atin and Ela espoused the cause. Finally, it is also evident here that the campaign for national liberation remained handicapped so long as the gender chasm was allowed to survive which also confirms the bard's steadfast commitment to gender equality. By raising these issues, the poet introduces the readers to certain debilitating sociocultural features which were deterrent to gender equality; and, by seeking to devise the mode to do away with them, he sought to create a mindset, which was immune from these well-entrenched retrogressive values and mores.

Divided Self

Char Adhyay has many twists in the plot. This is not a story that unfolds seamlessly. As shown above, despite being in love with each other, Ela and Atin are debarred from thinking of getting married as this was contrary to the oath they had taken. Ela likes Atin and expresses so, and yet, does not force him to go for a nuptial bond. Ela is persuaded to believe that Atin has a bigger task to fulfil which would remain unaccomplished if he was confined to her. Ela's argument is very clear: Since Atin is meant to work for the nationalist goal he should not get bogged down to have a conventional life which Ela explains by saying that his 'wings would have been restless in the small world of my love, and my trifling offering would have seemed like dregs' (1106). Just to create conditions in which Atin is allowed to be free to devote himself to the cause for which he was chosen by his master, she further says, 'that's why I . . . give you up wholeheartedly to my country, so that, your abilities will not be restricted by lack of space.' (1106). Now, one witnesses a twist. Given his upbringing in a patriarchal milieu and also perhaps by nurturing patriarchal prejudices, Atin reacts violently. Expressing his disenchantment, he retorts:

> [W]ho are you to offer me to the country or to anything else? You could have offered the gift of your charm, your grace, your love—which are truly your own; call it what you will: serving or blessing. … In the glory of womanhood, you could have gifted the wealth of your heart; but you withdrew that and said that you bestowed me to the country. You can't do that, no one can. The country can't be passed from one hand to another. (1106)

Besides articulating that Atin is not free from the socially nurtured patriarchal bias, the poet also highlights the helplessness of a woman when she is subject to views which are far from what she meant. The situation is a vivid description of how an Indian male behaves once his female companion offers a counterargument to defend her point of view. This did not seem to be at variance with the prevalent sociocultural ethos. At a more subtle level, Atin is unable to comprehend the reasons for Ela's decision though he is confident of being loved by her. There is another critical point that is subtly made, namely, that the love for country is instinctive and cannot be generated. Hence, he charges Ela as 'a naïve woman' (1106) who is also disillusioned with the role that she is expected to play in the group. The dialogue between them brings out a fundamental idea that Rabindranath espouses in his novels—*Ghare Baire*, *Gora*, among others— that dealt with the nationalist struggle. In Ela, Rabindranath finds a voice, a powerful voice indeed, to identify the lacuna that revolutionary nationalism had despite having inspired many youths to even make the supreme sacrifice. By comparing a woman's love which was 'small, but the depth of it is unfathomable [and] it is not a cage' (1106) with the nationalist campaign at their behest, Ela characterises their idea of India as a country as nothing but 'a cage [in which her] own strength does not find expression their [and] it gets warped' (1106) because it was their construct which was highly patriarchal. As a result, 'when [she tries] to give expression to what is not genuinely [her] own, the madness of it shames [her, and] … nobody realises that [her] wings are clipped and [her] legs are shackled' (1106). This is one aspect of the argument; the other equally important aspect relates to the mechanical model of the revolutionary nationalists in which they were instructed to abide by the master's instruction; they were not allowed to think independently since disobedience to the master was tantamount to the betrayal to the cause which leads Ela to call every member of the group, puppets: they dance to the tune being played by someone else and in the making of the tune, they are denied any role. This was likely to be a source of discontent among those who selflessly devoted themselves to the nationalist cause. Here again, the poet expresses his strong views against such a harakiri venture since, as Ela argues,

> human puppets can't dance for long. Perhaps human nature can be changed but it takes time. It is a mistake to think that by destroying human nature and making puppets of human beings, the work would be easier. One must recognise the power of [the] human spirit. (1107)

What emerges is the bard's appreciation for the unshackled human spirit that can be chained, only with detrimental effects. What Amalya of *Ghare Baire* mentions when Bimala asks about Sandip's lifestyle is reiterated here. Sandip never allows Bimala to speak to any member of the group to sustain supreme control over the way the swadeshi campaign was organised. Similarly, when Binoy of *Gora* refuses to take food cooked by Lachhmia, the Christian cook, he undermines the human spirit simply to satisfy his false ego of being a true Brahmin. Ela too sees Atin in two contradictory selves: on the one hand, he is persuaded to believe in the finer human sentiments while, on the other, his being oath-bound leads him to challenge the same beliefs to honour his commitment to the goal that the group has pledged to achieve. It is very clearly articulated by the poet when Ela says that 'your imposed self believes what your inner self does not since [the former] has got [the latter] inducted in the chess of the organization' (1107). It is a perfect assessment of what Atin undergoes. His divided selves move from one choice to another and remain indecisive regarding what would give him happiness. At the same time, he is aware that there was no escape from the group. This shows that despite being persuaded by Ela, his commitment to the group's cause does not allow him to desert his colleagues. The dilemma is resolved when Atin finally makes up his mind to permanently leave Ela by saying that 'I am walking a road that is narrow like the edge of a knife, there isn't enough to walk together' (1108). Nonetheless, the suspicion that Atin forcibly opts for this choice is confirmed by the latter part of the novel: This shows that his concern for humanity does not seem to have faded completely. He is forced to opt for a choice that appears to him to be preferable as per the oath that he took to serve the nation. Justifying his act as appropriate under the circumstances, Atin draws on an analogy from the Mahabharata where Krishna 'asked Arjuna to do the duty of the brave in spite of it being distasteful' (1117). Being baptised in revolutionary nationalism, Atin is expected to say this. Nonetheless, Ela feels that by following this path, Atin seems to have failed to realise that bravery and humanism are not contradictory but complementary to each other. Those who were brave have remained so because they always fought for 'protecting the weak' (1117), argues Ela. She further elaborates her point by saying that

> he who fights the powerful … for the weak … contributes to the preservation of humanity. But I saw men of exceptional nature lose their humanity. No loss can be greater. Although I knew that they would laugh at me, or taunt me in anger. I told them that if we do as much wrong as the wrongdoers, it is defeat. Before we lose, before we die, we must show them that we are superior in our humanity, otherwise why are we fighting a battle that we are sure to lose? Some of them did see my point, but there were very few. (1117)

Atin appears to have been swayed because, after having had many interactions with Ela, he also understands that bravery is an espoused ideal so long as it is protective of humanity. But, for him, it is a no-win situation since he can neither be dissociated nor is equipped enough to achieve the goal by resorting to violence given the fact that he had

> learnt for sure that if we use force against the powerful in this unequal battle, we can't win. Illness is bad for everyone but fatal for the weak. Those who are in power can abandon humanity and continue by the use of force, but we who are in a weaker position can't do so. We shall be tainted, totally defeated, and then disappear into the darkness of disgrace. (1117)

It was a reality check for those combatting a superior coercive power with access to the most advanced weaponry and also a strong base for the governance that evolved at the behest of the British. It was surely a difficult task. What upsets Atin is the demeaning he has to face despite being ready to make the supreme sacrifice. Here the debate reaches another height. Being appreciative of the selfless sacrifice of youths as they are drawn to serve the motherland, Ela identifies it as strategically suicidal because they had to fight a well-organised state power. Under these circumstances, one's patriotism is not adequate to accomplish the goal—patriotism was an energy that needed to be harnessed, equipped and given direction to effectively combat the enemy. Mere concern for the country—which was also one of the ingredients of patriotism—might not be enough to reach one's destiny. For Atin's group, patriotism was a cloak to hide their weaknesses. Hence Atin admits that he is not what is usually defined as a patriot because

> there is something greater than patriotism [and] those who don't agree use patriotism only as a vehicle, like crossing a river on the back of the alligator. I see clearly that their lies, meanness, distrust of one another, intrigue for power and spying on others, will pull them under slime. I can't guard my honour and do anything worthwhile in this ugly hold, in the polluted air of lies. (1118)

Here Atin's dilemma is clear for he, being unable to steer the nationalist campaign in accordance with his priority, is captive of an organisation that hardly allows him to be independent. He realises that patriotism is reduced to being a vehicle for aggrandizing one's achievement and is illustrative of the vacuous nature of the claim. The limitations are ingrained in the concept since it was conceived without reference to reality—a serious constraint for the entire campaign that Indranath sought to steer to fulfil the revolutionary nationalist goal. Here, Rabindranath reiterates his powerful critique against the exclusionary and prejudicial nature of nationalism. Atin argues that in a socioculturally disparate India, it is, instead of cementing a bond among the diverse people, a deterrent. While elaborating his argument, he also argues strongly against nationalism as a mode of bringing people together. It is the bard's opinion that finds voice when Atin articulates his scathing critique of nationalism by saying that

> nationalists the world over are declaring with brute force the terribly lie that by destroying the soul of a country, the country can be saved. My protest against it churns in my mind. I could have said it loudly truthfully, and it would have been much more worthwhile and enduring that this convert, underground attempt the free the country. (1118)

We note here three significant points. Two of them are very straight while the third one is an implicit appreciation of the Gandhian campaign that appeared to have gripped the country because it had also captured the mass imagination. First, the views are a clear condemnation of nationalism which, by seeking to hegemonise identities, were simply inadequate to a socioculturally diverse India. So, keeping in mind that India was socioculturally disparate, nationalism, instead of being a cementing device, was likely to create a fissure among the Indians. Second, despite having realised the limitation of working from underground, Atin remains quiet as he is, he admits, not strong enough to express what he feels so strongly internally. He however does not want to be excused for this folly because he realises that the method they adopted is futile in awakening the population belonging to different sociocultural zones. Finally, here the poet admires the Gandhi-led nationalist campaign by contrasting his style of national awakening with that of the revolutionary nationalists. Despite not being persuaded by many of his arguments, as is well-known, Rabindranath found in the Gandhian battle for political freedom what he espoused in many of his creative writings, including the famous essays on nationalism (1916). According to the poet, it was Gandhi who, having realised that an effective nationalist campaign was possible only by bringing people together—something which was not possible within the conceptual framework of nationalism that sought to essentialise identities, an anathema in the Indian context. What is most tragic is Atin's realisation that it is not possible for him to leave, being oath-bound to remain with the group regardless of the consequences. Entrapped in a situation which is largely his own creation, Atin is caught in a maze, from which there is no escape. Although this point appears to be peripheral to the main argument, it is illustrative of the bard's disgust with revolutionary nationalism for being narrowly conceived and also heartfelt satisfaction with the Gandhian mode of anti-British campaign for being inclusive, as he openly said in many of his critical essays.

Unified Self

Char Adhyay stands out for multiple reasons. Besides being a fine literary work, the novel, drawn on the poet's basic conceptual premises on nationalism, is a powerful articulation of those premises which shaped the contemporary nationalist responses, contrary to the Gandhian non-violent struggle for political freedom. To be precise, Rabindranath strongly opposed the revolutionary nationalist variety that flourished in Bengal before the advent of the Gandhian non-violent mode of protest: Tagore did not approve of the espousal of ideas in support of violence and efforts towards undermining the finer human sentiments. Second, the novel is distinct in terms of many plot twists. As the aim was to show how humanism prevailed over other narrow ideational goals, Rabindranath devoted much of his attention to this aspect. Being a priest of universal humanism, this does not seem odd. Nonetheless, by reiterating the importance of the human self in the novel, he reinforced his own concern and also emphasised that the efforts towards dividing, if not sacrificing, humanity for narrow politico-ideological goals needed to be fiercely opposed as they struck at the foundational roots of humanity. Presumably because of this, the bard establishes the point by focusing on the dialectical interactions between Atin and Ela who hold contrary views on this issue. A careful reading of the dialogues reveals that despite being forceful in their arguments, both Atin and Ela appear to appreciate, that in the end, humanity prevails over politico-ideological preferences. As shown before, Ela happily gives up her love for Atin since she is oath-bound to remain celibate till their political goal remains unfulfilled. Ela is now a divided self who, despite having surrendered to her instinctive feelings, is deterred from responding to Atin's urge. This is the storyline till the third chapter. In the final chapter, Atin fails to carry out the order of the master to kill Ela which again confirms how humanism acts as a determinant of his decision, being prior to narrow ideational beliefs.

The novel ends with a poignant note privileging humanism over narrow and sectarian ideational belief championing the revolutionary national goal. The relationship that thrived on love between Ela and Atin is hardly constricted by their allegiance to revolutionary nationalist aims though they are reticent about it, given their oath to the master. In view of his undiluted commitment to universal humanism, the bard hardly wavers from clearly articulating his preference when, in order to be true to his faith, he brings Atin closer to Ela despite the harsh consequences not only from his colleagues but also from the administration for being fugitive with an ulterior motive of throwing out the British yolk. Despite his exterior self which appears to be devoid of human sentiments, Atin displays finer human sentiments which are evident at the end of the novel when he unhesitatingly declares his love for Ela; when she gave the flower bouquet to him in private, in the terrace, it was 'the real starting point in the relationship [which he failed to realise so far because his] education, intellect and reserve gradually sank into a fathomless self-oblivion' (1124). Here, there is a further twist in the plot. Given Ela's involvement in killing a woman since she recognises her while robbing the latter of her money, the former knows that she is likely to be caught. Having been informed of this, the leader, Indranath, orders Atin to kill her; he apprehends that on being tortured by the police, Ela would put the group in peril by disclosing everything she knows. As soon as Ela comes to know about this, she completely surrenders to Atin, conveying her genuine love for him: 'Antu [as she was fondly addressed by her], please kill me with your own hands and it would be a blessing. ... Don't hesitate, Antu I am yours, entirely yours even in death. Don't let soiled hands [of the police] touch me. Take me, I am yours' (1125). Being unable to carry out the order of Indranath, Atin requests Ela to leave the place to avoid being caught by the police; she forcefully declines his request, refusing to leave him alone. What prevails is the appreciation of human concern of one individual for the other and vice versa. *Char Adhyay* remains not just a simple Atin-Ela love story; it proves that humanity is the most important resource for human existence and commitment to ideational preferences seems to be fragile if contrary to the core principles of humanism.

Concluding Observations

The novel *Char Adhyay* does not appear to be as complex as *Chaturanga*; nonetheless, it also dwells on Tagore's own take on gender issues: first, it is a reiteration of the priorities that the poet clearly articulates in other novels, and second, it also suggests that Tagore put forwards a discourse on gender that is consistently argued and persuasively adumbrated. Unlike *Ghare Baire* and *Chaturanga*, *Char Adhyay* stands out because here Tagore appears to develop a format of argument which is less complex or far more clearly stated.

Char Adhyay is a continuity of the viewpoints that Tagore developed in *Chaturanga*, where he dealt with Damini's suppressed sexuality, Jagmohan's compassion, Sachhis' quest for truth and Sribilash's loyalty.

They were the main protagonists of his concern for humanity which the bard referred to in *Char Adhyay* but dealt with in its entirety in *Chaturanga*. In *Char Adhyay*, he delved into the peculiar texture of human behaviour that could hardly be moulded in a specific fashion. Being devoted to the nationalist cause, Ela, for instance, restrains herself when Atin proposes to her; the radical behaviour manifestation of Ela at the end of the novel brings forth a nuanced picture since Ela, being deeply in love with Atin, is willing to go ahead which is not an unusual human feeling; however, the situation is reversed since Atin is then not keen to accept Ela as his wife. The story has not been narrated in black-and-white terms; instead, it has epitomised the complex tensions that human beings underwent in a real situation; Tagore was not free from this as the characters Atin and Ela show how human decisions are made; and to understand them in their peculiar socioeconomic contexts, one needed to be receptive to the influences which were neither fixed nor static, but were outcomes of an equally complex interplay of social, economic and political processes. What is striking in Tagore's creative writings is the fact that despite being an author who remained sensitive to the milieu in which he was born and raised, his messages were transcendental in appeal because what he sought to convey continues to be relevant even after the lapse of more than a century.

By following the conventional narrative style, *Char Adhyay* does not seem to be very different from Rabindranath's other novels or those written by his contemporaries. But, content-wise, *Char Adhyay* stands out because of the blueprint that it provides for humanity with reference to novel sociocultural messages and politico-ideological visions. Ela is an apostle of gender equality while Atin represents concerns for change regardless of adverse political and social consequences. Indranath of *Char Adhyay* and Lilananda of *Chaturanga* are voices of opposition resisting attempts at undermining their hegemony.

While *Char Adhyay* is primarily a political novel where the man–woman relationship is tangential to the main narrative *Chaturanga* is, for instance, clearly a social novel since it focuses distinctly on human relations in their manifold manifestations with reference to how they evolve in the prevalent sociocultural milieu. Presumably, because the bard aimed to study the complex interpersonal relations, he might have avoided referring to the specific political context linked with the British rule though the unconditional submission of two English-educated atheists, Sachhis and Sribilash, to Lilananda is indicative of the frustrations of Bengali educated youths under the discriminatory foreign administration. There is also the argument in defence of *Chaturanga* being a nationalist voice as well which is justified by drawing on the claim that Jagmohan and not the British teacher, Wilkins, introduced Sachhis to the libertarian ideas of humanism. This argument is forcefully made by the bard to show that intellectually Indians were no less than their British counterparts given the fact that service to humanity figured prominently in the ancient Hindu texts, especially the Vedas and Upanishads. *Chaturanga* and *Char Adhyay* are thus not just stories, but an unfolding of the bard's ideational preferences that evolved dialectically by challenging the mindset sustaining established views and practices.

References

Bose, Suddhasatva. 1979. *Rabindranather Char Adhyay* (Bangla). Calcutta: Bharati Publications.

Tagore, Rabindranath. 1908. *Swadeshi Samaj*. Kolkata: Visva-Bharati.

———. 1950. *Char Adhyay* (Four Chapters). Kolkata: Visva-Bharati.

———. 2009 (rpt). *Char Adhyay* (Bangla) Kolkata: Visva-Bharati Granthan Bhivag.

———. 2009 (rpt). *Char Adhyay* (Four Chapters). Kolkata: Visva-Bharati.

———. 1418 (Bangabda). *Char Adhyay*. Kolkata: Visva Bharati, Kolkata.

———. 2011. *Four Chapters* (English Translation of *Char Adhyay*). New Delhi: Penguin Books.

Part II

HUMANISING HUMANITY

Rabindranath was humanist par excellence. In his 1904 tract, *Swadeshi Samaj*, the poet strongly argued that mere political freedom was futile unless it was complemented by human emancipation from hunger, caste prejudices and sociocultural shackles crippling human beings. Hence, he insisted on exhibiting concern for others, especially for those hapless individuals who remained at the lower rung of society. It was possible, he argued further, by being compassionate towards one another despite the sociocultural distance. It is only by adopting the motto of serving others regardless of their sociocultural locations that one can identify with the objective that the bard had in mind. Besides upholding this motto, the bard also emphasised the creation of an independent mindset to understand sociocultural reality. This was a scathing critique of blind imitation by the Bengali elite of the English way of life; the aforesaid class considered it a passport to the British cultural world. In very firm language, the poet argued that those who felt so lived in a fool's paradise because imitation would take them nowhere; instead, they would become a laughing stock of the British. Even if one tried one's level best, one failed to become an Englishman because of the contextual differences in which an Indian and a Britisher were raised. On the other hand, there is a fundamental point that the poet articulated by condemning those who always upheld Western discourse as the most persuasive mode of conceptualising humanity: Tagore attributed this attitude to ignorance about intellectual discourses that had emerged in India since time immemorial. Here, Rabindranath referred to the 4 Vedas and 18 Vedantic texts or Upanishads. In fact, the Upanishads had helped him get to the bottom of most of the issues responsible for India's sociocultural decay.

According to him, humanity and civilisation ought to develop in tandem; if it was otherwise, the consequences were both devastating and harmful to the growth of human civilisation. This was evident in his admission that his admiration for the British civilisation waned as 'imperialist greed [brought about] so ugly a transformation in the character of so great a race' (Tagore 1996: 725). The consequences were disastrous because, as the poet further argued,

> the demon of barbarity has given up all pretence and has emerged with unconcealed fangs, ready to tear up humanity in an orgy of

> devastation. From one end of the world to the other the poisonous fumes of hatred darken the atmosphere. The spirit of violence which perhaps lay dormant in the psychology of the West, has at last roused itself and desecrates the spirit of man. (726)

Being critical of the West for destroying the foundational beliefs on which humanity rested, the bard minced no words in condemning the colonial powers for being so brutal to mankind simply because they remained indifferent to their responsibility towards humanity. Perennially optimist, he was hardly dissuaded in believing that

> like the sun, humanity can be clouded, but never extinguished [and] … to continue to ignore the claims of humanity is a sure process of suicide; it was a temporary phase in human history for the spirit of the age will be incarnated in a complete human truth and the meeting of men will be translated into the Unity of Man. (523)

There is no denying that the bard was a great priest of human emancipation for whom the idea of coming together regardless of sociocultural differences was of utmost importance. By focusing on *Gora* (1910), *Chaturanga* (1916), 'Balai' (1928) and *Muktadhara* (1922), this part is an elaboration of Rabindranath's approach to humanity and also his distinct articulation of what he meant by human emancipation: This is the one common underlying thread that links these creative texts. Gora of the novel *Gora* realised that humanity was prior to anything else when he was told that he was born to Irish parents; being a hardcore Hindu, he failed to understand why Anandamoyi never dismissed Laachmia despite being a Christian. As the novel progresses, one comes across many instances which show that Rabindranath did not undermine humanity for narrow religious considerations. The same idea reverberated in Sachhis when he happily married a widow, Damini, notwithstanding severe opposition from his peers: This further confirms that this novel, too, was based on pointing out the importance of human values, such as love and care, in cementing a bond between two human beings. 'Balai' and *Muktadhara* belong to a different genre since they dealt with the bonhomie between human beings and ecology; here too, the mental agony of Balai's aunt when the cotton tree that Balai planted was cut represented the same human sentiments of love and care—sentiments that established a bond between Balai and his aunt. Similarly, Dhananjay Bairagi in *Muktadhara* represented a voice that combined concern for humanity with his powerful critique of efforts that destroyed ecological balance by erecting a dam to stop the flow of water from the mountain springs to the neighbouring village, Shiv Tarai. A perusal of Bairagi's role brings forth the bard's condemnation of the ruthlessness of Ranjit, the king of Uttarakut; by depriving the villagers of Shiv Tarai, the king subjected them to immeasurable miseries. Thus what is reiterated here is the bard's unique conceptualisation of human emancipation and humanity on the whole.

Reference

Tagore, Rabindranath. 1996. 'Crisis in Civilization', in *The English Writings of Rabindranath Tagore*, ed. Sisir Kumar Das, Vol. 3. New Delhi: Sahitya Akademi.

3

Rabindranath Tagore's *Gora*

Rearticulating Nationalist-Humanist Discourses

A devout priest of universal humanism, Rabindranath Tagore was governed by three fundamental principles while articulating his views. First, being a disbeliever of hierarchical human existence, Tagore strongly argued for the eradication of divisions among human beings on any axis. Reverberating the idea that the renowned French philosopher Jacques Rousseau offered by suggesting that despite being free, man is everywhere in chains, he was persuaded to hold an identical view. Human beings are chained due to caste restrictions, ingrained prejudicial assessment of fellow human beings and also sustained attempts to subjugate the poor by the rich. Instead of creating circumstances for freedom, the Indian society generates conditions for unfreedom. Second, the chain was so strong, as Tagore argued, that it appeared to be difficult for the people to break it. This suggests that there were hardly any ways and means to develop circumstances in which human beings were allowed to enjoy freedom in its true sense. According to Tagore, it was surprising that while the Upanishads unambiguously highlight human freedom, there were many other conceptual texts justifying artificial segregation of one set of people from another, either due to religion or caste or any other segregating criteria. Third, a creative thinker who also gave a clarion call for breaking the chains, Rabindranath also inspired the victims to raise their voices against oppression and exploitation which a socioculturally degenerate society was likely to give birth to. Implicit here is the concern that Tagore categorically expressed to argue that a degenerated society was not naturally born but was constructed by a select few for fulfilling their partisan goals. Such a society was temporary, and human beings were equipped to start afresh by dint of their sincerity, honesty and truthfulness. His goal was to lay the foundation of a new era in which cardinal human values like care, concern and empathy were privileged over anything else. Selfishness was thus an anathema in Tagore's conceptual universe. By arguing strongly against the mental derailment of the colonised, the bard devoted his energy to create a universe in accordance with his ideological preferences.

One of the distinct features of Tagore's distinct sociocultural ideas was that, despite being emotionally charged with Upanishadic ideas, he was also sensitive to Western discourses. What was critical here was his upbringing in a cosmopolitan family in which Hindu ideational values were as significant as those from Islam and Christianity. He was a product of an age in which the search for indigenous roots was complemented by exposure to the British mode of conceptualising humanity. Instead of completely surrendering to Enlightenment philosophy, by paying adequate attention to the Upanishadic and Sufi traditions, Tagore evolved a new mode of thinking which was neither completely derivative nor exactly indigenous but was a creative blend of multiple politico-ideological priorities. It is thus safe to argue that there are many conceptual elements, which constituted what is accepted as the sociopolitical thoughts of Rabindranath Tagore.

One should also comment on the medium in which he spread his unique ideas. Tagore is generally identified as a poet par excellence which is perfect, but not a complete description of what he was. Based on an analytical dissection of ideas that he put across through his creative writings and critical essays, it appears that Tagore was perhaps one of the most creative thinkers of his generation. There was always an organic link between his novels, plays, dance dramas, poems and songs with what he maintained in his critical essays on specific sociocultural issues. In other words, one hardly misses the connection that one finds between his critical essays and creative writings.

There is one final point that needs attention before one explicates specific novels. Situated in the contemporary socioeconomic and political contexts, the novels are just a persuasive statement on a particular theme that he chose to elaborate on. Tagore's creative texts were not just written for pleasure reading: they were directed to put forward a socioculturally relevant point of view. In other words, a careful reading of his novels, short stories, dance dramas, etc., shows that each of them was impregnated with those ideas that the poet always espoused for pursuing his specific politico-ideological views. Not a nationalist activist like Gandhi and his colleagues, but an opinion-maker, Rabindranath represented a specific way of thinking which was, he felt strongly, complementary to the struggle that the mainstream Congress activists had launched. Because he believed that the political remained integrally connected with the social, divorcing them was conceptually myopic and practically debilitating. This was perhaps the main reason why the principal protagonists in his creative texts were divided into two incompatible groups championing contrasting views. The model of pursuing an argument corresponds with that of the Bhagavat Gita where Krishna and Arjuna represented two different modes of thinking: one was unwilling to take part in the war as it led to the killing of near ones while the other person, Krishna, was engaged in providing logical justification of Arjuna's participation in the Kurukshetra War since it was needed to establish dharmic justice. While making his point, Tagore followed the methodology, though a little differently, because his object was to do away with those noxious relics of antiquity. To him, caste was thus strongly criticised: not only did it divide humanity but it also allowed exploitation to continue; similarly, his scathing critique of anti-Muslim sentiments which caused a permanent fissure between Hindus and Muslims was also derivative of his voice against artificially created social schisms.

This chapter also makes a very specific point given the fact that each creative text is linked with his concern for universal humanism. For instance, the novel, *Rajarshi* (1886) dwells on non-violence which the poet highlighted, exemplified through the determination of the ruler of Tripura, Govindamanikya. The novel revolves around this point along with other peripheral concerns such as the intricate relations between husband and wife, king and priest or brothers; while strongly arguing against violence manifest in the animal sacrifice before the family deity, the bard also drew on the subtle changes in relations within the palace and outside it that this decision brought about. In a similar vein, *Ghare Baire* (1916) epitomised Tagore's scathing critique of the Swadeshi Movement (1905–1908) though it focused equally on the interpersonal relationship involving Sandip, Nikhilesh, Bimala and Amulya, among others. It was a powerful political treatise since it dealt with the nature of a political campaign that was organised to revoke the first partition of Bengal of 1905; it was also an attempt to articulate gender justice which was manifested when Nikhilesh created an ambience in which Bimala had an independent voice. One should not forget here the disenchantment that Bimala experienced when she found an incongruity between what Sandip said in public and what he practised in private. Rabindranath's creative texts are full of ideas which may appear peripheral though they contribute to the wider argument that he offered.

By keeping in mind the broader points made earlier, this chapter focuses on *Gora* (1910), which was a powerful sociocultural commentary on human relations that engulfed Bengal. This is a novel that revolves around an individual, Gora, and the novelist dealt with some of the most contentious issues that appeared to have shaped human relations in contemporary Bengal. The novel is largely a narrative though, on occasion, it becomes dialogical to establish a point out of the discussion when two contrasting points receive equal attention. Like many of his novels, Gora is about the definite understanding of social relations and how they are critical in articulating human behaviour. It is therefore a novel that does not seem to be very different in terms of the basic texture of other novels, except perhaps that aspect of human relations which are easily visible in day-to-day interactions. When Gora visited villages, he understood how caste segregation functioned and how the incongruous social relations between Hindus and Muslims in Bengal villages shaped human behaviour in their day-to-day interaction with one another. This was a revelation to him. So, the narrative moves around two axes It was about how an individual reacted to the prevalent sociocultural scene and contemporary political movements; it was also a comment, on how interpersonal relations were guided by both individual and collective prejudices.

Gora: Debate, Humanism and Freedom

Gora is about humanism and freedom in the context of the first decade of the 20th century when these ideas were subject to minute scrutiny because of the radical sociopolitical transformation following the consolidation, primarily, of sectarian identities: Hindus were mobilised as Hindus while their Muslim counterparts resorted to Islam as a cementing tool. Historically speaking, the success of the Congress nationalists in revoking the first partition of Bengal was critical to the increasing importance of identity politics. Without Muslims being part of the campaign, the idea gained ground that they no longer were important in so far as the nationalist mobilisation was concerned. It was a failure on the part of the Congress, as history demonstrates, to realise that the Muslim alienation was the outcome of coercive tactics in which the Hindu mobilisers indulged. *Ghare Baire* is illustrative here. With the foundation of the Muslim League in 1906, the Muslims of Bengal had an institutional platform to voice their views and grievances against the administration. A new era was ushered in when Congress no longer remained the only political mouthpiece for the colonised. Along with this, newer ideas gained momentum, which subjected the Congress strategies to severe scrutiny. It is also to be remembered that, unlike the Muslim League, the Congress was never a communal party, at least in theory, since it was open to all irrespective of religion. Nonetheless, the failure of Congress to erase its communal tinge did not allow it to become a platform for all. Even Gandhi was challenged by M.A. Jinnah and B.R. Ambedkar in the second Round Table Conference in 1932 when he claimed that he represented the country as a whole. Here, the purpose is not to dwell on historical currents but to lay out the context in which Rabindranath penned *Gora* which was published in 1910.

That Gourmohan or Gora, as he was fondly called, was favourably disposed towards his Hindu identity was evident when he happily agreed to become the president of the Hindu welfare society. He stood out in the crowd because of his physical build: his eyes were 'small but sharp, their arrowlike gaze seemingly fixed on a remote, invisible target, yet capable of turning instantaneously, like lightning, to strike an object close at hand' (Tagore 2011: 293). This is how he was introduced by Tagore in the novel. Since the method in which the poet articulated his views was dialectically constructed, he needed Binoy, a close friend of Gora, who generally countered the latter to establish a point of view. At the beginning of the novel, it was evident when Gora appreciated his friend, Abinash's denigration of the Brahmos as 'a sign of ... good health' (293). Being in absolute agreement with Abinash, Gora expressed his annoyance when Binoy did not find it so striking:

> [Y]ou are not only prejudiced, but have also lost reason. It's not natural for members of a society to adopt a calm, rational stance towards a group of people who violate social restrictions to act in a contrary fashion in all matters. Society is bound to misunderstand them, ascribing perverse motives to their straightforward actions, viewing as evil whatever they regard as good. So, it should be. It is one of the penalties to be paid for deliberately breaking social laws. (294)

Gora, being a hardcore Hindu, was likely to criticise the Brahmos because the Brahmo sect evolved as a voice of protest against Hindu orthodoxy. When he was criticised by his friend Binoy that his discomfort was neither logical nor expected, he retorted to defend his point of view that 'those who fancy the heroism of becoming Brahmos must experience this pain of being ... denounced by the Brahmins' (294). So, for Gora, the criticism against those clinging to the Brahmo faith was obvious because it was a deliberate attempt to divide Hindus on the basis of preferences which did not correspond with the core values of Hinduism. It was thus a vacuous protest, argued Gora. The debate about how Brahmos viewed women continued; according to Gora, the respect that a man accorded to a woman was just to fulfil partisan desires. Binoy challenged this by referring to the fact that the Hindu shastras also held women in high esteem: they were worshipped 'for they light up our homes'. Gora was not persuaded since he believed that the word 'worship' was misleading for 'the kind of respect English culture accords to women when they light up the hearts of women' hardly corresponded with what it meant in the real sense of the term. Gora reinforced his point by elaborating on it:

> in the English scriptures, all that hyperbole about women conceals one inner motive, sexual desire. We should worship the female sex at the mother's chamber and the virtuous housewife's holy shrine; when women are worshipped elsewhere, such adoration conceals an element of degradation. (295)

Based on his strong dislike of the Brahmos for being deviant from the fundamental ethos of Hinduism, Gora developed a strong critique of Brahmoism which did not seem to be ahistorical as the campaign led by Radhakanto Deb at the behest of the Dharma Sabha assumed massive proportions when the Brahmo Samaj emerged on the scene in the 1840s with initiatives from Rammohun Roy and Rabindranath's grandfather, Dwarkanath. Aghast at the initiatives that the orthodox Brahmins undertook to justify inhuman practices, including sati, for instance, the Brahmo Samaj was a beacon of light which brought many disgruntled Hindus closer to the proponents. For obvious reasons, it was strongly criticised by those who dismissed the initiative as a sinister design against Hinduism. Being a devout Hindu, it was natural for Gora to vehemently oppose the Brahmo endeavour. Second, as the discussion between Gora and Binoy shows, the former was not even inclined to accept the Brahmo argument for feminist concern for freedom because it was a shield to hide the real objective of those who were championing women's liberation. According to Gora, it was a design to fulfil one's sexual desire which was defended in the English cultural voice by characterising women as sources of 'light', which figuratively means knowledge. Here too, Gora's target of attack were the Brahmos for they allowed women to come out of purdah to freely mix with their male counterparts. Rabindranath had shown this in his 1916 novel *Ghare Baire* by taking Bimala out of the conventional household restrictions in which she had been, so far, placed. As shown in Chapter 1, Bimala was a liberated woman though she later repented when Nikhilesh, her husband, was severely injured: she attributed his predicament to her deviation from the well-established cultural norms. Nonetheless, by raising the same point in the debate between Gora and Binoy, the poet recounted those conceptual beliefs which he held so dear to his heart. Thus, the poet did not extend unqualified support to gender parity though he endeavoured to do so in many of his creative texts; this confirms that he was too constrained by the prevalent social limits, though by raising his voice for women's freedom, he evolved a new genre of thinking in favour of his politico-ideological beliefs. As evident in the available literary sources, the issue of gender gained importance in the sociopolitical discourses, and it was Rabindranath who hardly wavered in putting across the views despite not being compatible with the dominant mode of thinking in then Bengal.

The aforesaid idea received further attention when Binoy, not convinced by Gora's argument of dismissal of the English cultural ethos on this issue, drew the latter's attention with the point that the indigenous cultural values were equally responsible for disallowing women to flourish as an independent individual. Given the fact that women were as important to society as men, it was unfair to develop different kinds of criteria to judge them. So, the argument for the complete renunciation of women did not seem to be normal. While making this point to counter Gora, Binoy thus argued that

> if the claims of English are false, so is our excessive insistence on renouncing the lure of women and gold (*kamini and kanchan*). To protect human nature from easy distractions some people poeticize the beautiful aspects of love, ignoring its darker side, while others exaggerate the evils of love, prescribing renunciation. These are merely two different modes adopted by two kinds of people. If you blame one, you cannot absolve the other. (295–296)

Being persuaded to believe that women and men were integral to human society, Rabindranath sharpened his criticism of orthodox Hinduism further by highlighting the discriminatory nature of the argument to deny the former their legitimate rights as human beings. The poet held the view that Binoy articulated while responding to Gora's viewpoints: it was fair to accept man and woman as essential to constitute a healthy human society. Neither of the extreme views was fair since it was not adequate to conceptualise the role of men and women as indispensable partners in building a well-knit social unit. For Rabindranath, both these views needed to be strongly criticised since they were both misleading and confusing.

Caste and Religious Prejudices

One of the perhaps most complex novels, given many plots and subplots and many contrarian ideas, *Gora* evolves in many layers to articulate a language of differences, if not protest, which one may not find in any other of Rabindranath's novels. Rabindranath's purpose was to highlight how prejudicial Hindu views and practices created a permanent fissure not only between Hindus and other religious groups but also between castes among the Hindus. A hardcore Hindu, Gora was thus rigid in his views and also the practices that he found integrally connected with his claim of being a pure Hindu. That Gora became so obstinate in nurturing his values was evident when he refused to eat in his mother's room simply because she employed a Christian maid. To her utter surprise, Gora's mother was stunned by his refusal because it was the same maid who had nursed Gora when he was a baby. It was made clear by his mother when she said that the maid, Lachhmia

> has always fed you by hand, reared you since you were a child. Until just the other day, you would not relish your food without the sweet dish made by her. I'll never forget the way Lachhmia nursed you back when you contracted smallpox as a child. (297)

Gora remained unperturbed and expressed his annoyance to his mother by saying that neither he nor Binoy 'can have meals in [his mother's] room until [she] dismiss[es] Lachhmia, that Khristani [Christian] maid of [hers]' (297). It was an expression of hatred against an individual simply because she belonged to a different religion. Anandamoyi was clueless as to why Gora had become a 'fanatic unlike Binu [Binoy] who was never reluctant to have food cooked by Lachhmia'. While scolding Gora, she also referred to the fact that he might have got this from her 'equally fanatical husband who, [in order to maintain] purity, refuses to eat anything but self-cooked food' (297). Here, Tagore built his critique against Hindu orthodoxy: his annoyance was expressed when Anandamoyi conveyed her disapproval of Gora's avoidance of having food in a room which had been cleaned by a Christian maid. This was a powerful statement against the narrow-mindedness of Gora which also confirmed that by being so protective of his orthodox identity, he was ready, even, to devalue humanity which caught her by surprise. Also, Hindu orthodoxy was not universally adored was evident by the opposition of Anandamoyi who was sandwiched between Gora, her son, and her husband because of the views they held to justify artificially created, segmented human existence. It was a very difficult situation for Anandamoyi to negotiate both as a mother, on the one hand, and as a wife, on the other. Nonetheless, by raising her voice against an illogical standpoint, she echoed the views that the poet held assiduously to combat orthodox Hinduism. Being intrigued by the sudden fascination for orthodoxy by her husband and son, Anandamoyi expressed her opinion even to their annoyance. She was clueless to fathom how her husband became so obstinate about his Hindu-Brahmin identity since when he worked in a British firm not only did, he happily dine with the British officers but was also reported to have appreciated the taste of cooked 'forbidden meat, like beef and pork'. While being perplexed at this change, she thus stated that 'now, in old age, having relinquished his job and acquired heaps of money, he has suddenly done an about-face, becoming very fastidious about purity' (298). Her sense of mental agony was manifested when she also mentioned that being persuaded by her husband, she had rejected those values which were superstitious and which she was unable to appreciate anymore since they 'cannot be retrieved at anyone's bidding' (298). Nonetheless, her motherly care for Gora prevailed over her logical mind when she expressed that 'never mind if you don't let me feed you in my room, but at least I get to see you in the evenings, and for me that's enough' (298). She also firmly conveyed that despite their reluctance to eat food prepared by a Christian, she 'will accept water from Lachhmia' (299). Perhaps, this was a voice of protest against religious orthodoxy which seemed unusual to her since she abjured orthodox beliefs only with the support that her husband extended in the earlier part of her life. Now, she was flabbergasted when she found that her son, Gora, was also following the same path. The poet boldly presented her as a person with strong views against superstitions. On the one hand, Anandamoyi was an epitome of a wave that flourished in Bengal, especially at the behest of the members of the Brahmo Samaj in opposition to the Dharma Sabha holding superstitious beliefs as integral to one's Hindu identity. On the other, by empowering Anandamoyi, Rabindranath also put forward his views on gender parity. Gora's mother was a voice that articulated the view that women were an independent agency and were capable of asserting themselves whenever it was required. This idea was reverberated in other female protagonists in novels like Bimala in *Ghare Baire*, Kumudini in *Jogajog*, Damini in *Chaturanga* or Prakriti in the dance drama, *Chandalika*.

The dialogue between Gora and his mother also reveals that despite being vocal, the female characters in Rabindranath's creative texts failed to assert themselves on occasions to the extent they should have, which proves that they were constrained by rigid sociocultural values. Given his unflinching commitment to Hinduism, Gora was not even willing to go beyond the surface of the argument that his mother made while being critical of her son. Here, Gora's friend, Binoy's, observation is worthwhile to understand this aspect of the poet's concern. While not being persuaded by Gora's complete dismissal of her mother's views, he thus highlighted the point by saying that

> because you [Gora] never look closely at anything in this world, you dismiss as fanciful whatever escapes your notice. But I tell you I have often observed that [your mother] seems to nurse a certain anxiety about something, as if there is something amiss that she can't put right, which causes some hidden pain in her domestic life. (299)

Here, the poet reinforced how the woman's voice was always suppressed due to gender discrimination, being practised over centuries, as if they were integral to social stability. This is evident in Binoy's endeavour to draw Gora's attention to an area of human behaviour which escaped his notice because of his obstinacy to look beyond what was known to him. Here, the poet, in a very poignant manner, articulated the pain that Anandamoyi was undergoing simply because she was emotionally close to them and it was thus not possible for her to completely ignore them. Nonetheless, by standing behind Lachhmia, she fulfilled two of her sociocultural objectives: on the one hand, she, being opposed to Gora's hatred for Lachhmia for being a Christian, challenged the segregation of humanity based on religious identity. This point was further emphasised when she, on the other, ventilated what she felt when, as Gora's mother, she was not allowed to express her strongly held views to maintain domestic peace. In other words, as a mother, she was helpless though she held the view that what Gora and her husband were doing was superstitious and detrimental to sociocultural transformation.

One of the important issues that the poet raised at the beginning of the novel was his idea of India or Bharatvarsha. For Binoy, the idea did not entail a mere geographical tract, but a platform for the co-existence of human beings regardless of their religious and social identity though it was never stated so clearly by him presumably because of the sociocultural context in which they were not likely to be appreciated. The issue was raised in his conversation with Gora with a query whether the 'Bharatvarsha that we know is real or not' (301) to which Gora replied that in his perception, 'Bharatvarsha is like the ships' captain who constantly bears in mind the port at the other end of the sea, whether he is feasting or revelling, at work or at rest' (301). What is evident here is uncertainty because of the British rule which was a deterrent to what Gora felt was adequate for creating an India of his choice. Aghast at the Bengali middle class for having accepted the British rule as a panacea, Gora was anguished for valid reasons. According to him, the appreciation for British rule was tantamount to mental servility which needed to be combatted to establish a Bharatvarsha which was meant to fulfil the sociocultural goals of Hinduism. The colonised were caught between the false honour bestowed on them by the rulers and the real happiness that one derived from one's labour. So, for Gora, Bharatvarsha was both a will to work for the betterment of humanity and also to build and strengthen this zeal by asserting their capability. Once that was accomplished, the captain would successfully navigate the ship towards the port of his preference. Hence, in his youthful exuberance to identify the real India, he thus exhorted that

> there is a real Bharatvarsha—a complete India. Unless we establish ourselves there, we can't absorb its true living essence into our minds

> and hearts. Therefore, I say, forgetting all else, discarding book-learning, the lure of prestige, and the temptation of odd profits, we must set sail for that very port, whether we drown or perish. (302)

This is one aspect of the idea of India that Rabindranath espoused since the publication of his seminal text *Swadeshi Samaj* in 1904. *Ghare Baire* was illustrative of this concern when Nikhilesh strongly argued for self-reliance as essential for India's liberation, which was not just political freedom but also entailed human emancipation from socioculturally constructed values and segmenting one section of the population from another. Here, the poet was very caustic in his remarks, given the unconditional surrender of the educated section of the Indians to the Britishers for mere material gain which was very sarcastically explained by Gora when he said that, 'even if the god of wealth, Kuber himself, were to offer the [colonised Indians] a boon, they probably wouldn't dare to ask for anything beyond the gilt badge sported by a governor's peon' (302). Gora felt that this was a matter of shame which did not rattle the colonised Indians ever presumably because that ensured a peaceful and trouble-free life. Under these circumstances, what was required to be done was to generate concern for one's country which lost her independent sociocultural identity presumably because of the intellectual servility of those who unconditionally supported the rulers even if that resulted in their self-degradation. So, the sole task was, according to Gora,

> to express unhesitating, undoubted, complete respect for everything swadeshi, to generate the same respect in the hearts of the unpatriotic. Ashamed of our country for so long, we have weakened ourselves with the poison of slavery. If each of us opposes this by personal example, we can claim a space for future work. Anything we attempt now proves to be a mere imitation, learnt from the schoolbooks of history. Can we truly devote ourselves wholeheartedly to such false pursuits? They would only degrade us. (303)

Besides showing his concern for his motherland, Gora was equally interested in exploring the ancient Hindu texts which, he always considered, were repositories of wisdom. Not bringing them to the public domain he thought was an extension of the colonisers' conspiracy to not allow the Indians to know their intellectual heritage and also to champion the Western intellectual discourse as the only available source of knowledge and wisdom. In order to fulfil his heartfelt desire, he employed a Sanskrit expert, Harachandra Vidyabagish, who introduced him to the Vedantic texts that produced 'such sharpness and breadth of intellect [that] was beyond [Gora's] imagination' (305). Furthermore, from Vidyabagish, he also learnt patience and the art of being provoked unnecessarily. He was fortunate to have had Vidyabagish as his teacher who was, as per Gora, 'so calm and patient, so forgiving and serene' (305). Here, one is reminded that Debendranath followed the same path: a teacher, Ramchandra Vidyabagish, was appointed to clarify the inner sense of the Upanishadic hymns: this, he enjoyed because it allowed him to get to the sources of indigenous knowledge. Rabindranath may have drawn on this when he created the character, Harachandra Vidyabagish, as a teacher for Gora. The parallel is very striking since following his exposure to the Vedantic texts, Gora followed in the same footsteps that the poet's father had undertaken. After having had the opportunity to comprehend the ideas in the Vedantic texts in their original version, Gora also realised that Hinduism contained many critical ideas which were useful for service to humanity. It was useful for him to denounce attempts by the foreigners to denigrate Hinduism though he was vehemently opposed to the so-called shastra-driven superstitions as they were sources of distortions in the Hindus' perception of the holy texts. His incense was manifested when he countered the allegations of the foreign authors against Hinduism which were defined as 'nothing but a compilation of inhuman practices' (306). Being vocal in his criticism, he thus began a column in a leading English daily against 'the foreigners' contempt for [the] Hindu community [because] it seemed to make him like a goad' (306). Based on his understanding of the Hindu scriptures, especially the Vedantic texts, he was not confident to logically defend his contention that Hinduism was based on high moral ideals which were nearly oblivious due to the Hindus' lackadaisical attitude to their rich intellectual past. As an intellectual counter to the argument that the Christian missionaries offered to defame Hinduism, he thus wrote a book, entitled *Hindooism* [sic], in which he declared that

> we shall not allow our country to be placed in the dock in foreign court and judged like a criminal by a foreign law! We shall earn neither shame nor glory in judging ourselves minutely by British ideals. We shall not feel ashamed in the least, either inwardly or before others, of the rituals, beliefs, scriptures and customs of our birthplace. We shall shield our country and ourselves from humiliation, boldly and proudly accepting all that our nation has to offer. (306)

Here, one notices a very subtle blending of Gora's nationalistic sentiments for the motherland with his concern for the foundational ideas of Hinduism. The poet seems to have carried forward the ideas that he clearly articulated through Sandip of *Ghare Baire*—who deployed typical Hindu imageries and ideas to mobilise support for the swadeshi campaign. Similarly, Gora, being a devout Hindu, had no qualms in identifying himself as a true Hindu who was also trained properly to understand the kernel of the Hindu shastras. Implicit here was also his belief that unless one was proud of one's sociocultural and intellectual heritage, one could never be well-equipped to serve the motherland. So, the poet's devotion to Hinduism reinforced, in turn, Gora's loyalty to Hinduism as it provided him with a specific religious identity; it was an identity which was drawn on very useful sources of knowledge which remained peripheral due to the colonisers' endeavour to stifle the indigenous voice. It was also a reiteration of the poet's faith in the Hindu intellectual past that helped him counter the deliberate design of a section of the Indians to distort the religious texts for their partisan gains. It was also an attempt to highlight the claim that the nationalist concern for the motherland remained handicapped unless one was confident of its sociocultural and intellectual basis. Here, Rabindranath reiterated that without being aware of one's roots, under no circumstances, could one be persuaded to be ready to sacrifice for one's country. One perceives a wave of thoughts which finally led to the consolidation of the Brahmo Samaj at Rabindranath's behest. As is argued earlier, while Dwarkanath and Debendranath did not categorically express their views against the British authority, Rabindranath was, at times, very nationalistic in his views and he also abjured the Knighthood in protest against the 1919 Jallianwala Bagh massacre. Gora was a symbol of this creative amalgamation that the poet endeavoured throughout his life. He was not a nationalist in the sense Gandhi or any of the mainstream political activists were; he was nationalistic since he adopted means to express his opposition to British brutality in a very unique way which his creative texts and also his various activities epitomised.

Rabindranath's loyalty to Hinduism was not an endorsement of the superstitious beliefs that were accepted as integral to the religion but was an effort to grasp the inner vitality of Hinduism by focusing on its intellectual legacies. Hence, to him, what was always prior were the ideas, particularly of the Upanishads, which always privileged humanity regardless of the artificial segregation based on religious identity or identities drawing on other markers of the socioeconomic schism. It was Gora who clearly articulated this view when he expressed pride in being a Hindu:

> I am a Hindu, after all. If I can't grasp the profound concepts of the Hindu dharma today, I shall master them tomorrow. Even if I never comprehend them, I must still follow this path. Because I could not shed the Hindu connections of my past life, I was born into a Brahman

> family in my present life. In this way, through a succession of births, it is via the Hindu religion and community that I shall ultimately arrive at the highest stage. If I ever forget myself and tend to follow some other direction, I must return to my faith with redoubled conviction. … By being born a Hindu I have already entered the main gate. Now, if I sustain my efforts, I can gradually move ahead. (307)

Here, that Gora was a devout Hindu is evident and he was ready to follow his faith religiously irrespective of sharp critiques from his father, in particular. At the beginning of the novel, the father–son rivalry over the latter's unconditional surrender to Hinduism shows that the poet appears to have been profoundly influenced by the neo-Hindus in Bengal who, in order to prove their true Hindu identity, seem to have sacrificed some of the basic concerns for humanity. Gora represented a tension between orthodox Hinduism and those values that did not seem to support the former though he always believed in the Hindu idea of *moksha* or salvation. By being strongly critical of Hindu orthodoxy, Gora demonstrated his concern for reforming Hinduism which lost its vitality because of the deliberate distortions of the fundamental values on which it rested. One is here drawn to Anandamoyi, Gora's mother, a very upright person who continued to keep Lachhmia as the cook despite Gora's vehement opposition to her being Christian. Defending Lachhmia, not because Anandamoyi was impressed by Christianity as a religion, but because of her humanistic concern, she articulated the poet's heartfelt concern for humanity as a well-knit collectivity when she mentioned that

> the entire world calls me a Christian, and many other things besides, but I accept everything, saying: 'Aren't Christians human beings, after all! If the [caste] Hindus were … so dear to the Almighty, why does He let you suffer defeat at the hands of Pathan, Mughals and Christians, in turn?' (309)

By providing a powerful argument, Anandamoyi draws our attention to an environment where there is a hint of gender parity. She was allowed to organise her life according to the practices that she held so dear since they upheld her concern for humanity. And, also by being caustic about the view of segregation of human beings in terms of various religion-driven modes, she also raised her voice against those who nurtured a divisive mindset with the false hope that it was a stepping stone towards receiving providential blessings. In other words, the logically pursued argument of Anandamoyi exposed many well-settled claims that the orthodox Hindus subscribed to fulfil their selfish goals and objectives at the cost of a larger section of humanity.

Gender as a Sociopolitical Marker

Set in the prevalent socioeconomic tapestry, *Gora* puts across the points through the main protagonists, Gora and Sucharita, that support the poet's inner conviction for gender balance in the country in a context of multiple contradictions which grew in importance largely due to a large number of archaic values and mores; it was a persuasive comment on the nature of Indian nationalism that did not become nationalistic in the true sense presumably because of the nationalists' failure to create a template of togetherness irrespective of religion, gender and one's socioeconomic location. The poet's idea of India was articulated in his insistence to generate togetherness irrespective of segmentation of any kind. Gora was his voice in this regard though he was not entirely persuaded by the exclusionary sociocultural design that the protagonist of his novel offered. On occasions, Gora's view of India coalesced with that of the poet. It was evident when Gora was introduced to Paresh Babu and his daughter, Sucharita, by his friend, Binoy. According to him, 'if Gora can unhesitatingly accept Hindu culture in its entirety, it's because he regards Bharatvarsha [India] from a very broad perspective,' argued Binoy. He said,

> Bharatvarsha appears in its entirety, all its features, major and minor, merged into a great unity, a vast harmony. Because all of us are not capable of such a vision, we constantly misjudge Bharatvarsha, seeing it in fragments and comparing it with foreign ideals. (314)

Implied here are three core pillars of Gora's conceptual universe that he conveyed to his friend, Binoy. First, Gora's inclination to the Hindu culture was complementary to his wider concern that Bharatvarsha was epitomised by being accommodative of myriad groups with different sociocultural identities. Second, his Bharatvarsha was a model of harmony regardless of any sociocultural chasm which also means that, to him, it was not merely an ensemble of parts, but one that, by merging differences, led to the rise and consolidation of 'a great unity'. This was also to reiterate that mere political freedom from foreign rule was not an end in itself, but a step towards realising the great unity that he aspired to build in his version of Bharatvarsha. Finally, being critical of the endeavour at conceptualising India in fragments, Gora evolved a notion of Bharatvarsha fragments that retained their distinct sociocultural identity as fragments and also contributed to great unity that he very passionately cherished. Therefore, Gora's creative model was not only inclusive in the sense of being accommodative of even contrarian sociocultural interests but was also a sharp critique of the Western design of nation that evolved a mode of togetherness by compartmentalising people in terms of their religion, language, culture and also by inculcating the idea of a common enemy. Rabindranath was opposed to divisive human existence which led him to sharply criticise the European civilisation as it was nationalistic in spirit and texture. At the same time, his opposition to see India in fragments also reveals his deep-rooted concern for bringing people together irrespective of caste, class and gender. This was stated very unambiguously by the bard when Gora mentioned that 'we see only half of Bharatvarsha [because] we see Bharatvarsha only as a land of men; we don't notice women at all' (357). Appreciating the English for having created a milieu in which women were treated at par with their male counterparts, Gora further added that 'like the English, we would like to see women everywhere, indoors and out, on earth, in water and in space, at meals, feasts and work, everywhere' (357). The reasons were not difficult to find since

> when members of a household gaze with long familiarity at women performing domestic chores, they don't really see the women at all. If we could view our nation's women outside our domestic needs, we would perceive our nation in its beauty and wholeness. We would see an image of the nation easy to die. At least we would never behave mistakenly as if the women of our country are nowhere to be found. ... We need to create a milieu [in which] ... our women can appear in public without loss of dignity [and we must be aware that] ... the seclusion of women has reduced our swadesh [country], our own nation, to a half-truth, incapable of infusing our hearts with love and power in their complete forms. (357)

The concern for gender parity is explicitly stated here: by not recognising women as integral to human existence, the prevalent views were prejudiced, Tagore unambiguously stated. They were indispensable for running a home though their role was hardly socially acknowledged. This conceptualisation of women being ignored despite having a critical role in domestic life is reflective of a part of wider prejudices which Tagore articulated by underlining that we saw 'the peasant only as farm-labour and the weaver only as fabric producer, we dismiss them as lowly and uncouth, not recognising them as complete beings, and this rich-poor divide weakens the nation' (358). Following this argument, he linked gender abuse with our attitude to demean women: 'if we imprison the women of our country within their routine of cooking and grinding regarding them reductively as merely the female sex' (358). This was the root of our decadence as a nation since one important half of our population was not only ignored but reduced to social entities without substance. This was the root cause of India's downfall as a country, and Rabindranath put forward a persuasive conceptual framework through Gora's friend, Binoy, to meaningfully generate ideas for common well-being; under no circumstances, he argued, could women's contribution be belittled:

> Man and woman represent two aspects of social power; man is power manifest, but the magnitude of his strength does not lie in its visibility; woman's power remains unexpressed, and to try constantly to express this secret power is to propel society towards swift bankruptcy by expending all its stored-up capital. That is why I say, if we perform the holy sacrifice while women take charge of the grain-store, the yagna ritual will be successful, despite the woman's invisibility. Those who try to expend all forms of power for the same purpose, at the same place and in the same way, must be insane. (358)

According to the poet, gender equality was possible to achieve, only when women were recognised as an integral segment of society and who needed to be taken into account most seriously. In other words, the aim here was to evolve a supportive environment where gender discrimination disappeared. It was easier said than done. Nonetheless, the main protagonist of the novel, Gora, an orthodox Hindu with prejudices against women, now realised that given their immense importance in society, it was not logical to dismiss them just as an appendage. In other words, with Binoy's intervention, Gora imbibed the concern for gender parity given 'women's special presence and influence in society' (358). Gora, thus, appears to have conceptualised his approach to gender issues at two levels. At the level of values, that women remained integral to human society was acknowledged; at the level of practice, he felt that this was a stepping stone for unifying India for it consolidated the foundation of Bharatvarsha drawing on sociocultural diversity which came out very clearly in his statement insisting on

> a vast, profound unity in many manifestations and multiple endeavours of Bharatvarsha, a unity that drives [him] wild with joy. Rejoicing at such unity, [he had] no hesitation in mingling with the most ignorant of Bharatvarsha's inhabitants, taking [his] place beside them in the dust. Some understand this message of Bharatvarsha, others don't, but never mind [he was] with everyone in Bharatvarsha—they are all my own people—within all of them [he had] no doubt, eternal Bharatvarsha's concealed presence is constantly at work. (377)

What is striking here is Gora's awareness of India or Bharatvarsha being one regardless of sociocultural diversity; he was able to mingle with everyone since he belonged to a nation (sic) that decried discrimination of any kind as it was a threat to the unity that had evolved over generations. The exhortation—'my own people'—appears to have captured the feelings of Gora that were unambiguously expressed. It was further clarified by Gora in his dialogical interaction with his compatriot, Binoy. According to him, since 'Hindus are a community, … it is impossible to express its essence by confining it to any label, … just as the ocean can't be described by its waves, Hindus can't be described as one either' (522). Being vehemently opposed to the design of conceptualising Bharatvarsha as one, he further elaborated his stance by adumbrating the view that it would be conceptually wrong to imagine that 'there is no diversity among human beings' (523). The sociocultural divide was a source of strength because it allowed people to learn how to survive and also flourish as a community amidst diversity. The forcible unity was harmful to the existence of human beings as human beings because by muzzling diverse sociocultural voices, the endeavour sealed their natural growth. Tagore's Gora thus spoke that

> the brigand races who believe it's best for the world if they vanquish all other races to extend their sole empire, who are too arrogant about their own power to admit that the distinctiveness of other races is of priceless benefit to the world, who spread only slavery across the world —how are you people different from them. (523)

This digression is not futile since it put forward Gora's *Weltanschauung* or world view which was an aid to comprehend his approach to gender equality. The argument is indeed a little convoluted because Gora's concerns for gender parity are part of this entire sociopolitical priority, which stemmed from his own experiences as 'a Hindu' and also out of constant dialogue with the Brahmos, especially the other protagonists in the novel. The role of Sucharita was also not insignificant because her direct or indirect encouragement helped Gora find a persuasive course of thought. A thoughtful woman herself, Sucharita adored Gora for his 'utterance which was no mere discourse, it resembled a new creation. It was so tangible over time that it could dominate one's whole mind and body … and she no longer retained the strength to determine how far her opinions coincided with Gora's' (524).

Gora, thus, not merely articulated a persuasive message of treating human beings as an equal set of multitudes regardless of division but he endeavoured to develop a design for all on the basis of his firm commitment to humanity. Gora was strongly opposed to socioeconomic schisms segmenting one section of the multitude from another. His exalted goal was to awaken the nation (sic) as one set of people with multiple sociocultural preferences. He thus declared that

> by professing my respect, I want to awaken the nation's heart to the greatness of our sacred philosophy, the profundity of our devotional tradition. I want to arouse its pride in its own riches. I shall not let the country bow its head in shame, nor make it blind to its own reality by generating self-hatred. That is my vow. … I constantly feel that Bharatvarsha cannot be completely represented through masculine perspective alone. Its existence will be fully realized only when manifest to the eyes of our women. I have thus no doubt that communion between man and woman remains a future, a strong future, for Bharatvarsha. (537)

There was not an iota of doubt that without a man–woman partnership, the future of Bharatvarsha was bleak. Nonetheless, Tagore's earnest call for radical changes in the social, economic and cultural fields created a template to build a model for furthering the goal that Gora held so dear to him. Despite being an orthodox Hindu by upbringing, Gora's endeavour towards attaining common well-being was the outcome of two major sources: These were Sucharita's influences which were supplemented by Paresh Babu's powerful intellectual inputs and his experience which he gained by extensive travelling in villages. Hence, Tagore noted that

> the deeper he penetrated the world of [the villagers], the more a certain thought began to trouble his mind. He observed that in India's rural areas, social restrictions were far more powerful than in educated, cultured society. In every household, food, sleep, rest, work, everything was conducted, day and night, under the unblinking gaze of society. Each individual had a very simple faith in popular traditions, never questioning such things. Yes, social restrictions and adherence to custom did not empower them at all in their fields of activity. It was doubtful whether such timid, helpless beings, so incapable of judging what was good for themselves, existed anywhere in the world. Beyond adherence to traditions, there was no other good that they wholeheartedly acknowledged, or were willing to understand. It was prohibition, enforced through punishment or partisanship, that they regarded as supreme. The awareness of what must not be done entrapped their nature in a net from head to toe at every step, through various forms of discipline. … There was no broad unity within them that could draw them all together in good times or bad. (575)

In a rather long argument, Tagore very grudgingly referred to the prevalent sociopolitical and cultural environment to argue that it was an impediment to fulfilling the objective of ensuring common well-being; the root cause was the mindset that was opposed to even recognising human beings as human beings. Caste segregation and the religious chasm between Hindus and Muslims remained a constant source of irritation to those seeking to create an ambience for ideologically justified socioeconomic and political equality. In other words, Bharatvarsha was divided not only along gender axes but also following the segmentation of caste identity. These are not new claims since Tagore had already elaborated some of them in his earlier creative texts. *Gora* was perhaps the most articulated version of Tagore's oppositional politics, seeking to reinforce views for equality for all. Nonetheless, what is a little perplexing was the nature of the approach that Tagore upheld to put his ideas in such a way as to generate support for the project that he proposed to carry out for ensuring good to all. Seeking to identify the roots of our failure to bring about radical socioeconomic and cultural changes, Gora was aghast when he noticed that

> humans were using the archaic practices as weapons to suck the blood of other human beings, brutally robbing them of their selfhood. How often he had observed that in performing social rituals, nobody showed the slightest compassion for anybody else! [He was appalled] … when the father of a poor man was seriously ill, … the villagers, instead of helping him, [attributed his illness] … to an unknown sin [forgetting that] the poor man had neither the resources nor any help that was forthcoming. (575)

Here too, Tagore expressed a general concern linked with his aims for gender empowerment. It was difficult to achieve the goal because of the widely held ideas in favour of ritual-based social behaviour. In a cruel society, as he noticed, there was hardly any space for compassion, empathy and care. As a result, human beings in general, and the villagers in particular, suffered immeasurably. Gora thus stated that 'this society did not help a man in times of need, nor supported him in times of trouble; it only used discipline as a threat to subdue him' (576). The idea here is very explicit: Unless a society is compassionate enough to engender the feeling of togetherness among fellow human beings, our existence is neither humane nor worthwhile. A powerful exhortation indeed, it was directed, at one level, to create conditions for evolving a level playing field in which discrimination of any kind was an anathema; at another level, along with a scathing critique of the prevalent sociocultural practices upholding supremacist mindsets, implicit here was also a call for change by involving those with likeminded attitudes and missions.

Unlike Damini in *Chaturanga* and Ela in *Char Adhyay*, who were not hesitant in displaying sexuality, Sucharita in *Gora* is a voice that was tempered but firm, decisive but polite and self-generated but contextual. Here, Tagore articulated his views on gender differently though the foundational concerns remain the same, namely, by characterising Sucharita as a fearless voice, he raised those issues which he felt needed attention. One of the distinct manifestations was the participation of the female protagonist, Sucharita, in discussions on sociopolitical and nationalist issues which, in then Calcutta, was exclusively a male domain. By encouraging her to speak out while debating these concerns, *Gora* also represented a voice which was complementary to the processes of women empowerment. Tagore was raised in an environment in which views and also practices supportive of gender equality were always appreciated, and attempts were constantly made to recognise them as integral to the family. As such, the Brahmos were pathfinders for many progressive endeavours: women's education, championing views against the purdah system of seclusion for women and involving them in events outside home, among others. Tagore was also a pioneer in many respects, as his experiments in Santiniketan and Sriniketan show.

A careful analysis of Sucharita's character also reveals that Tagore was not free from being paternalistically biased. While Damini and Ela were primarily guided by their instinctively nurtured desires while justifying their acts, Sucharita was encouraged to speak out by Paresh Babu and Gora; her dislike of Haran Babu, her suitor, created an ambience which enabled her to say unhesitatingly what she felt. It is also true that Damini and Ela—products of an environment in which gender parity was the norm—exhibited a fearlessness that was also context-driven. But in the case of Sucharita, the male protagonists in the novel are seen to have encouraged her to share her views in the deliberations which was certainly a persuasive input that helped her build an independent personality and also create conditions favourably disposed towards her. In other words, by giving her a respectful place in the forum for discussion, the poet not only created an opportunity for her to express her views but also a design seeking to institutionalise the processes for sustenance for the future. This also means that, for Tagore, it was not a one-time device, but one that was likely to contribute to the generation of a mindset in support of gender equity and a voice against gender discrimination. Gora's highly prescriptive approach to moral issues led him to espouse an unusual marriage of views; his Hindu orthodoxy bloomed alongside his abiding commitment to gender equality. This was one of the main reasons that brought Sucharita out of her patriarchally mandated shell throughout various fiery deliberations on sociopolitical issues that she participated in at home. Sucharita's character is, therefore, to a significant extent, a product of various paternalistic influences in her life, which was typical of the era. By being sensitive to them in the novel, Tagore, in *Gora*, also created a legitimate space for progressive voices regardless of gender.

The Idea of Bharatvarsha

There is one common thread in the corpus of creative texts that Rabindranath left for posterity: given the inchoate sociocultural and politico-ideological diversity, the conventional idea of nation was hardly adequate to meaningfully comprehend the idea of Bharatvarsha or India. In his perception, one of the reasons for this is located in the fact that the collectivity that India represented was not brought together by 'a political power' (Tagore 2013: 79); it had come together by being appreciative of 'the divergences among the communities inhabiting a common socio-cultural space' (79). This was a unique way of bringing people together despite differences since the 'identical civilizational ethos [that] generated in them a concern for common well-being' (79). So, it was an example demonstrating that the civilisational bond was equally strong to build a well-knit community irrespective of sociocultural differences. The underlying force was the intense desire to come together and sustain the unity that evolved by inculcating the sense of living together. Imbibing the spirit in which Bharatvarsha was conceptualised by the poet, Gora testified this by saying that although

> Hindus are a community … it is impossible to express its essence by confining it to any label [because] so immense is the community [which is] just like an ocean [that] can't be described by its waves, Hindus can't be described in a straightjacketed format. (Tagore 2011: 522)

In contrast with the ideas espoused by the Brahmos who left Hinduism for being so narrow and ritualistic, Gora, as a hardcore Hindu, delineated his views to defend his notion of Bharatvarsha as a place for all religious groups and not merely Hindus. Since India was a melting pot, other religious groups learnt to appreciate the idea of diversity through the mode of coalescence. Questioning the Brahmo Samaj's exclusionary design, Gora exhorted when Sucharita, being a Brahmo, endorsed the philosophical justification of the new sect primarily to oppose Hindu orthodoxy, by saying that 'Do you want to impose your own party's sole authority upon everyone else? Do you wish to turn a blind eye, imagining there is diversity among human beings, that everyone is born into this world only to enlist with the Brahmo Samaj?' (523).

By forcefully arguing his point, Gora, while castigating the Brahmos for being divisive, if not arrogant, came out with a clear statement in support of his belief. It was a battle of ideas between Rabindranath and those who, within the Brahmo Samaj, privileged their anti-Hindu views without even recognising the diversity that Hinduism, unlike any of the religious faiths, accommodated. This is also illustrative of the poet being appreciative of some of the fundamental ethos that sustained Hinduism despite constant attacks on Hindus from outside. What was perhaps striking to the bard was the resilience of the Hindus to retain the inherent concern for sociocultural diversity notwithstanding sharp critique by many against ritual-based Hinduism. Given the peculiar nature of Hinduism, it was better to describe the faith as not just a sect but a way of life nurtured over generations regardless of the continuous threat to its existence. Gora was aghast at Sucharita's steadfast commitment to Brahmoism which was clearly a design to cause a fissure among the Hindus:

> it is not your Samaj alone that has created the twenty-crore people of Bharatvarsha. … On what ground do you seek to utterly flatten out this vast Bharatvarsha, by forcibly seizing the responsibility of decreeing which course of action is suitable for these twenty crores, or which belief and practices would ensure sustenance and strength for all of them! The greater the hindrances you encounter in your impossible attempt, the more angry (sic) and disrespectful you will feel towards your own country, and the more your contempt will alienate the very people you wish to help! (523)

Fundamental to Gora's argument is his concern for humanity which, if divided, was likely to be debased by the effort that the Brahmos had undertaken. Conceptually, this is a very useful intervention since it was contrary to the sectarian views that many Brahmos upheld—a clear deviation from the core values on which the Brahmo Samaj rested. What is significant here is to note that the poet did not seem to have been happy with the consolidation of ideas among the Brahmos who, instead of being involved in eradicating segmentation among human beings, openly expressed their hatred towards the ritualistic behaviour of Hindus which contributed to the Brahmo–Hindu chasm. It was sharply argued by Gora when he responded to Sucharita's defence of Brahmo Samaj as the only way to serve humanity:

> [I]f you see the people of Bharatvarsha as non-Brahmos you will distort their image and regard them with contempt, and constantly misunderstand them. You will never get to see them from the perspective that allows one to see them as a whole; … they think in

> many different ways, act in many different ways, follow many different beliefs and customs, but underlying this is a basic humanity; within all this is something that belongs to me, to Bharatvarsha, something that, when viewed from a true perspective, will pierce its outward shell of pettiness and incompleteness to present before us the vision of a great, noble entity. … The people of this Bharatvarsha have accomplished many tasks, and to imagine that all that has become utterly futile is to show disrespect for the truth, and that itself is atheism. (523–524)

By being critical of the Brahmos who endeavoured to separate themselves from the wider Hindu society, Gora drew attention to the rich heritage that Bharatvarsha represented; at the same time, being appreciative of the visible sociocultural diversity in India, he also made a strong case for this specific landmass for being a place where many views blossomed naturally. According to him, diversity was immanent in human civilisation since human beings were born as socioculturally separate entities:

> The Lord who made human beings so diverse, who wishes to preserve their diversity, is the very One you imagine that you worship. If all of you truly believe in Him, why are you unable to recognize his decree? Why does pride in your own intelligence and your own party prevent you from accepting its significance? (523)

Here Gora's scathing critique of Brahmo Samaj was based on his unflinching belief in Hinduism which drew its sustenance from a providential design supportive of the multiplicity of faith and beliefs. This was unique to Hinduism which never attempted to gloss over sociocultural diversity as it was an endorsement of the creator's will. Despite being a Brahmo, Rabindranath argued for sociocultural diversity as being inherent to humanity, and attempts at compartmentalising human beings were neither humanistic nor complementary to their evolution as one close-knit entity. It is also evident that the poet seems to have been persuaded by the Hindu appreciation for diversity which was not artificially generated. It was an outcome of being nurtured in a society being respectful to human beings with separate sociocultural identities. Gora articulated the idea when he forcefully argued that

> the Hindu faith has tried to nurture people of many attitudes, many views; in other words, the Hindu faith alone has acknowledged people as human beings, not as members of some group. The Hindu faith

> accepts the illiterate as well as the learned—and not just a single facet of learning, but the growth of knowledge in many dimensions. (524)

In order to hone his argument, he made a comparison of Christianity with Hinduism which was probably a response to the growing importance of Christian missionaries in India and also their success in large-scale conversion of Hindus into Christians. What was tacitly stated here is also the point that the Brahmos, by being abusive to Hinduism, belonged to the same sectarian groups that flourished at the cost of the Hindus. To clarify the views, Gora's argument is worth quoting. According to him, since

> Christians don't wish to acknowledge diversity, [they fail] to recognize that Hinduism strives to perceive the One through the medium of the many. Unless our minds break free of the fetters of Khristani (sic) learning, we cannot claim the glory of understanding the true nature of the Hindu Dharma. (524)

Gora's argument comes full circle. Three important points deserve attention here: First, Gora was proud of his Hindu sociocultural roots. For him, Hinduism was more than a religion or religious sect since it dealt with the common well-being of humanity as one. Second, Gora was aghast at the growth of the Brahmo Samaj that artificially divided the Hindus because of their failure to conceptualise Hinduism from a proper perspective. It was also reinforcement of the argument that Hindus, notwithstanding being socioculturally different, remained united by being respectful to the One that created them. Finally, Gora's argument that Brahmos were separate from their Hindu counterparts was obvious since it was drawn on the Christians' arrogance in identifying themselves as a unique version of humanity. What he hinted at here is the fact that the Brahmos were blindly imitating derivative religious traditions with no organic roots in India's sociocultural ethos. Hence, it was a faith that could hardly be a source of inspiration to the people belonging to Bharatvarsha.

Disillusionment

Being raised in a metropolitan city like Calcutta, Gora was secluded from the villages where one came across a completely different kind of Bharatvarsha that hardly corresponded with the view that he had so assiduously nurtured so far. On his many trips to the villages in the vicinity of Calcutta, he came in touch with a reality which was completely alien to him. As one who hid his caste identity, Gora easily mixed up with the villagers indiscriminately though it was a cause of suspicion for them. Nonetheless, he continued exploring the peripheral areas of India which added various new but surprising dimensions to the sociocultural existence of human beings that were hardly known to those confined to the city.

> [T]he deeper he penetrated into [the villagers'] world, the more a certain thought began to trouble his mind [because] … in these rural areas, social restrictions were far more powerful than in educated, cultured society. In every household, food, sleep, rest, work, everything was conducted, day and night, under the unblinking gaze of society. Each individual had a very simple faith in popular traditions, never questioning such things. Yet, social restrictions and adherence to custom did not empower them at all in the fields of activity. It was doubtful whether such timid, helpless beings, so incapable of judging what was good for themselves, existed anywhere else in the world. (575)

These are perhaps the most explicit graphic details of how artificially drawn social boundaries sustained divisions among the villagers. It was not unusual as the poet lamented that Indians, by virtue of the environment in which they were raised, considered such division as integral to life. In his critical essay, 'Shudradharma' (2018 rpt: 281–287), Rabindranath attributed the continuity of this mindset to a deliberately created social system in which the so-called Shudras were taught to be dutiful to their socially assigned duties as a means for their salvation. As the poet explained, 'Hinduism has made them believe so over generations because without their support the high castes would be deprived of the comfort of the life in which they were accustomed to' (285). What surprised Rabindranath was the mechanism through which this servility continued to exist in India: the hegemonic influence of religion and acceptance of these restrictions were shown as divinely ordained. The restrictions were allowed to remain 'hegemonic because the so-called Shudras endorsed their mode of serving the people in specific ways as they naturally accepted their existence as inferior to the upper caste Hindus' (285). This social design to keep them perennially under servility was deliberately created by 'the self-proclaimed social leaders primarily for protecting their benefits because of the accident of birth' (285). Age-old prejudices deeply embedded in the social fabric remained so powerful that attempts at reversing them were not only remote but also impossible which Gora realised when he expressed that

> beyond adherence to tradition, there was no other good that they wholeheartedly acknowledged, or were willing to understand. It was prohibition, enforced through punishment or partisanship, that they regarded as supreme. The awareness of what must not be done entrapped their nature in a net from head to toe at every step, through various forms of discipline. (Tagore 2011: 575)

What the poet said in his critical essay corresponded with what Gora mentioned while explaining the helplessness of these lower-caste people; it was bondage from which there was no escape, and over time, it became an integral part of their existence which remained unchanged as those championing partisan interests resisted attempts for reversal. These prejudicial practices had emerged because of (a) lack of powerful opposition and (b) the failure of the victims to raise their voices. To his utter dismay, and also surprise, Gora thus expressed how it was possible for 'humans to use these practices as weapons to suck the blood of other human beings, brutally robbing them of their selfhood' (575). His blood boiled when he found that 'in performing social rituals, nobody showed the slightest compassion for anybody else!' (575). To substantiate his point, he referred to an example of a dying man, who was forced to hold a big feast to propitiate the almighty to lessen the sin that caused his permanent illness. No one bothered to find out whether it was financially possible for him to spend money for this feast but, as Gora exhorted, 'there was no forgiveness' (575). Similarly, in the case of a marriage, 'the bridegroom's party would adopt every strategy to make the burden intolerable for the bride's father, without the slightest pity for the wretched man' (576). He was not only disillusioned but also clueless as to how to make these hapless people stand on their own, given the long-standing crippling practices which were upheld by those suffering due to their acceptance as appropriate. Even in death, the forcibly imposed rituals were 'a greater source of affliction for the offspring of the deceased that the death itself' (575). It was a society which was inhuman since 'this society did not help a man in times of need, nor supported him in times of trouble, but it only used discipline as a threat to subdue him' (576). A devout Hindu who was always proud of his religious identity, Gora was exposed to the ugly side of Hinduism during his trip to the villages. It was a source of terrible disappointment to him which was evident when he categorically stated that 'the dharma that gave everyone strength, energy and wellbeing in the form of service, love, compassion and self-sacrifice, was nowhere in evidence' (576). That his ideas were sternly rejected by those belonging to the lower castes caught him by surprise.

He, however, realised that opposition to the upper castes would not only invite trouble for them but also create conditions where they would be deprived of the financial loan that they got from the local moneylenders. It was, according to Gora, 'the net of indebtedness, the moneylenders' bond [and] not the bondage imposed by a king' (575). This is reflective of how the poor villagers suffered due to their caste identity and also because of the well-nurtured ploy to keep them under chains by evolving a mode of behaviour which was accepted as natural by the victims. Gora was troubled by the nature of this Hinduism as it developed in the villages as an instrument to justify the personal gain of a select group of people. Here, the poet intervened and explained the helplessness of Gora who, despite being willing to generate self-esteem among the deprived, remained just a bystander! As the bard so poignantly explained,

> the practices that only drew boundaries, divided people and tormented them, that would even deny the intellect and keep love at arm's length, were the ones that constantly hindered everyone in every respect, in every moment and activity. (576)

His contact with the villagers was considered by the poet as his 'rebirth [which helped him clearly understand] the harmful effects of this foolish compliance ... are an impediment to the recognition of human beings as they are' (576). It was a rebirth in another sense as he also realised that there was a hiatus between what he so far believed and the reality that he confronted which led him to a natural conclusion that it 'became impossible for him to continue deluding himself with the illusion of abstract thought' (576). Three points need attention here: First, Gora, while being critical of the caste hierarchy, represented what Rabindranath articulated in his many critical statements which he frequently made to question the artificial segregation separating one section of humanity from another. For him, it was an endorsement of his wider conceptual concern for human emancipation. Second, by being fiercely critical of the vicious social circle that had emerged out of the holy alliance between the upper caste and also the rich, the poet also hinted at how the poor villagers survived in rural areas where they had no option but remained socially chained due largely to the consolidation of a social system by those motivated to gain at others' cost. In later years, B.R. Ambedkar evolved a powerful critique of Gandhi's fascination for villages more or less in the language in which Rabindranath articulated his distinct perception opposing hierarchical human existence in rural areas. Finally, through Gora, the poet also showed how one's knowledge was governed by the context: As Gora was a city-bred individual, he remained captive to the ideas of Hinduism which was, to him, a religion of humanity regardless of division around any of the human-made axes. Once he landed in the villages, his carefully nurtured thought processes received a serious blow—whatever he had learnt so far about Hinduism was hardly realistic because it was a deterrent to the fulfilment of his mission.

Gora's acquaintance with the sociocultural texture of village life was an eye-opener because it put him face to face with 'the nation's profoundest weaknesses' (576). He was appalled by the social distance between the Hindus and Muslims which Rabindranath conveyed in categorical terms in many critical essays in *Kalantor*. What however struck him was the religious bond that brought the Muslims together unlike the Hindus, who failed to generate togetherness given the caste hierarchy and division around many other axes. In his words, 'Muslims possessed the unifying element that could draw them together … in times of trouble or difficulty in the village … [in contrast with] the Hindus who would never close their ranks to stand by each other' (576). This was painful since Hindus always remained segmented; it was a source of curiosity how, despite being part of an identical sociocultural milieu, the Muslims developed themselves as a well-knit collectivity. 'It pained his entire being to acknowledge that', Gora admitted, 'Muslims were united by their dharma [Islam], not merely by their practices, [which instilled in them] those human values by which they could, at a single call and in a single instant, stand together and readily surrender their lives' (577). One could perhaps locate the conceptual roots of M.A. Jinnah's two-nation theory that finally led to India's vivisection in 1947 on the basis of the argument that Muslims, given their separate religious identity cohesively joined them with one another, needed their homeland. Contrarily, Hindus, in view of being divided around many axes besides caste, always remained heavily segmented. So, they could never be united like their Muslim counterparts. This is one aspect of the argument seeking to identify the reasons why Hindus were segregated due largely to some of the deliberately nurtured sociocultural prejudices against their own brethren and, of course, against the Muslims. The other aspect of Gora's argument relates to those loyalists who were mesmerised by the British authority which was certainly an impediment to the rise of India as a close-knit unit of humanity. While persuasively seeking to defend his standpoint, Gora explains that

> because a section of his own countrymen was hostile to the country, because they viewed all aspects of their country in a negative light, they appear to have knowingly absorbed the humiliation of this self-detached view by trying day and night to cover his country's entire image with a dazzling emotional aura. (577)

Gora's aim here was to generate a sense of being proud of one's motherland which was sadly missing not only among those living in the city of Calcutta but also those who were on its periphery. A patriot par excellence, it was not acceptable to Gora, who endeavoured hard to instil the sense because he believed that without 'renewal of his countrymen's respect for their own motherland' (577), no effort towards emancipating India was likely to succeed. Given the sociocultural practices and also the prevalence of an alien rule, the task was not so easy; however, it was not impossible which led Gora to declare that by generating respect for the motherland, he

> wants to awaken the nation's heart to the greatness of our sacred philosophy, the profundity of our devotional traditions; [he] wants to arouse its pride in its own riches [and he] shall not let the country bow its head in shame, nor make it blind to its own reality by generating self-hatred. (536)

Here, the novelist reminds us of the philosophical values of the indigenous discourses that his grandfather, Dwarkanath, and his father, Debendranath, had inculcated in him. Being proud of the indigenous philosophical discourses, Rabindranath designed a model of togetherness irrespective of differences in terms of class, caste and ethnicity. Neither xenophobic nor orthodox in his understanding of the prevalent sociocultural reality, the poet was receptive to those influences, which, he felt, were of relevance to awaken a moribund nation. Opposed to the nationalist conceptualisation of human multitudes, the poet fought for united human existence by attacking those impediments which impaired unity.

The novel *Gora* was also a persuasive explanation of why India lagged behind the Europeans notwithstanding her rich legacy. Once Gora decided to go to the villages to see for himself 'the country … outside the social worlds of the respectable bhadralok, the educated and the Kolkata dwellers' (400), he confronted another side of Bharatvarsha which was

> fragmented, comprising narrow-minded and feeble individuals [who] are utterly unaware of their power, ignorant and indifferent about their interests [because] they are heavily constrained by many self-created and imaginary obstacles … by clinging to every prejudice and superstition. (400)

Hindus were divided because of those nurtured superstitions and prejudices which created an unbridgeable gulf between one section of their community from another. Gora hadn't had an opportunity to confront such a Bharatvarsha while being in Calcutta where the schism did not seem to be as open as it was in villages. The views that Gora held were echoed in Rabindranath's assessment of the situation which he articulated in his address to the staff and students of Visva-Bharati on 20 September 1932, where he said that 'the social inequities upon which all our enemies find their principal support have time-honoured loyalty making it difficult for us to uproot them' and 'the dismemberment of Hindu society is certainly fatal to its wholeness'.[1] To support his contention, he further mentioned,

> if we cheaply dismiss [this mission] with some ceremonials to which we are accustomed and allow the noble life to be wasted with its great meaning then our people will passively roll down the slope of degradation to the blankness of utter futility. (327)

Appalled by the lack of serious protest against division in Hindu society, the poet designed a model on the basis of his understanding of the problem. Knowing well that it was not an easy task since it involved a radical transformation of the dominant mindset governing the Hindu mode of life, Tagore first provided a sharp critique of those Hindus surviving, if not thriving, by defending superstition and then charted out his blueprint for doing away with this system. In his tribute, Swami Sharadhananda (1856–1926) who was a social reformer, elaborated his scheme by underlining that

> it is for us at once to set to work to examine where our Hindu system is at fault, and unflinchingly to remove every loophole that has been left for weakness to enter. For the weak tempt the strong into the path of sin. If when the Musslamans grow violent, we tamely submit to their violence, we must know that this has become possible mainly by reason of the weakness born out of our lack of unity. To appeal to them to be good, not to be cruel; to point out that no religion can be based on murder, is as ineffectual to prevent aggression on the weak by the strong as it would be to avert a storm whenever a part of the atmosphere has become lighter than its surroundings.[2]

1 Rabindranath Tagore's speech on 20 September 1932, reproduced in Das (1996, 327–328).

2 Rabindranath Tagore's tribute to Swami Shradhananda, 25 December 1926, reproduced in Ghosh (2008, 556).

There are two complementary aspects to this argument: On the one hand, by providing a scathing critique of Hindu society, Tagore made it very clear that the purging of these crippling features, not ingrained but created, involved collective effort; what was required was introspection as to why it had happened which would help us understand the reason behind the alienation of Muslims from the Hindus. The assessment was based on his own experience of how the majority of Hindus treated the Muslims as a landlord in an estate in East Bengal in which Muslims were demographically preponderant. To transform the Hindu mindset, the poet, on the other hand, suggested that Hindus needed to launch a serious campaign to put across the point that violence was futile and only through bonhomie between the two communities, it was possible to develop communal amity.

Rabindranath was equally perturbed by the ill-treatment that the caste Hindus meted out to their lower-caste counterparts. Being appreciative of the endeavour that the Mahatma undertook, the bard had no hesitation in conceding that inhuman social practices were also a serious weakness of Hindu society and needed to be meaningfully addressed and done away with. In this effort lies a political design that the poet appeared to have devised. Being interested in building a model for human emancipation, the poet strongly felt that unless the carefully nurtured divisive tendencies were eradicated, no scheme for developing humanity as a well-knit collectivity was possible. As he believed,

> the true path to emancipation lies in man's unity: our political dependence is nourished by the innumerable sects and divisions that keep our peoples apart. The day has come when human civilization must move forward breaking through the fetters of the Ages—towards broader understanding based on mutual faith and love. (Das 1996: 333)

How was it possible? Here the poet urged those opposed to caste discrimination to join the campaign that Gandhi spearheaded to attack the age-old system of social degradation whereby one section was being continuously humiliated. Besides insisting on 'mutual faith and love for one another', he expressed his uncritical support for the Mahatma's untiring efforts in removing 'the burden of Ages', which was, he further characterised, 'the burden of disrespect upon the bent back of those who have been stigmatised for the accident of their birth, the sin of willful denial to a large body of our countrymen of sympathy which is the birthright of all human beings' (335–336). Here too, Rabindranath articulated a political voice when he insisted on uniting the countrymen for the cause of humanity. Unlike the Mahatma, who always couched his arguments in an unambiguous political mound, the poet can be said to have contributed to the consolidation of a platform of togetherness irrespective of social, cultural and differences around any other axis. A successful attack against 'the burden of history' led, according to the bard, not only to

> the casting off the chain of India's moral enslavement, but also indicating a path for all humanity [because] we are challenging victimization wherever and whatever form it may exist, to stand the test of relentless questioning of conscience which Mahatmaji has brought to bear upon our day. (336)

Thus, the Mahatma's aim of evolving a united opposition against foreign rule could not be achieved without doing away with the indigenous sources of sociocultural division. While denigrating those practising social distance from one section of Hindus, given their low caste, the poet participated in the offensive campaign that Gandhi launched amidst opposition even from some of his trusted colleagues. This was Rabindranath's realisation which was based on his interactions with his Muslim and lower-caste subjects on his landed estate. Gora testified some of these ideas during his trip to the villages. Not only did he confront schism between the Hindus and Muslims and upper-caste Hindus and their lower-caste counterparts but he also found, though rarely, how humanism surpassed these artificially created barriers in a village that he visited. As Gora narrated, the Hindu–Muslim divide disappeared and a Hindu couple took care of a Muslim child when his father, Pharu Sardar, was jailed following an attack by a group of Muslims under his leadership on the representatives of the indigo planters. Opposing the forcible cutting of paddy that the villagers grew for their survival in a climate of near-famine, Pharu Sardar 'had dealt such a blow to the British police officer's right hand that it had to be amputated at the clinic' (Tagore 2011: 401). This was an unprecedented event because 'never had this area witnessed such a daring feat' (401). The consequences were however disastrous because, following this, 'the police torture had spread like wildfire through every neighbourhood; they left nothing intact in the tenant-farmers' house, and the honour of women in their homes were jeopardized' (401). It did not seem to be unexpected since whenever there was opposition to the whimsical acts on the part of the indigo planters, the villagers had the same fate. Gora was surprised to hear this and was also perplexed to find that the menfolk had absconded which left their wives in perpetual hunger and other difficulties. Pharu Sardar's wife had the same plight and Gora was surprised to know that 'her only garment was so tattered that she was ashamed to emerge from her house' (401). But another surprise was awaiting Gora when he found that Pharu Sardar's wife and his young son were being looked after by a Hindu barber because 'seeing them starving, the barber's wife spontaneously came forward to provide them' (401) though they also lived hand-to-mouth. It was an example of how humanism prevailed in circumstances when one needed another. There is another aspect which also shows the poet's hatred towards those supportive of caste hierarchy and extended unconditional assistance to the ruling authority. In the same village, when the villagers were asked about night stay, they recommended the local tehsildar (a government officer responsible for maintaining law and order and also collecting rent from the cultivators), Madhav Chatujje, a Brahmin, thinking Gora, being a Brahmin, would be reluctant to stay in non-Brahmin households. To their surprise, he decided to spend the night with the barber's family though he cooked his own food with the supply from his host; he refused to stay with the tehsildar for Chatujje was not only a collaborator with the British but also a hardcore champion of caste and religious segregation. It was a revolutionary step which caught the barber by surprise since, in his perception, an upper-caste Hindu spontaneously accepting their hospitality was inconceivable given his low-caste origin. Here the novelist was at his best when he justified Gora's decision to not accept Madhav Chatujje's request to stay in his bungalow by saying that 'the more [he] thought about having to accept the hospitality of the vile, unjust Madhav Chatujje just to preserve his caste purity, the more intolerable the prospect appeared' (403). Gora's rebellious persona surfaced when he mentioned with anguish that

> what a great heresy we are committing in Bharatvarsha, making purity a matter of appearances alone! It would save my caste purity to dine at the home of a man who torments Muslims by creating all sorts of trouble, but I would lose my caste status in the home of a person who accepts such torment to protect a Muslim family and is even ready to suffer social condemnation for it. (403)

Gora did not seem to be comfortable with caste hierarchy which is clear when he rejected Chatujje's offer of hospitality; also, by being appreciative of humanism, he clearly expressed what Rabindranath had been espousing in his creative essays and other creative texts. That he had been, so far, blinded by an imposed identity was established when he saw that a poor couple was hardly perturbed with the threat of social ostracism for their help to Pharu Sardar's wife and kid. What we hear is the poet's voice that he always raised against artificial segregation on the basis of religion which he believed was created to sustain vested interests in society. Gora's articulation of the issue was thus refreshing and also an endorsement of the humanistic concerns that Rabindranath held so dear throughout his life.

The novel ends with a plot twist which reinforced Rabindranath's concern for and faith in indivisible humanity. It happened when Gora was told by his mother, Anandamoyi, that he was born to Irish parents who had died: While his biological father died in the mutiny, his mother passed away after he was born. Given the circumstances, Anandamoyi happily took the responsibility of raising Gora as her son which her husband, Krishnadayal, also joyously accepted. As soon as Gora came to know that they were not his real parents, he felt that

> [I]n a single instant, his entire life becomes like an extraordinary dream. The foundation of his life, developed over all these years since his very infancy, was utterly destroyed. What he was, where he was, he did not seem to understand. As if behind him there was nothing called a past, and before him, the future, so purposeful and clearly determined for such a long time, had completely vanished. As if he was simply floating like a momentary dewdrop on a lotus leaf. He had no mother, no father, no country, no caste, no name, no family gotra, no deity. All that he had was a No. (600–601)

Completely disillusioned, Gora now questioned his belief, his faith and the seriousness in which he was, so far, pursuing his commitment to Hinduism when he was not a Hindu himself. He seemed to have lost his face to Sucharita, whom he wanted to marry; given his religious affiliation to Christianity by birth, it might not be possible. In a melancholic tone, he vented his frustration:

> I am not a Hindu. I was informed that … I am foundling from the days of the Mutiny. My father is an Irishman. So, from north to south across the whole of Bharatvarsha, all temple doors are now closed to me. In this whole country, there is no place for me, at any level, to sit down for a meal with others. (602)

He was perhaps reminded of his folly when he declined to eat food prepared by Lachhmia despite Anandamoyi's repeated requests because, according to him, a true Brahmin was, for maintaining his caste identity, not allowed to do so. The same Gora now realised that his insistence on being a real Brahmin acted as a deterrent to emerging as a human in its true connotation. In his dialogue with Sucharita's father, Poresh Babu, he thus admitted:

> all these days I strove wholeheartedly to realize the idea of Bharatvarsha [which was tantamount to] a struggle for a compromise between the

> obstacles, stemming from his allegiance to Hinduism, and [his] sense of respect. ... That is why, when I tried to serve Bharatvarsha while viewing it in the light of what I learnt as a Brahmin, I repeatedly turned back in fear. (603)

That he was beginning to understand India's real sociocultural texture and complexities which cannot be formatted in a single mould was evident in the above confession. He was, as if, under chains which vitiated his perspectives and also vision because he tended to see prevalent social reality through a prism that sustained caste hierarchy and thus acted as an impediment to conceptualising humanity as one. Rabindranath was at his best here by putting forward, in words, the emotional stress that the main protagonist of the novel underwent. As one who was a great priest for universal humanism, the poet unambiguously stated his position when Gora exhorted that

> [T]oday in a single instant my imaginary fortress has evaporated like a dream. Set completely free, I have suddenly arrived at the heart of a great reality! All Bharatvarsha's virtue and flaws, joys and sorrows, knowledge and ignorance, have come directly close to my heart. Today I have gained the right to true service. The real field of action now lies before me. It is not the arena of my heart, but the actual site for promoting the welfare of those hundred crore people in the world outside. (603)

It was a rebirth for him since he was able to see human beings as they were. Given his assiduously nurtured caste prejudices, he failed to see beyond his indoctrinated mode of existence. He was one of those rootless individuals who remained disconnected from the world around him; that was a constructed world in which the prejudices based on the accident of birth appeared to have prevailed in shaping the individuals' interactions with one another. Being a proud Brahmin, Gora hardly realised that it was futile to segregate human beings in compartments unless one was keen to serve one's partisan interests. That he had wrongly pursued a course of action which was contrary to universal humanism was evident when he forcefully stated that

> [T]oday I have become what I earlier strove day and night to become but without success. Today I have become an India—Bharatvarshiya. In me, there is hostility towards any community, Hindu, Muslim or Christian. Today, I belong to every community of this Bharatvarsha [and] I accept everyone's food as mine. (603)

According to Gora, it was 'a new birth after destroying all the falsehoods and impurities that had enveloped me since infancy' (603). While questioning his earlier dispensation as a hardcore Brahmin, he was now ready to uphold the core values of universal humanism. What Rabindranath wanted to show through Gora was his assessment of the prevalent sociocultural context in Bengal. As shown in *Ghare Baire*, one of the reasons for the fundamental chasm between the Hindus and Muslims in Bengal was the deliberately generated hatred by the former of the latter. Being boastful of his Hindu identity, Sandip never saw eye to eye with Nikhilesh who always endeavoured to develop communal amity irrespective of religious identity. The political scene became complex once the Muslims found the Muslim League, founded in 2006, a platform for ventilating their grievances which led to the consolidation of an apprehension that Hindus were meant to protect their brethren's interests. Being opposed to political segregation, the bard expressed his views when Gora insisted on being initiated:

> [T]oday into the mantra of deity who belongs to everyone, Hindu, Muslim, Christian or Brahmo, whose temple doors are never closed to any community or any individual, who is not merely a deity for Hindus, but the deity of Bharatvarsha. (604)

Rabindranath was never persuaded to believe that India was meant to be a Hindu-India since it was a space which always championed sociocultural togetherness, irrespective of diversity on many counts. India was a template for the coexistence of myriad communities with distinct sociocultural voices which was argued very poignantly by Gora; so, in the development of Bharatvarsha, their role could never be undermined. It is the crux of the argument that the poet advanced in many of his creative writings by also raising his cudgels against discrimination of any kind. Repenting his behaviour when he declined to eat food cooked by the Christian Lachhmia, Gora realised that Anandamoyi epitomised the real India since she was hardly deterred from supporting Lachhmia to the chagrin of Gora: 'the mother I sought everywhere was waiting in my own house. You have no caste, no discrimination, no contempt for anyone. You are the very image of goodness. It is you who is my Bharatvarsha' (605).

The novel comes full circle. There are many plots and subplots, but underlying these remain an idea of Bharatvarsha which is respectful of sociocultural diversity. What is unique in this novel is the poet's distinctive way of couching the argument in a narrative in which social and political are dialectically connected. Gora was thus a phenomenon that evolved in conjunction with the nationalist campaign amidst an organised threat to Hindu orthodoxy that was manifested with the foundation of the Brahmo Samaj. Being his alter ego, Sucharita and also her father, Poresh Babu, upheld the Brahmo point of view while challenging Gora's argument in favour of those supportive social prejudices, defending segmentation among human beings on the basis of religion and also caste. A careful reading of dialogical interactions between them reveals that it was also a battle of ideas. What is commendable in these interactive dialogues was the poet's understanding of the prevalent sociocultural context in Bengal in which Hindu orthodoxy remained a predominant force at the behest of Radhakanto Deb-led Dharma Sabha though the Brahmo Samaj caught the imagination of a large section of those Hindus who were persuaded to view Hinduism in fresh conceptual parameters. *Gora* was thus an articulation of Bengal's social history in the form of fierce debates over Hindu sociocultural practices that gained salience in the transformed nationalist discourses, especially following the rise of Gandhi as an undisputed leader of the mainstream freedom struggle.

Concluding Observations

Gora is not just a novel, but a voice, first of endorsement of conventional ideas, and later, one of protest. Rabindranath weaved multiple threads of a narrative to firmly establish his model of universal humanism. On the one hand, the novel begins with Gora's uncritical faith in the Western idea of nationalism which, he thought, was conceptually tenable and instrumentally effective to bring disparate Hindus together, given their allegiance to Hinduism. As the focus of the novel shifted to the villages, a doubt emerged in his mind which led Gora to assume that what he conceived as real was, in fact, far from reality. The Hindus were themselves divided around many social axes besides their alienation from the Muslims. It also came to his mind that his idea that the Hindu concern for humanity was the same everywhere was also flawed. In a way, he, being persuaded by the unifying capability of the idea of nationalism, put forward the view that an identical religious identity naturally corresponded with uniform sociocultural togetherness. Once disillusioned following his visit to the village, Char-Ghoshpur, he confronted a completely different sociocultural reality which ran contrary to what he had nurtured so dearly, so far. Here one comes across conceptual compatibility between what Gora realised and what Rabindranath argued while condemning nationalism as an idea by underlining the fact that 'the Nation has thrived upon mutilated humanity' (Tagore 1985: 26). The changing Gora's concept of nation underwent a vast change through his confrontation with a reality in Indian villages that was completely alien to him because he was raised in the city of Calcutta. Although, as long as he was enamoured by his Hindu identity, he hardly spoke about it. His adopted mother Anandamoyi forcefully argued the point that what he conceived as India was faulty given its inherent sociocultural diversity. She defended her point by not conceding to Gora's insistence on removing Lachhmia, her Christian maid. Her 'Indianness' was far more realistic than Gora's 'pure, disinfected, masculine version of Indianness and Hinduism' (Nandy 1994: 41). Here too, the conceptualisation is drawn on the poet's critique of nationalism which tends to homogenise people, an idea which does not fit into the Indian reality given its inchoate sociocultural diversity. Under these circumstances, what is required to be done is to devise a design of togetherness in which the distinct sociocultural identities of the communities need to be indiscriminately respected. Hence, the poet rightly mentioned that

> the thing that we have to think of is … to remove those social customs and ideals which have generated a want of self-respect and a complete dependence on those above us—a state of affairs which has been brought about entirely by the domination in India of the caste-system and the blind and lazy habit of relying upon the authority of traditions that are incongruous and anachronistic in the present age. (Tagore 1985: 68–69)

In fact, this is an idea that Rabindranath pursued in his dance drama, *Chandalika* (1938), where the low-caste Prakriti was socially ostracised simply because of the accident of birth; the poet challenged this by showing that for a Buddhist monk, it did not matter and he happily drank water given by her. In *Gora* too, his adopted parents, Poresh Babu and Anandamoyi, had been hardly restrained from adopting Gora despite his Christian birth: humanity prevailed though there were reasons for them to be swayed by the sectarian vision of Hinduism. That they remained unaffected also underlines that the spirit of India was hardly manifested uniformly. The idea reverberated in B.R. Ambedkar's last speech in the Constituent Assembly on 25 November 1949 where he attributed the possibility of the evaporation of democracy to the existence of caste, which was contrary to fraternity and was thus 'anti-national'. Ambedkar made a very perceptive theoretical formulation that matches that of Rabindranath when he said,

> since caste was divisive, [it] was anti-national [because] in the first place they bring about separation in social life, and [secondly] because they generate jealousy and antipathy between caste and caste [and] … in these circumstances, the fundamental principles of democracy —liberty, equality and fraternity—would be no deeper than coats of paint. (Ambedkar 1949: 980)

The nationalist mode of conceptualising India is, therefore, neither apt nor has an explanatory value given the inherent sociocultural diversity in which Indians are nurtured since birth. The religious differences and caste schism notwithstanding, there also exists a linking thread that helps evolve a template for togetherness. It can thus be argued that when Gora went through his climatic transformation to accept India's multicultural persona as integral, he can be said to have adopted the Gandhian mode of reconciliation of conflicting sociocultural interests. The reborn Gora thus realised that the social humiliation of a section of Indians was no less insignificant than the insult that the colonial rulers meted out to the colonised.

Gora is therefore a critique within a critique because, in this novel, Rabindranath endeavoured to provide a design for the collective urges to come together for a common cause, which is based on his understanding of the limitations of the idea of nationalism. Gora realised this once he came out of Calcutta and confronted a new sociocultural reality in the villages. The other critique evolved out of the poet's disgust against the artificially created caste division that was not only unjustified but was also contrary to his concern for universal humanism. In other words, he was persuaded to believe that India's political freedom remained elusive so long as the idea of living together separately struck organic roots. What is suggested here is the idea that since sociocultural diversity is integral to India's rise and existence as a compact of people, it needs to be respected to develop a unified collectivity for fulfilling the nationalists' political goal. *Gora* is thus an unambiguous statement of how to cement a bond among socioculturally disparate people. Unlike *Ghare Baire*, where the author raised the issue of a Hindu–Muslim chasm being responsible for weakening the nationalist campaign, *Gora* provided a clear-cut design to address sociocultural cleavages. With many plot twists since Gora was introduced in the novel as a hardcore Hindu, who was perfectly indoctrinated in the core tenets of Hinduism which he completely discarded once he realised that prioritising one specific religious identity was divisive in view of India being a kaleidoscope of multicultural and multireligious inputs. By beautifully presenting the main protagonist of the novel, *Gora*, the poet created a new template of India to support his view that India was not just a community but a community of communities which did not receive adequate attention in the nationalist discourse till Gandhi appeared on the country's political scene in the second decade of the 20th century.

Appreciative of universal humanism, also championed by the Enlightenment philosophy, *Gora* was an engagement with the nationalist discourse seeking to build and consolidate a Hindu cultural national identity. Here, being critical of nationalism as a mode of organising humanity, the poet linked Gora's fascination for nationalism with a mindless surrender to the Western discourse which was 'ultimately a victory of the West over Indian civilization' (Nandy 1994: 49). Resorting to a dialogic mode of argument, the bard pit in a limited, divisive and communalist Hindu ideology against an open, liberal and alternative Hindu selfhood for India which conformed to the universal humanist perspective that he propounded at the end of the novel. The idea was articulated very clearly in his poem, 'Bharat Tirtha' (The Indian Pilgrimage), when he described India as the confluence of all civilisations, the concourse of all of the people of the world. According to him, India was thus 'more than a country, it is a microcosm of the entire world, it is a symbol of the universal' (Sarkar 2009: 45). In a fascinating way, the poet had shown radical metamorphosis in Gora's perception of patriotism when he realised that multiple sociocultural identities were integral to India out of his experience in the villages; he immediately understood how vacuous was his claim for an exclusive Hindu-Brahmin identity—that the division among the Hindus around many sociocultural axes was futile and an irrelevant way to awaken mother India. It also dawned on him that it was the people whom he must love and he must love them in all 'their squalor, misery and contradictions' (45). For Gora, it was therefore not a nationalistic but a patriotic resolution of the issue that Rabindranath grappled with throughout the novel to persuasively argue for universal humanism by juxtaposing it with the narrow Hindu identity that gained an ideological salience in the early part of the mainstream nationalist campaign in Bengal. Gora's patriotism was not just love for the Bharatvarsha, but for those hapless sections of humanity that remained peripheral due to the prejudicial mindset; it was both a fight for justice and a step towards empowering the disempowered. Hence the orthodox Gora was appalled at the barriers that the caste Hindus created within its castes and against other religious communities and also the intolerance of the Brahmos vis-à-vis the Hindus. This was 'ludicrously irrelevant when seen in the extent of the diverse religious influences that [became] part of India's history, its population, politics and everyday life' (Jahan 2005: 71). In the end, Gora, while conceptualising India as a compact, rejected the argument in support of prioritising one specific religious identity by declaring that 'today, I am really an Indian! In me, there is no longer an opposition between Hindu, Mussulman and Christian. Today every caste in India, the food of all is my food' (Tagore 2011: 603). *Gora* was thus a persuasive comment that the poet offered on the transition of Indian nationalism from being sectarian or exclusionary to being an all-inclusive design of togetherness.

As a novel, *Gora* introduces a new genre of conceptualising Indian identity in contrast with what Bankim Chandra Chattopadhyay sought to inculcate in his *Anandamath* (1882). Instead of paying attention to the multicultural and multireligious texture of India, Bankim's notion of Hindu identity was premised on the construction of the Muslims as the hated Other. In contrast, Rabindranath, who initially put Gora as a hardcore Hindu, upheld the view that the Hindu, given its civilisational connotation, could never be explained in terms of the narrow meaning of religion because it was also a way of life that evolved by being accommodative of multiple sociocultural and religious groups. His aim was to develop a Bharatvarshiya Samaj as 'a platform on which the differences among many religious, sectarian or racial identities could be transcended' (Dutta 2021: 14). This belief was based on the idea that the Hindu identity, instead of being restrictive, was 'a liminal identity between or belonging to the national and the universal' (14), which is drawn on Rabindranath's conceptual belief that in Bharatvarsha, 'the abiding purpose, the undying truth ... is national as well as universal'.[3] Against all odds, linked with the contemporary sociopolitical milieu, the bard endeavoured to build an identity which was an admixture of concerns for the indigenous sociocultural traits with the appreciation for humanity as a whole. It was not, at all, exclusionary, but drew its substance from 'an empathic and non-hegemonic national-universal identity' (Pandit 1995: 207) that Gora most persuasively defended once he confronted the deliberately created social distances in the villages between Hindus and Muslims and also among the Hindus around caste axis and later, when he discovered that he, being born to Irish parents, was not, at all, a Hindu. *Gora* thus dealt with a *problematique* that gradually gained precedence in the post-Swadeshi Movement era when Hindu–Muslim sociocultural incongruity and also the chasm between the caste Hindus and their lower-caste counterparts became a source of serious concern for the nationalists. The message that the novel conveyed was not merely relevant to the nationalist cause; it was an exhortation that remains pertinent even today when humanity is heavily fractured on counts which the bard highlighted so clearly in his many creative writings, including this novel.

3 This is Rabindranath's own argument which he elaborated in a letter of 1911, which is referred to by Pal (1993, 287).

References

Ambedkar, B.R. 1971 (1949). *Constituent Assembly Debates, Book no. 5.*

Das, Sisir Kumar, ed. 1996. *The English Writings of Rabindranath Tagore*, Vol. 3. New Delhi: Sahitya Akademi.

Dutta, Ashim. 2021. 'Tagore's Exploration of Hindu Identity of Gora'. *The Journal of Commonwealth Literature* 14.

Ghosh, Nityapriya, ed. 2008 (rpt). *The English Writings of Rabindranath Tagore*, Vol. 4. New Delhi: Sahitya Akademi.

Jahan, Husne. 2005. 'Quest for All-Indian Identity in Rabindranath Tagore's *Gora*'. *South Asian Review* 26 (2): 71.

Nandy, Ashis. 1994. *The Illegitimacy of Nationalism: Rabindranath Tagore and the Politics of Self.* New Delhi: Oxford University Press.

Pal, Prashanta. 1993. *Rabindrajibani*, Vol. 6. Kolkata: Ananda Publishers.

Pandit, L. 1995. 'Caste, Race and Nation: History and Dialectic in Rabindranath Tagore's Gora'. In *Literary India: Comparative Studies in Aesthetics, Colonialism and Culture*, ed. P.C. Hogan and L. Pandit. Albany: State of University of New York Press.

Sarkar, Tanika. 2009. 'Rabindranath's Gora and the Intractable Problem of Indian Patriotism'. *Economic and Political Weekly* (25 July): 45.

Tagore, Rabindranath. 1985 (rpt). *Nationalism*. Delhi: Macmillan India.

———. 1996 (rpt). 'With Mahatmaji in Poona', 24 September 1932. In *The English Writings of Rabindranath Tagore*, ed. Sisir Kumar Das, Vol. 3. New Delhi: Sahitya Akademi.

———. 1996 (rpt). 'On Mahatmaji's Birthday', 27 September 1932. In *The English Writings of Rabindranath Tagore*, ed. Sisir Kumar Das, Vol. 3. New Delhi: Sahitya Akademi.

———. 2011 (rpt). Gora. In *Classic Rabindranath Tagore*. New Delhi: Penguin Books.

———. 2013 (rpt). 'Bharat-Itihas Charcha' (Bangla). In *Itihas*. Kolkata: Visva-Bharati.

———. 2018 (rpt). 'Shudradharama'. In *Kalantor*. Kolkata: Visva-Bharati.

4

Situating *Chaturanga* (Quartet)

Conceptually, *Chaturanga* (1916) and *Char Adhyay* draw on identical concerns. As shown before, *Char Adhyay* was a response to the nationalist mode of political mobilisation that the poet never appreciated since it was contrary to his firm belief in universal humanism. Rabindranath raised some questions to understand the nature of revolutionary nationalism, and also endeavoured to respond to them with reference to his understanding of contemporary politics which had undergone a sea-change with the arrival of Gandhi on India's political scene. The novel stands out because not only was it a scathing critique by the poet but it was also a voice for gender parity which Ela articulated. By dwelling on the issues that figured in *Char Adhyay*, the 1916 publication, *Chaturanga*, can be said to have reviewed them from a different perspective. Structurally, this novel corresponds with *Ghare Baire* in which each chapter focuses on the main protagonists of the novel—Nikhilesh, Bimala and Sandip since the four main characters, Sachhis, Sribilash, Jagmohon and Damini are dealt with in four different chapters which were also published separately in four consecutive issues of *Sabuj Patra* (November 1915–February 1916). Etymologically, *Chaturanga* is claimed to be the precursor of the board game, particularly chess. The word is also found in the epic Mahabharata where it refers to the four-fold divisions of the army into infantry, cavalry, elephantry and chariotry. These four characters represent different politico-ideological priorities which, the poet characterised by metaphorically labelling them as four different approaches to reach the same goal. By raising questions than answering them, they also referred to the human uncertainties which probably captured the poet's doubts while seeking to comprehend the nature of the nationalist struggle that unfolded at the behest of the contemporary Congress ideologues. Besides being severely critical of the strategy that the political class adopted, Rabindranath opposed nationalists since they completely derecognised the importance of humanism in bringing people together.

Chaturanga is the story of a love that is caught between conflicting worlds of ideas. Sachhis, the protagonist, was in constant search of an anchor, missing out on the truth for ideas that found no explanation in a world of reason. Sribilash, on the other hand, a highly-educated scholar, did not believe in anything beyond the world of reason and tried to act as Sachish's conscience-keeper and sounding board. Jagmohan, being a hardcore humanist, always upheld the utilitarian belief in 'the greatest good for the greatest number'. Damini stood out as the only character who was definite about what she did and did not want. She was not afraid to ask disturbing questions that even Leelananda Swami failed to answer. She never endorsed her dead husband's right to will away the house, her jewels and even herself to Leelananda Swami's religious cult, without her permission. She also questioned Swami's right to accept her custody without asking whether she agreed to the proposal. She was not afraid to express her physical desire for Sachhis who reciprocated this but was afraid to either confront or acknowledge it. As the summary of the novel shows, each character is a tragic metaphor of the time they lived in, unwitting and ignorant victims of a social structure they had no role in shaping into what it had become.

Unfolding of the Ideas

Both *Char Adhyay* and *Chaturanga* appear to remain closeted into one broad conceptual idea, namely, the poet's humanism and its reflection in pure and simple concern, love, care and empathy for others which, as he felt, lost their appeal first with the strengthening of social barriers and consolidation of colonialism. As shown above, the novel *Chaturanga* revolves primarily around five characters: Sribilash, the narrator; Sachhis; Jagmohon or uncle as he is referred to since he was the elder brother of Sribilash's father, Harimohon; Lilananda, the religious guru of Sachish; and Damini, the widow who was given to Lilananda after her husband's death. Rabindranath unfolded those ideas which he held so dear to put across his concern for universal humanism. At the outset, the poet introduced the person who could be considered a link with the mental universe that he subscribed to: Uncle Jagmohon, who did not like his elder brother largely because of his worldly way of thinking and his obsession with his elder son, Purandar, who always upheld his father's wishes, notwithstanding his dislike. Contrarily, Sachhis, being persuaded by his uncle, Jagmohon, was baptised in a thought process which taught him to question the views and social practices that were readily accepted, given well-entrenched sociocultural roots despite being divisive in character. With Jagmohon as his mentor, Sachhis was introduced to the liberal discourses by being acquainted with the writings of Jeremy Bentham and J.S. Mill. 'With his brain cell kindled by Mill and Bentham', thus argued the poet, 'his atheism began to glow like torch' (Tagore 2011: 618). There was another important characteristic which drew Sachhis to his uncle: He always behaved with Sachhis as if he was of the same age because he considered 'reverence for age an empty convention that confirmed the human mind in servitude' (618). Known for his curt words, Jagmohon always espoused the idea that respect needed to be earned and chronological age was just a matter of digits which could never be a source of respect. It was evident in a letter in which he castigated his relative, who informed him of his wedding and addressed the letter 'to your auspicious feet'. As Jagmohan wrote,

> what it means to describe the feet as auspicious, I do not know; nor do you; it is therefore sheer nonsense. Then again, you have completely ignored me and addressed my feet instead. You ought to know that my feet are a part of my body cannot be seen as separate from me as long as they are severed. Further, they are neither hand nor ear; to make an appeal to them is sheer madness. Finally, your choice of the plural number over the dual with reference to my feet may express reverence, given a certain quadruped is an object of devotion to you, but it bespeaks an ignorance of my zoological identity that should, I feel, be removed. (618)

Explicit here is Rabindranath's social vision which was based on his sharp critique of the so-called archaic practices. There are imprints of the Derozians who led a campaign against Hindu orthodoxy and which also influenced Tagore's father, Debendranath Tagore, to a significant extent. Critical is the point that the desire to follow the age-old segmental social customs was detrimental to humanism since they drew sustenance from those deliberately constructed designs for continuing orthodoxy. This is one dimension which separates *Chaturanga* from *Char Adhyay*; it was an attempt to establish the importance of humanism in building human bonds, and unfortunately, the then-nationalists did not seem to be sensitive to this aspect. Here the poet laid the foundation of the novel on his firm views against social orthodoxy. Being inherently rebellious against what was transmitted to him as given, the bard also evolved 'a new genre of thinking to champion the humanistic goal and ideal' (Kakkar: 2012: 18) which was not readily accepted as they were contrarian. Nonetheless, it generated enthusiasm among the youth like Sachhis, who always questioned the ideas that his father, Harimohon, forced on him. Jagmohon's baptisation of Sachhis in rationalism immediately created an unbridgeable gulf with his elder brother which he, of course, knew since it meant not only a serious challenge to his well-nurtured sociocultural views but also the alienation of his son. As a narrator with emphasis on details, Rabindranath also explained the purpose for which Jagmohon raised his voice against his brother by insisting that 'service to humanity was an important aspect of Jagmohon's atheistic creed [and] the chief delight in such altruism lay in the fact that it brought nothing save financial loss—no award or merit, no promise of [reward] … nor did it placate any irate deity [which further means that] … there is nothing in it for me' (Tagore 2011: 619).

Atheism and the concern for humanity remained integrally connected with the poet's thought processes though he was aware that it was a difficult task since the former and morality were Siamese twins. Hence Jagmohon warned that 'being atheists requires us to be morally impeccable [and also] … because we don't obey anything we ought to have greater strength to be true to ourselves' (619). Being persuaded to question the artificially generated Hindu–Muslim schism, the uncle–nephew duo fought happily for the rights of the Muslim workers against those controlling the tannery industries in their neighbourhood; this further infuriated Harimohon since it was blasphemous to him. In other words, by challenging the carefully maintained social distance between these two major communities, they deviated from the norms that upheld Rabindranath's concern for humanity as an indivisible collectivity. The point was reiterated when, to Harimohon's chagrin, Jagmohon invited many of his Muslim neighbours for a feast in which the food was cooked and served by the Muslims as well. Once Harimohon expressed his anger to his brother for this, Jagmohon defended his decision as tantamount to serving his god. According to him, since he never questioned his brother on his daily food-offering to his gods, Harimohon should stay away from abusing his gods too. Unlike his elder brother's gods who never ate the offerings, his gods in the form of the invited Muslims never disappointed him. As he explained to Harimohon,

> You will notice that among all deities they are distinguished by a remarkable ability to [eat] whatever eatables are placed before them. None of your gods can do that. I love to watch this miracle, so I have invited my gods into my home. If you weren't blind to true divinity, you would be pleased at this. (620)

In terms of their approach to humanity, Jagmohon and his younger brother, Harimohon, were poles apart. While the latter held the views which were predominant among the Hindus, the former was free from the prejudices that the mainstream Hindus held against the Muslims and untouchables; he was also different from the Brahmos who believed in the formless and indivisible deity. Questioning the worship of deity as 'a deception', Jagmohon, a firm believer of humanism, was not afraid to say when his brother filed a legal suit against him to deprive him of patrimony. He unequivocally stated that 'he didn't believe in gods and goddess; didn't care for scriptural restrictions on diet; didn't know from which part of Brahma's anatomy the Muslims had originated; nor saw any objections to dining or mixing with them' (620).

As per the argument made by Jagmohon, he epitomised the universal humanism that the poet espoused. Free from religious and caste prejudices, he was a rare voice in then Bengal who always championed the views against social division on the basis of religious identity. Being raised in a locality in which Muslims were also integral, Jagmohon understood that without taking them on board, the argument for a Hindu–Muslim social bond became vacuous. This is one aspect of Jagmohon; the other aspect was his concern for the hapless which was evident when he took care of Nonibala, an orphan lad who had nobody to look after her. As soon as Sachhis rescued her, Jagmohon agreed to give her shelter because a guardianless woman was easy prey which was also illustrated by the fact that she was raped by her cousin brothers; later, when she was housed with Jagmohon, Harimohon's elder son, Purander, also exploited her sexually. Even after she conceived, on Jagmohon's advice, Sachhis conceded to marry her though she committed suicide before the actual wedding. Besides cursing the society that failed to take care of the helpless beings, Jagmohon also castigated those who enjoyed at someone's expenses by saying that 'the heartless creature who fathered the child, I'll never call a father [because] … that fellow only put the girl in trouble but does not face any trouble himself' (624). That he always prioritised humanity was also shown when, despite the serious risk of being affected by the fatal disease, plague, Jagmohan plunged into action when the Muslim tanners in his locality were down with the disease. Not willing to leave the place when Harimohon asked him, he devoted himself to taking care of his ailing Muslim brethren. Since the government was reluctant to provide adequate medical care, nobody wanted to go to the plague hospital. As evidence shows, Bal Gangadhar Tilak was incarcerated since he was critical of the government policy to contain the plague epidemic that broke out in Maharashtra in the late 1890s. Tilak's *Kesari* raised the voice against the government's indifference. The mob was furious in Puna and the plague commissioner, W.C. Rand (1863–1897), was assassinated by the Chapekar brothers (Damodar Hari Chapekar [1869–1898] and Vasudeo Hari Chapekar [1873–1899]) in 1897. Rabindranath also wrote essays in *Bharati* criticising the failure of the government to take care of the plague-infected people in Calcutta besides raising funds for the plague victims. The government's indifference was evident when Jagmohon poured out his grievance by questioning, 'should the sick be treated as criminals' (628). In order to serve the affected individuals,

Jagmohon thus converted his house into a hospital where Sachhis and some of his friends came forward to help him. Unfortunately, Jagmohon died of the plague, leaving Sachhis an orphan since his uncle was not only his mentor but had also raised him with those politico-ideologically progressive world views that his biological father miserably lacked. There is an important query that the author raises: Did Sachhis become what he became due to his uncle's influence or it was his professor of literature at college, Wilkins, who transformed him into a social rebel. Being disappointed with most of his students, Wilkins asked Sachhis to come to his residence for instruction in literature which was described by his classmates as his racist preference for the fair-complexioned Sachhis. The poet himself resolved the confusion by underlining Jagmohon remained critical of Sachhis being endowed with ideas championing universal humanism (628). Having spent most of his time with Jagmohan, he saw his uncle very closely and this instilled in him those ideas that his uncles espoused so dearly. It was, therefore, easier for him to understand that atheism and service to humanity were both sides of the same coin. Jagmohon's concern for the hapless Nonibala and also those Muslim tanners who were deprived of medical care also made Sachhis believe in what his uncle stood for. Not only did he say what he believed but also practised what he said. For Sachhis, it was an eye-opener; he realised that despite not being formally trained in any philosophical discourse, his uncle instinctively imbibed those ideas supportive of universal humanism unlike his teacher, Wilkins, who acquired atheism and its concomitant ideas after having been formally taught in a specific format of education. Wilkins reached his conclusion following his experiences of human brutality, drawn on artificially nurtured prejudices of one section against another; he was drawn to these ideas probably because of the formal training that he received by being a part of the system of education that prevailed in England.

Now, there is a plot twist. There was no news of Sachhis for more than two years before he was located in Chittagong in the company of a mystic sannyasi, Lilananda. It was inconceivable to Sribilash who had been very intimate with Sachhis during his college days; Jagmohon had always dissuaded the latter to stay away from these individuals who flourished by deceiving innocent individuals:

> These sannyashis are like the fake coins, useless in life's transactions. Yet they go around saying that they have renounced the world. If one is of any use there's no way one can slip out of the world of samsara; they are trash, after all, like the dry leaves that fall from the boughs because the tree shakes them off. (629)

It caught Sribilash by surprise when he found Sachhis who was Jagmohan's protégé, to be under the magic spell of the mystic Lilananda. His friends were thunderstruck when it was intimated to them. How did Sachhis readily accept what he hated from the core of his heart? It was inexplicable. Nonetheless, given Sachhis' devotion to the sannyasi, it was also difficult to surmise that the former accepted the latter under duress. An argument was offered by one of Rabindranath's biographers (Pal 2016) that the character Lilananda corresponded to a significant extent with Ramakrishna (1836–1886), the great Bengali mystic, who cast a magic spell among the educated Bengalis in the 19th century. Many of the educated youths regularly visited Dakshineswar where the mystic Thakur, as he was commonly known, lived as a priest in the Kali temple, founded by a philanthropist landlady Rani Rashmani in 1855. Many members of the Brahmo Samaj came to him for mental solace, and this popularised him among the educated Bengali youths. Foremost among them was Vivekananda who, despite being agnostic at the beginning, became his disciple; the leading Brahmo Samaj members, including Debendranath and Keshab Sen, among others were also among those who dropped in to listen to his advice. A rational Rabindranath was clueless as to how this mystic Ramakrishna mesmerised these young minds. By portraying Lilananda, the poet perhaps endeavoured to conceptualise the phenomenon which was beyond comprehension in the conventional mould of thinking. In other words, Lilananda was perhaps an attempt, on the part of the poet, to understand how the most rational Sachhis agreed to surrender to him despite being a true follower of an agnostic Jagmohan.

An analytical dissection of how Lilananda became a significant influence in radically transforming Sachhis does not seem to be a difficult task since the poet, in the novel, gave us enough input in this regard. At his first meeting with Lilananda, Sribilash got a hint of his philosophical moorings when the former advised him 'to leave the floor of the ocean of knowledge and come to the shore' (Tagore 2011: 630) which probably indicates that instead of hovering around in a makeshift world, he was asked to enjoy his worldly existence. It was further clarified by his statement that diver who 'goes down to the seabed to look for pearls [needs] to come to the surface for oxygen' (630). Here, there is a clear imprint of Ramakrishna's teachings. According to him, one gains salvation by staying within the family; there is no need of becoming an ascetic who gives up worldly enjoyment for reunion with the almighty. That Sachhis was simply spellbound by the mystic Lilananda was evident when he defended his unconditional surrender to his spiritual guru with reference to Jagmohan's conceptual universe. He thus argued that,

> when Uncle was alive, he gave me the freedom in the sphere of life's activities, and this was like the freedom a child enjoys in the playpen. With his death he set me free in the ocean of ecstasy (*rasa*) which offers the freedom of a child finds at its mother's breast. Having enjoyed the freedom of daylight, why should I now forego the freedom of the night world [which means that] Uncle has had a hand in both. (631)

This was not the answer Sribilash expected from Sachhis who impressed him as his classmate in college by being so clearly tilted in favour of rationalism. It would have made Jagmohon unhappy since his uncle's conceptual backing would not have allowed him 'to massage his legs and his hookah' which Sachhis was seen to have been doing so happily to obey the instruction of Lilananda. Here too, instead of getting angry, Sachhis justified his acts as a follow-up action to what his uncle taught when he insisted that one was required to use one's limbs for the service of mankind; it was necessary to utilise the acquired knowledge as and when it was possible. The view was categorically stated when Sachhis argued that,

> now I am in the ocean of ecstasy, where a boat's moorings are its guarantee of liberty [meaning thereby salvation]. That is why the guru has bound me like this to a life of service; by massaging his legs I am making my way across the ocean. (631)

So, Sachhis accepted what he was doing happily because it was a means to attain salvation. The idea of attaching stings did not appear to be valid given his natural inclination of serving his guru, Lilananda. In other words, by allowing Sachhis to massage his legs, the guru actually prepared the path for Sachhis to enjoy the ecstasy of life which would have remained elusive otherwise. Despite not being persuaded at the outset, the rational Sribilash saw in his friend's endeavour a positive step towards realising 'the Universal soul, an idea that inheres in all beings' (631). Here is a plot twist since Sribilash stuck to his distinct identity though he joined Lilananda's group presumably because he too was persuaded to believe that this was how one realised the universal soul. By insisting that he wanted to safeguard himself, he separated himself from the rest to avoid being 'a mere ripple in a flood of Sameness [because], after all, I am me' (631). Here too, there was a constant struggle between the two contrarian selves of Sribilash: on the one hand, Sachhis ingrained in him the idea of realising the universal soul as important in human life; Sribilash could not restrain himself because to him, 'the idea is like wine and it will clasp anyone to his breast' (631). On the other hand, being proud of his distinct identity, he hated to share 'the inebriate's joy' (631) though it was, he also realised, a source of ecstasy. The magic spell of Lilananda also drew Sribilash to his retinue which was a little surprising as the latter had condemned Sachhis' downfall by being deviant of what he had learnt from Jagmohon. But, at the same time, his desire to attain salvation convinced him of the importance of a guru in this regard. Here, there are reasons to believe that by allowing Sribilash to be swayed by the mystic influence of Lilananda, the poet probably sought to capture the growing inclination of contemporary Bengali youths to follow the path devised by Ramakrishna: 'Having roped two formidable English-educated atheists into his fold, Swami Lilananda's fame spread far and wide' (631), which led him to make his base in Calcutta.

Having shifted to Calcutta along with Lilananda and his group of disciples, Sribilash experienced that he had changed beyond recognition. It was difficult for him to change the frame of mind that had its roots in the 'delirious wanderings from village to village' (632). Calcutta was no longer as attractive as it had been in the past presumably because of the heavenly pleasure that he derived by being part of a different kind of life which he defined as

> a realm of ecstasy, where the cosmic Female and consciousness-pervading Male made love endlessly; the music of that cosmic romance filled the village pastures, the peepul-shade at the river-crossing, leisurely afternoons and evening pulsating with the chirp of crickets; it was like a dream in which I floated without hindrance in the open sky. (632)

Being appreciative of the pastoral beauty of village life, the poet always longed for his return to the villages. Here, the melancholy that Sribilash expressed was that of the poet himself since he did not seem to enjoy being in Calcutta which he found to be mechanical and devoid of human sentiments. Rabindranath endeavoured to capture the joy of being together with a purpose. Lilananda was also a means to enjoy an ecstatic life comprising men and women with more or less similar mindsets. Here too, one witnesses an imprint of the philosophical ideas of Ramakrishna who always tried to build bridges among human beings regardless of gender, caste and religion. With his idea of a common union of man and woman, Lilananda articulated a design that was similar to that of the mystic Thakur of Dakshineswar.

To Sribilash, Calcutta was no longer the city he aspired to live in since it was no longer as self-fulfilling as in the past. He found the city lacking in the charm that he enjoyed in abundance in the villages. He failed to adjust though he

> tried desperately to sustain the trance of lachrymose ecstasy amidst crowds tossed about by hunger and thirst, pleasure and pain, and the baffling problems of good and evil. At times I felt I was too weak, I was straying, my devotions lacked concentration. (632)

Sacchhis however gained confidence when he turned to Sribilash he saw 'in his face no recognition of the fact that Calcutta had a position in geographical space; to him, it was all shadow' (632). Tagore was agreeable to the idea that there was hardly a uniform source of pleasure for all; the human self could never be conceptualised as a well-knit unit. Different upbringing and capacity to absorb knowledge-driven ideas differed radically from one individual to another: It was conceptually myopic to even pursue the thought. At the same time, the receptivity quotient also undergoes a radical metamorphosis as one grows up. We do not know how Sachhis became a disciple of Lilananda though it was clear that he enjoyed being in his company since it was an entry to a world, which had so far remained unreachable. But the story of Sribilash was different. Once he found Sachhis in the company of the mystic guru and his retinue, he, despite having expressed his distaste for the philosophical moorings that gained precedence, happily associated himself with them. This was an illustration of Rabindranath's claim that change was inevitable in response to stimuli of various kinds: One might give up a mode of thinking by being exposed to a different conceptual vision; this was likely if one reached a different level of thinking in the same theoretical mould. Being raised in a cosmopolitan family and also having exposure to rural Bengal, the poet had first-hand experience of myriad human behaviours as part of the collectivity and otherwise. In other words, being an articulation of human drama in its most complex forms, *Chaturanga* was, like any of his novels, an attempt to capture the seamless unfolding of human life in response to multiple influences which are not always easy to fathom.

The Feminist Voice: Damini in *Chaturanga*

Damini, the female protagonist of gender issues in the novel, represented Tagore's ideas of sexuality and gender freedom in a fashion that was simply inconceivable in then Bengal. She was a woman with a voice, asserting her individual preferences for what she deemed appropriate for her in social circumstances that were not exactly in her favour. In a nutshell, Damini was a vision that Tagore articulated in *Chaturanga* to argue for women's independence as an agency even if that disturbed the social equilibrium. What is also striking is to unambiguously put before his readers the inner feelings of women who were forced to accept the conditionalities as inescapable. Like Bimala in *Ghare Baire*, Damini was also a rebellious expression: While Bimala, on occasions, did not appear to have been sure of what she preferred, Damini was confident about explicitly raising issues of sexuality which were usually avoided in public discourses. A change was thus visible; the reason may be identified in the locations of these two novels: Bimala was not always categorical in expressing what she wanted presumably because the novel was set in rural Bengal where the idea of gender equality did not seem as prominent as in metropolitan cities, like Calcutta and Bombay. The issue of sexuality was thus frankly discussed by Damini who was a city-based woman. It was unambivalently stated by Tagore when Sachhis, one of the main characters, stated that there were two forms of universal feminism: One was articulated by Nonibala, who represented one form of

> the Universal Feminine who by [taking] upon herself the stigma of sin, who sacrifices her life for sinner's sake, who, dying adds to the contents of life's cup of ambrosia. [In Damini], the universal feminism assumes another form. She has not struck with death, she is a celebrant of the vital force. Like a spring garden she is always brimming with waves of lovely fragrance. She doesn't want to renounce anything in life; she is unwilling to play host to ascetics; she has sworn not to pay a single paisa in homage to the cold north wind. (633)

By creating Damini as a fearless woman being hardly restrained by the social shackles while seeking to fulfil her desires, the poet carved an independent space in the discourses championing gender equity. Damini was a free woman who, in other words, represented a new wave of thinking that Tagore articulated by contrasting with the conventional notions of feminism which were restrictive and also repressive. Within this conceptual format, the poet expanded her argument by graphically illustrating what Damini undertook to fulfil her carnal desires when she surrendered to her beloved Sachhis. In his diary notes, Sachhis frankly expressed what he felt when Damini initiated an intimate interaction with him in a desolate place. As he elaborated,

> ... then something clasped my feet. At first, I thought it was a wild animal [because the incident took place in a cave surrounded by a deep forest]. But a wild animal is hairy, this creature wasn't. My entire body shrank at the touch. It seemed to be an unknown snake-like creature. I knew nothing of its anatomy—what its head looked like, or its trunk or its tail—nor could I imagine how it devoured its victims. It was repulsive because of its very softness, its ravenous mass. I was

> speechless with fear and loathing. I began pushing the creature away with both feet. It seemed to place its face on my fee—it was breathing heavily—I didn't know what sort of face it was. I began to kick at it. Eventually, I came out of my trance. At first, I thought the creature was hairless; but suddenly I felt a mass of hair, as from a mane, fall on my feet. (637–638)

So, Damini was not afraid though Sachhis was not as forthcoming as she had expected. In Sachhi, Tagore had shown how two contrasting pulls arising out of the prevalent social context put him in a dilemma. To him, surrender to a woman did not seem to be desirable, given the social context though he did not seem to be disinclined to respond to Damini's call. Being sensitive to the contextual constraints, the poet was perhaps unable to think differently. It is also possible to argue that in view of his primary concern, namely to deal with suppressed women's sexuality, Tagore opted for this: Sachhis was made less forthright than Damini. There are reasons to persuasively argue this point if one refers to the confession that Damini made to Sachhi when she met her alone. She did not appear to have hidden her desire as a woman when she mentioned that as 'a woman, … it is our nature to devote ourselves body and soul to caring for the body. The task is entirely the responsibility of women. That's why when we see the body being neglected our hearts cry out' (655–656). The hint was subtle but clear; Damini's desire for Sachhis was attributed to her responsibility for care for her beloved. It also provoked Sribilash, another character who held the conventional notion of being desirous of sex as taboo, to be drawn to Damini who castigated him for being indifferent to the importance of the body in human relationships which she characterised as 'weird' (656). In response to Damini's questioning, Sribilash felt what he lost when in a soliloquy he admitted that 'the longing of your sex for the weird is boundless. … O Sribilash, earn enough merit in this world so that you can be reborn as one of those weirdos' (656). This is one aspect of the argument suggesting that human carnal desires can be suppressed as it is socially engineered and also justified; the other aspect is highlighted when Sribilash was asked to be restrained by being drawn to the fact of women being calculative and also cunning when it concerned the pursuance of their personal goals and objectives. Characterising his weakness for Damini as surrender to 'Nature's fatal charm' (643), Sachhi endeavoured to hold him back by saying,

> the beautiful form with which it has bewitched you will disappear like a mask as soon as she has realised her purpose; when the time comes, she will remove this very desire which has clouded your vision and made

> you see as greater than anything else in the universe. When the trap of illusion is clearly laid, why walk straight into it with bravado? (643)

Sacchi and Sribilash depict those characters who, being largely governed by social mores and values, were not clearly persuaded to appreciate gender parity unconditionally. They being favourably disposed, did not always express their priorities unambiguously presumably because of their inability to break the social barriers. There is no way that one can be very sure of one's stance since it had its roots in the prevalent socio-economic circumstances. Women could be deceptive though the poet was confident that once they made up their minds regarding what was appropriate for satisfying their needs, they hardly wavered. In view of her unconditional love for Sachhis, her womanly concerns made her 'most intolerable' (648) when he was made to suffer by others. Furthermore, the fact that 'she would try to thrust herself forward to take Sachish's task on herself' (648) also suggests how deeply she was in love with him. By strongly arguing that Damini was right when she expressed her desire and also undertook steps for its gratification, Tagore showed significant advancement in so far as championing the cause of gender equality was concerned. It was not single-way traffic since Damini's effort was likely to succeed once the socially engendered practices and values were effectively challenged, and, if possible, discarded. The task, which the bard vividly described, was easier said than done by outlining the nature of the dilemma that Sachhis and Sribilash underwent.

Nonetheless, the novel has a happy ending which highlights the importance that the poet accorded to finer human sentiments, expressed through love, care and empathy of one individual for another. By agreeing to marry Sribilash, Damini also respected those values which were integral to humanity. Her primary aim was to make Sribilash happy also by taking care of the concerns that he always nurtured; of these, the concern for Sachhis was, of course, primary since both of them happily undertook the same journey to realise the core values of humanism. Being happy to contribute to the family by deciding to do the household jobs, she also expressed sharing the burden with her husband who, she felt, was 'working to the bone' (663) to ensure happiness for her. It was a venture in which both of them participated out of their love for each other and which made Sribilash characterise their endeavour as 'a mingling like the confluence of the Ganges and Jamuna' (663). Furthermore, when Sribilash saw that Damini started giving sewing lessons to the Muslim girls in the neighbourhood, he also felt that 'she seemed to have vowed not to be outdone by me' (663). Here Rabindranath, being a priest of gender equity, established that women also contributed to the well-being of the family which was a revolutionary claim since the role that they played was hardly recognised or acknowledged. In other words, a strong critique of gender discrimination due to the well-entrenched patriarchal mindset, the poet minced no words to firmly argue his points for gender parity which did not, for obvious reasons, receive approbation since it disturbed the applecart, nurtured so carefully over generations. Nonetheless, his appreciation for love-based bonds remained an important aspect of his creative writing. It was, therefore, not surprising when the ecstatic Sribilash described their joy as a couple by saying that 'Calcutta became Vrindaban and our daily struggle became the nimble Krishna's flute, but I lack the poetic talent to express this simple truth in the right key. Let me just say that the days that went by didn't walk or run, they danced' (663).

Besides highlighting the pleasure that Sribilash derived out of this union with Damini, the above statement also represents the critical role of 'social conscience' (Radice 2000: 417) which was manifest in what Damini did to ease his burden. This may seem a commonsensical claim on the surface, but in view of the prevalent sociocultural milieu, it was an exception since women's contribution to the family was hardly recognised. Apart from highlighting this relatively under-publicised aspect of the role that women discharged, by dwelling in detail on the importance of love that brought Sribilash and Damini together, the bard also conveyed that, to him, love was

> one supreme thing [that he] understood from [his] own inner experience: only through love can all conflicts be resolved. Those who cut themselves to pieces in arguments, or who fight over actions, those who don't want to agree at all, can reach agreement through love. Those who, whether in the fields of debate or activity, are always ready to destroy each other like gods and demons, become brothers to each other through love. (Tagore 1961: 467)

The driving force was love that brought two unknown individuals together to develop and cement a bond between themselves. By responding to Sribilash when he sought her as his companion, Damini represented a voice of freedom which allowed her to say what she strongly felt. It was possible since the outside world had undergone a sea-change, claimed the poet. Under these circumstances, that women's servility at home was likely to be seriously challenged was too obvious to mention; they, thus, became independent agencies of change. While insisting that old ideas supportive of gender discrimination would disappear naturally, the poet also created a milieu in which women themselves 'realised that they needed to be proactive given the obvious opposition of the vested interests that thrived by keeping women under male thumbs' (Tagore

2008: 362). Here, the poet's argument was an inspiration to those, men and women alike, who started questioning the age-old beliefs defending gender discrimination. At another level, the bard articulated a profound idea in support of gender parity, namely, 'the endeavour towards changing the well-entrenched habits was likely to be vehemently opposed since it was a threat to patriarchy ... which should not have been a deterrent since modern impulses should not be discarded merely in view of the adversaries capable of being harmful' (365). He showed how freedom or absence of restriction was critical to the unfolding of human personality regardless of gender. What he reinforced was, in other words, his belief in universal humanism which became irrelevant unless gender disparity was completely eradicated.

Chaturanga was a powerful statement that Tagore made to elaborate and also justify his unique conceptualisation of gender parity which drew on the spirit in which his predecessors, especially Rammohun Roy and Vidyasagar, strongly argued against gender discrimination. This was a novel set in an urban locale which was reflected in the differentially structured responses to the gender questions. Contrasting with Bimala of *Ghare Baire* will illustrate the point. Bimala was less vocal though she dealt with sexuality in a way which was satisfactory to her. Being raised in Calcutta, Damini had a completely different take on this issue; She was not only uninhibited but also expressive in her choice. It was evident when she completely surrendered to Sachhis in the cave; She was shackle-free and courageous when she decided to go ahead with the plan regardless of the consequences. Here, gender freedom was shown to have been won by her fearlessness and also her willingness to pay the price, if any, for this. By marrying Sribilash, who was not her first choice, she again asserted her independence by following what she deemed appropriate for her. She had also shown that she did not want to remain an appendage to the family. It was thus not surprising that she also happily shouldered the responsibility, to whatever extent possible, to ease the financial burden on Sribilash. At the same time, she also expressed her commitment to her husband since she was deeply in love with him. The poet articulated her feelings when she mentioned that 'my longings are still with me. I go with the prayer that I may find you again in my next life' (Tagore 2011: 663). What Damini said reverberated in Ela of *Char Adhyay* when she earnestly requested Atin to kill her because it would help her happily die with the feeling that he loved her. Was it merely a feminine sentiment? Probably not, because by constructing the female characters in a specific mould, Tagore endeavoured to show that love remained supreme in humanity; once it was otherwise, human civilisation was reduced merely to man–woman physical existence just like animals in their natural habitat.

Concluding Observations

Chaturanga is a narrative that unfolds with many plot twists. There is, of course, a steady storyline based on Rabindranath's subjective preferences. Nonetheless, the intermittent plot twists trigger surprise since the reader is hardly prepared to experience these. As per the first chapter 'Uncle', the interaction between Sachhis and his uncle, Jagmohon, reveals that both of them rejected those ideas which were, according to them, irrational. Hence, Sachhis was persuaded to accept the views of his uncle as most appropriate when he invited the Muslim tanners for a fest at his paternal home. Both the uncle and his nephew did not restrain themselves since it was nothing but a service to humanity. The decision of Sachhis to marry the hapless Nonibala, who conceived as his brother raped her, was also further proof of humanity being prioritised. It is also argued in the novel that what Sachhis learnt was not derivative of the instruction of his teacher at college, Wilkins, but was based on his involvement with his uncle in many of his activities. In Jagmohon, one may find the imprint of many of the Derozians, who always challenged the archaic practices, especially the deliberately created social distance between the Hindus and Muslims, but also perhaps the influence of his father, who devoted his life to the service of hapless individuals. In a nutshell, Jagmohon can be said to have combined many of the ideas that evolved in the wake of social protests, at the best of the Derozians and also the Brahmo Samaj.

Sachhis' emotional bond with the mystic Lilananda caught the readers by surprise since what he believed by being appreciative of Jagmohon's intellectual training did not restrain him from joining the retinue, of which Lilananda was the supremo. It was difficult to imagine that a person with a rebellious mind surrendered completely to attain salvation (*moksha*) as he believed that was the final goal for all. On a surface reading of such change in Sachhis, one may end up suggesting that he was confused. But a contextual reading will lead one to support another contention. There are reasons to believe that Sachhis represented that wave of thinking which justified the urge of many of the members of the Brahmo Samaj to visit the mystic Ramakrishna, the priest of Dakshineswar Kali temple, to derive mental solace. It must have been a source of surprise to the poet since it was difficult for him to comprehend why most of the enlightened members of the Brahmo Samaj frequented the Dakshineswar temple. That they opted for this consciously was also beyond doubt which made the poet realise that the human mind was unpredictable and there was hardly a persuasive conceptual format to devise scientific criteria to assess why humans behaved as they did. Being aware that she was a victim of archaic patriarchal prejudices, Damini articulated a voice for gender equality which was similar to that of Ela who hardly remained reticent about her liking for Atin. Here too, Damini made a choice in favour of Sribilash once Sachhis refused to concede to her request for wedlock with her. The interaction of Damini with Lilananda was full of ideas that the bard offered to reinforce his conceptualisation of gender parity. Even after marriage to Sribilash, she maintained her independence which was manifested when she forcefully argued that she was also equipped to contribute financially to the family's upkeep along with her husband. Damini, by insisting on her equal role in running the family, questions the stereotypes of man–woman identities. At the collective level, Rabindranath also established the argument that the society was conscious of gender equality, and the endeavour of Damini and Sribilash was to be merely identified as exceptions to the rule. *Chaturanga* is therefore a design for transforming the predominant mindset sustaining patriarchy and also ushering in a new era free from prejudices against women being inferior.

References

Kakkar, Sudhir. 2012. *In the Inner World*. New Delhi: Oxford University Press.

Pal, Prasanta. 2016. *Rabijibani* (Life of Rabindranath), Vol. 3. Kolkata: Ananda Publishers.

Radice, William. 2000. 'Atheists, Gurus and Fanatics: Rabindranath Tagore's *Chaturanga*'. *Modern Asian Studies* 34 (2): 417.

Tagore, Rabindranath. 1961. *Samanjasya* (Balance). In *Rabindra Rachanabali,* Vol. 13. Calcutta: Visva-Bharati.

———. 2008 (rpt). *Nari* (Woman). In *Kalantor*. Kolkata: Visva-Bharati.

———. 2011. *Chaturanga* (Quartet). In *Classic Rabindranath Tagore* (English Translation). New Delhi: Penguin.

5

Rabindranath and Environment: 'Balai' and *Muktadhara*

Rabindranath Tagore's notion of inclusive development does not merely involve the growth of human beings as a well-knit and also discrimination-free collectivity but also a seamless existence between humans and their natural environment. Based on his belief that mankind and nature should coexist to create a world of his choice, Tagore took ample care in protecting nature. In his perception, nature is like a caring mother who protects her children even by happily undergoing pain and discomfort. The poet strongly felt that nature and human development were complementary to each other; this led to the poet's displeasure and emotional vacuum once he found the indiscriminate depletion of forests in the country and elsewhere to create space for industries to grow. It was a condemnation of the haphazard growth of industrialism in India and elsewhere at the behest of the colonial rulers in collaboration with indigenous support. The bard's voice reverberated in Edward Carpenter's seminal work, *Civilization: Its Cause and Cure and Other Essays* (1899) in which he expressed his disenchantment with the spiralling growth of industrialism at the cost of humanity. While providing a critique of Andrew Carnegie's defence of wealth creation for common socio-economic betterment, which he argued strongly in his *The Gospel of Wealth* (1889), Carpenter did not seem persuaded with the argument that the industrialists, by ploughing back a portion of the profit from industries, were to contribute to the society at large. One of the primary pillars of his critique was that the destruction of nature could never be compensated by mere help to those who needed to be helped. Deforestation had devastating consequences, foremost among them being the disruption of the delicate ecological balance. The idea was most forcefully pursued by Gandhi in his *The Hind Swaraj* of 1909 which was a sharp critique of Western civilisation and was also, on the other, an explanation of the invincible nature of colonialism by indulging in ruthless industrialisation. For instance, Gandhi, like Carpenter, also provided a sharp critique of industrialism which was meant to cause a permanent fissure in humanity by segregating the beneficiaries of industrial civilisation and those who were deprived. According to him, industrialism was far more dangerous than snake bites since it adversely affected everybody in contrast to the latter which harmed only one individual. Critics like Carpenter or Gandhi questioned uncontrolled industrialisation as it was disastrous to human existence in the long run. This was a mode of thinking that flourished in Europe and gained momentum in the nationalist writings, especially of Gandhi and Rabindranath, because both of them realised that the campaign for industrialisation was a ploy to protect the socioeconomic interests of one section of the people at the cost of the other. Both of them raised the cudgels against industrialisation since it drew its sustenance from a discriminatory mindset, seeking to permanently segregate the haves and have-nots. Furthermore, they were appalled by the increasing importance of cities with industries because of the flow of people from the villages to the cities to work there. It was true that because of the lack of sources of livelihood, the villagers preferred to leave their homes, which however led to the alienation from their roots. Hence, both the Mahatma and the poet devised an alternative plan of action for the revival of the villages, both as places for generating adequate income for the inhabitants and also as a platform for bringing people together regardless of socioeconomic and cultural divisions.

Gandhi's 1909 tract, *The Hind Swaraj* or *Indian Home Rule*, is a powerful comment on how brutal industrialisation dehumanised human existence besides being a ruthless attack on the fundamental civilisational ethos on which humanity rested so far. One of the primary pillars of his sharp critique of Western modernity was based on his understanding of the civilisation that flourished in the wake of the Industrial Revolution. The booklet was a manifesto of Gandhian politics that evolved out of his sharp critique, especially of Western civilisation, that also created conditions for ecological disbalance due to indiscriminate depletion of forests. In other words, he felt that industrialisation was futile in so far as India was concerned because, instead of addressing the basic concern of rural poverty, it acerbated the circumstance. In his interaction with Maurice Frydman in August 1936, Gandhi articulated his views on the revival of villages by saying very unambiguously that it was

> possible only when it is no more exploited. Under these circumstances, it was beyond our imagination [because] … industrialisation on a mass scale will necessarily lead to positive or active exploitation of the villagers as the problems of competition and marketing come in.

> Therefore, we have to concentrate on the village being self-contained, manufacturing mainly for use.[1]

Explicit here is a sharp critique of industrialisation since it was exploitative of the villagers and meant to contribute to the well-being of those who had no role in so far as where village reconstruction was concerned. What Gandhi thus favoured was a system of production that was of use for the villagers and also for the environment; otherwise, industrialism would bring human civilisation to the brink of destruction. Hence, Gandhi prescribed a system of production appreciative of the need of the villagers and 'there would be no objection to the villagers using even the modern machines and tools that they can make and can afford to use; only they should not be used as a means of exploitation of others' (241).

The mechanisation of production was thus an instrument for the exploitation of the hapless villagers; not only did they have no environmental protection but they were also deprived of the sources of their livelihood following the introduction of the machine, which being less labour-intensive, created circumstances in which villagers were deprived of opportunities for utilising their labour for productive work. Gandhi supported mechanisation when

> the hands are too few for the work intended to be accomplished; but is an evil when there are many hands than required for the work, as is the case in India. … The problem with us is not how to find leisure for the teeming millions inhabiting our villages. The problem is how to utilise their idle hours, which are equal to the working days of six months in the year. That's why every mill generally is a menace to the villagers. (Gandhi 1934: 356)

Before the advent of the mechanisation of production following the industrial revolution, human beings had the means to survive which were not exactly detrimental to the ecological balance. Nature created avenues for fulfilling their daily needs; although they had difficulties, they were free from what industrial civilisation unleashed both in the form of diseases and also mindsets championing greed and enmity with one another. Reverberating the concern of Edward Carpenter, Gandhi was keen to develop the unity of human beings with nature which was a casualty once the industrial civilisation gripped humanity. With the consolidation of the idea that nature was also a source of property, the rat race for grabbing forests assumed massive proportions and hapless

1 Gandhi's interaction with Maurice Frydman, 25 August 1936, *Harijan*, 29 August 1936, reproduced in *The Collected Works of Mahatma Gandhi*, pp. 63, 241.

inhabitants, who, so far, had protected them, became just mute observers. So, for Gandhi, industrialisation was a source of devastation not only by erecting a barrier among human beings but also by instilling a sense of selfishness consolidating the chasm into an unbridgeable gulf.

Being persuaded to believe that machine-driven civilisation was harmful to humanity, Gandhi thus characterised industrial civilisation as 'a great sin' (Gandhi 2005: 81), which was already visible in Europe because 'ruination is now knocking at the English gates' (81). Hence, he strongly argued against industrialisation which, instead of improving human life, was a stepping stone towards large-scale destruction of human existence. While elaborating his point of view, he thus mentioned that

> the workers in the mills of Bombay have become slaves. The conditions of the worm working in the mills is shocking. When there were no mills, they were not starving. If the machinery craze grows in our country, it will become an unhappy land. (81)

Convinced that machine-based civilisation was a source of human downfall from which it was difficult to recover, Gandhi defended buying Manchester clothes because 'it were better for us to send money to Manchester and to use flimsy Manchester cloth than to multiply mills in India' (81). A nationalist Gandhi who was soon to give a clarion call for abdicating foreign clothes, preferred to buy foreign products because, as he said, 'by using Manchester cloth we only waste our money; but by reproducing Manchester in India, we shall keep our money at the price of our blood, because our moral being will be sapped' (81). Thus, Gandhi directed our attention to the moral degradation that industrial civilisation brought in by generating competition instead of cooperation which was suicidal for humanity. His support of the Manchester textile industries was to relieve the Indians of the evil consequences of industrialism. In other words, Gandhi, under no circumstances, appreciated industrialisation as it was disastrous for mankind: It caused a permanent fissure among human beings because industrial civilisation led one section of humanity to become appallingly rich at the cost of the rest of their brethren, and instead of generating sources of sustainable development, industrialism, by destroying natural wealth, altogether ruled out that possibility.

Gandhi's critique of industrialism hovers around his condemnation of human desire to make quick money which machine civilisation was capable of. By comparing the urge to make money with a snake bite, he reinforced the argument that the former was more poisonous because 'it destroys the body, mind and soul of communities [whereas] the snake-bite harms the body of one individual' (82). Hence machine-civilisation was a far greater evil to human existence which came out very sharply when he further argued that 'machinery is like a snake-hole which may contain from one to hundred snakes. Where there is machinery there are large cities; and where there are large cities, there are tramcars and railways; and there only does one see electric light' (83).

They all caused irreparable damage to human health which he justified by referring to the views of British doctors who argued that 'where means of artificial locomotion have increased, the health of the people suffered' (83). Being confident that the machine was nothing but a powerful instrument of destroying humanity by weakening society's moral fabric, besides harming the protective natural ecological balance, Gandhi left no qualms to express his strong reservation for industrial civilisation. It was a testing time for humanity since machines helped them attain the goal as instantaneously as possible which attracted most of us to industrialism though we tended to forget that, as a result, we were losing some of the permanent sources of comfort for goodness. Being aware that it was a difficult path, Gandhi was engaged in developing a mindset that was vehemently opposed to the mechanical way of getting things done. One accepted that 'nature has not provided any way whereby we may reach a desired goal all of a sudden': whatever was expected to be speedily achieved was not possible in a natural environment. This was likely to generate support for machine-driven human existence. At another level, his concern for nature-based sustainable development for mankind was based on strengthening the critique against industrialism which was possible only with the realisation that 'machine is bad' (Gandhi 2005: 83), which the Mahatma elaborated further by suggesting that 'if, instead of welcoming machinery as a boon, we should look upon it as an evil, it would ultimately go' (84). So, it was a long-term plan for the revival of a life that disappeared with the hegemonic influence of machine civilisation, and Gandhi was persuaded to endorse the view that it was likely to be regenerated with the rise and consolidation of a mindset in favour of human existence that drew its sustenance from nature by vehemently opposing the artificial machine-dominated civilisation.

Rabindranath and the Politics of Environment

Unlike Gandhi, who in his *The Hind Swaraj* espoused a view opposed to industrial civilisation since it was a deterrent to the unfolding of humanity in its natural fashion, Rabindranath was far more subtle in pursuing his approach to the environment through an identical concern for ecological equilibrium remained dominant in their views. While Gandhi focused more on the adverse consequences of haphazard industrialisation at the cost of nature, the poet endeavoured to create a mindset appreciative of ecological balance as essential for healthy human existence. They thus differed from each other in terms of their ideational approach though their aims remained the same. Gandhi's concern was much broader since his ideational universe revolved around the harmful consequences of rabid industrialism on humanity as a whole. He also felt, and rightly so, that colonialism would not have flourished had there been no industrial revolution for the latter required raw materials as well the market for selling the machine-produced goods. Once the British lost North America as a colony, they were required to expand their colonies elsewhere, and India became a prized possession. It contained a huge market and useful raw materials for running the industries back in England. In his *The Hind Swaraj*, Gandhi referred to these facts to persuasively argue in favour of a dialectical interconnection between colonialism and industrialism. It was obvious that colonialism and industrialisation were complementary to each other, and India played a critical role in the consolidation of industrial civilisation in England. By contrast, Rabindranath focused on nature as complementary to his micro-concerns for the environment and integral to his conceptualisation of human beings who were interdependent on nature. His conceptual universe, although drew on issues which Gandhi hardly took into account, was based on his deep-rooted belief that without adequate care for nature, humanity was likely to be doomed in the days to come. He was keen to generate love for nature which he clearly articulated in his many creative texts. The set of practices that he instilled in the ashram was guided by his concern for nature because not only was it a source of human sustenance but also a source of joy. It was evident in his songs, poems, short stories, plays and novels, among others. Fundamental to his understanding was an idea of interdependence between nature and humanity and vice versa.

A careful scan of the views that Gandhi and Rabindranath offered with regard to nature and humanity reveals that both of them were, knowingly or unknowingly, heavily influenced by Edward Carpenter's seminal work on the adverse impact of industrialisation on the environment and also human beings. Gandhi provided a critique of industrialisation in pursuance of the ideas that he imbibed from Carpenter; the poet, instead, realised that without being sensitive to the importance of nature in the existence of humanity, no endeavour towards protecting the human civilisation was likely to succeed. Critical to Rabindranath's thinking was a design to evolve a form of existence which bound human beings with nature as a close-knit unit. While Gandhi was appalled by the disastrous impact of industrialism, the poet devoted his energy to reviving those ideas which were critical to the generation of concerns for nature. Dialectically construed, the relationship between nature and human beings was conducive to the healthy growth of human civilisation. One of the reasons which led the poet to understand the importance of nature was his experience of being in rural East Bengal to manage his landed property. Appalled by the heartless activities of the villagers in destroying the forest cover in the villages and the continuous excavation of the river bed for sand, the bard raised his voice in opposition. In his regular meeting with the villagers, he drew their attention to the devastating impact of ecological disbalance on their lives. Being disturbed by the recurrence of floods every year, he asked the villagers to be vigilant about the excavation of sand from the river bed and also the depletion of forests to avoid floods devastatingly damaging the villagers and their properties.

Illustrating the Poet's Concerns

Rabindranath was not a political thinker per se though he had views which were pertinent to the conceptualisation of contemporary politics. He was anti-British—though in a subtle way—since he believed that political freedom was futile unless it was accompanied by radical social metamorphosis in the sense of wiping out artificial sociocultural differences, segregating one section of the population from another. Similarly, the symbiotic network involving nature and humans remained an important source of strength to humanity. The poet expressed his delight in the change of seasons heralded by new life forms—the blossoming flowers, growing plants and myriad living creatures. For Rabindranath, the shifting of seasons and the arrival of new life in the form, sometimes of unknown creatures, was illustrative of the bountifulness of nature. It helped him evolve newer ideas and ways of appreciating the change of nature that was independent of human intervention. So, since in the natural unfolding of nature, human beings had no role, they committed a crime when they disturbed the ecological balance. Implicit here is another powerful voice for restraining human beings from undertaking activities harmful to nature. Acknowledging the benevolent role of nature and calling it a source of joy, the poet, through his writings, argued for the dialectical unity of human beings and the natural world.

Rabindranath developed some core ideas to justify his love and care for nature. It is difficult to refer to innumerable texts from the huge corpus of literature on this theme that Tagore left for posterity; this chapter has chosen a short story, 'Balai' (1928), and a play, *Muktadhara*

(1922), to understand how the Rabindranath conceptualised the complex inter-relationship between nature and humanity and also to comprehend the political texture of his views in this regard. Here, the term political is used not in its instrumental sense but as part of the epistemology in which it connotes a specific power relationship. In the poet's perception, in grasping the complex interconnection between nature and humanity, political, in the sense of being a type of power relationship, shall be of help because his concern was to conceive of nature as integral to humanity. Given this logic, nature was not independent of humanity, and a relationship being appreciative of each other was necessary, if not essential, for the continuity and thriving of the civilisation as a whole.

The story 'Balai' revolves around a young boy, Balai, who was raised by the poet's brother after the child lost his mother. His father was working elsewhere, which meant that the entire responsibility for nurturing Balai rested with Rabindranath's extended family. Characterising the story of humankind as nothing but a creative blending of 'many chapters' identifying the distinctive features of humanity, Rabindranath dealt with one critical chapter of humanity through the main protagonist of the story, who built a universe of thinking around his concern for plants and trees. It is a conventional story about how a young boy was instinctively drawn to nature; at the same time, it is a narrative of how the poet conceptualised a dialectical unity between nature and humanity. Here, Balai is a nodal point because, in the narrative, he is shown to have articulated the views that the poet espoused while setting out his priorities in this regard.

Unlike boys of his age group, Balai was peculiarly passionate about nature: He deviated from many of the conventional ways in which boys of his age charted out their day-to-day activities. Instead of roaming here and there, Balai preferred to stand alone to minutely observe the movement of clouds and never bothered to get to a covered place to avoid being drenched by rain:

> [W]hen dark clouds massed themselves in layers in the eastern sky, it was as if his soul became dense with the moist fragrance of the forest; ... when the rain came thrumming down, his whole body would listen to what it said; when the sunshine lay on the roof in the afternoon, he walked about bare-chested, as if gathering something into himself from all the sky.[2]

Superbly articulated, it was Rabindranath's own description of how he felt when nature presented herself in such a way. As available evidence suggests, the bard used to roam around in the natural forests in Santiniketan to

2 Rabindranath Tagore, 'Balai', English translation, available at https://parabaas.com/translation/database/translations/stories/gBolai.html, 1.

enjoy the bounty of nature, alone; he felt disturbed in the presence of anyone else since it was, for him, 'an impediment to talk to the trees the way he desired' (Tagore 2009: 90). Here lies the root of unique thinking on education, the aim of which remained unrealised unless the kids learnt to appreciate nature as integral to human life. He thus lamented that 'from our very childhood habits are formed and knowledge is imparted in such a manner that our life is weaned away from nature and the world is set in opposition from the beginning of our days' (90). The idea is very clear for without being part of nature, one is deprived of real education. Being disappointed with the system of education that flourished in British India, the poet thus caustically remarked that

> [W]e rob the child of his earth to teach him geography, of language to teach him grammar. His hunger is for the Epic, but he is supplied with chronicles of facts and dates. He was born in the human world, but is banished into the world of gramophones, to expiate for the original sin of being born in ignorance. Child nature protests against such a calamity with all its power of suffering, subdued at last into silence by punishment. (90)

This was Rabindranath's philosophy of education. 'Balai' is the poet's own expression underlining the importance of direct interaction with the surrounding environment as integral to the type of education that he held so dear to his heart. Questioning the type of education that did not allow the child to explore nature and its beauty, not only did the bard consider it a sin but also an attempt to muzzle the natural desire for knowing the unknown. Instead of encouraging learners to get lost in nature, British education created a reign of terror by threatening punishment; this was also an attempt to take humanity away from human beings. 'We must not surrender to this conspiracy,' argued the bard further by insisting that 'we must solely deal with living ideas, have faith in life; otherwise, our learning shall have no meaning' (Dutta and Robinson 1997: 252). Insisting that learning emerged out of love, care and empathy, he conveyed the idea that Balai could appreciate nature, which always remained a source of joy and happiness for humanity. It was reinforced when he mentioned that in Santiniketan, he enjoyed life to its fullest manifestation because here 'life forms around beautiful nature' (253). He was unhappy in Greenwich village in the US simply because he considered himself in the prison of city life: 'My soul is being choked in this atmosphere where … nature was banished altogether' (253). As is well known, the poet was opposed to the building of a concrete jungle in Santiniketan and was in favour of sustaining its original beauty by keeping the forest cover as it was. Hence, his advice was to not disturb the natural environment by cutting trees or clearing the forest unless it was necessary for creating space for the university: 'Let me not bring fetter of gold for my ashram but freedom of spirit with its wedded companion Poverty, the pure, the simple, the tender and yet austere' (253). This was possible, according to Rabindranath, without the barrier between the environment in which life grew and human beings. Given the brutal ascendancy of industrialism, the relationship appeared to have been snapped, the poet apprehended.

'Balai' is thus a statement seeking to comprehend the very complex interplay of forces involving nature and human beings. Here, the story is not just about an individual but represents a collection of ideas that forms the poet's politico-ideological inclinations in favour of a particular system of thought highlighting how he felt when nature changed its texture. For the protagonist of the narrative, nature was always expressive; it was our failure to understand her language.

> When the mango trees bloomed in the month of Magh [January–February], a deep happiness would enter his blood, in memory of something inexpressible; his nature would spread itself in all directions, like a grove of sal trees [available in plenty in Santiniketan and its vicinity] flowering in Phalgun [February–March], would become suffused, become deeply coloured.[3]

His joy knew no bounds once he saw the growth of mango from the flowers. At these times, he preferred to spend a larger part of the day 'talking to the mango trees' because he felt that 'they do not enjoy being left alone' (1). Balai shouldered this responsibility and shared 'the fairy tales that he knew with them' (1). Balai had another habit that struck the poet. He often saw him walking in the garden 'with his head bowed, searching for something' (2). When he was asked, he would invariably reply by saying that he was trying to gauge the growth of the saplings that had appeared the other day. Unable to bear the pain once a flower was plucked from a plant, he immediately complained to the poet and requested him to stop this. That he cared for nature as a whole was evident when the grasscutters came. Because his concern for nature was undiluted, he never fancied for any specific plant because he believed, as Rabindranath felt, that it was his moral duty to protect nature which was also manifested in the grass or other non-fanciful saplings. When the poet refused to concede his request, he placed his appeal before his aunt, 'Please do not let the grasscutters cut down my

3 Rabindranath Tagore, 'Balai', English translation, available at https://parabaas.com/translation/database/translations/stories/gBolai.html, 1.

plants' (2). His views were not respected and he remained melancholic throughout the day; he realised that 'there were some griefs that were his alone [because] they sounded no chord in anyone else' (2). Behind this statement remains a profound truth that Rabindranath most clearly stated by emphasising that without nature around us and care for mother earth's creations, especially life in various forms, human life would have become impossible. 'Balai' represented a concern which was articulated millions and millions of years ago, which the bard explained by underlining that

> the boy's age was the age, those millions of years ago, when, for the womb of the ocean and newborn layers of mud, the earth's would-be forests rose and first cried out; that there were no animals, no birds, no babble of life; on all four sides only rock and silt and water. The trees leading all other creatures on the path of time, raised their hands to the sun and said, 'I shall stay, I shall survive, I am the eternal pathfinder; after death and amidst death, endlessly, I continue my pilgrimage of growth, my journey in sun and cloud, through night and day.' Even today that murmur of the trees in every forest, on every hill and grassland; and from their branches and leaves, the life-breath of the earth speaks out, again and again: 'I will stay, I will stay.' These trees, the mute foster-mothers of earth's life, have through endless aeons milked the heavens to gather into the earth's nectar cups the radiance, the essence, the grace and power of life itself; and endlessly they raise their eager heads high: 'I will stay.' (2–3)

While explaining the growth of life on Earth, Rabindranath underlined the tremendous importance of trees which survived despite sustained attacks on them for reasons connected with human need, if not greed. Being 'the mute foster mothers of earth', the trees remained critical to the survival of life in any form. He also appreciated the contribution of natural forests in fostering human life by drawing nectar from heaven, which illustrated the dependency of human existence on the survival of trees and plants. This is an obvious truth because, without oxygen which trees help produce, no life would be able to survive; we do not feel this because nature always remains kind to living creatures notwithstanding the constant attacks on forests for fulfilling human greed in the form of heartless appreciation for industrialism. Balai was, to the poet, a rare voice that, having internalised this eternal truth, rearticulated the concern which hardly received adequate attention because of the reckless march of industrial civilisation across the globe. In the poet's words, 'Balai had heard that call of the earth-being, heard it in his blood' (3).

By pursuing an inductive method of reasoning, the poet concluded the short story by highlighting the extent to which human beings failed to surpass the beliefs that evolved over generations. The point revolves around the growth of a silk-cotton sapling which came to Balai's notice when it was just a shoot; for him, it had been 'an infant's first incoherent word'; he had nurtured the shoot till it was a visible sapling, and he had felt that the shoot needed extreme care just like a child who always depended on a mother's care to grow. The sapling grew under his careful supervision and became a cynosure of the poet's eye as it became a large tree in the middle of the gravel path. The poet was in favour of cutting the tree since he neither found justification for a big tree causing obstruction nor was he persuaded to keep it to respect Balai's wish. He was, however, restrained by his wife from destroying the tree since it was linked with Balai's sentiment although he was annoyed because 'the tree grew shamelessly large [and] ... the plant began to look more and more loutish to me [which led him to propose] ... death penalty for it' (3). Balai never agreed to this even when the poet suggested replacing the plant with high-quality rose bushes. The story, however, ended on a painful note because Balai left his uncle's place to join his father in Shimla and later went to England for higher studies. Before he left, he asked his aunt to get a picture of the silk-cotton trees which, he thought, must have become a big tree by then. To her dismay, the tree was cut down by her husband exactly for the reason that he wanted to see it. She was shocked because (a) Balai's father took him away, which was tantamount to 'breaking off the umbilical cord' (3) and now (b) with the uprooting of the tree, she permanently lost a symbol of Balai's memory.

In this very brief short story, Rabindranath conveyed many poignant messages in a very nuanced manner. It was a story of the intimate connect between humanity and nature. 'Balai' is a voice for safeguarding nature, given its utility in helping life grow and prosper. On another level, this short story also represents a battle in which life-saving trees get destroyed without taking into account their critical role in the survival of humanity. Here Balai's uncle epitomises that force which hardly bothers about the irreplaceable role that forest cover plays for the living creatures to grow and thrive. The story is also instructive for it is an attempt to instil a concern for nature among the young kids who, being part of the school in Santiniketan, were also taught to appreciate nature in simple words. Childhood was the best time to appreciate reality as it was since, as the poet analysed, 'it is the only period of life when a civilised man can exercise his choice between the branches of a tree and his drawing room chair' (Tagore 2009: 91). Disappointed by the prevalent pedagogy that flourished during the British era, Rabindranath prepared an alternative road map which was articulated with the foundation of Patha Bhavana as a school in Santiniketan. He was aghast when students of Botany were taught about plants without first-hand knowledge about what they looked like or how they grew into trees. Critical of a teacher's approbation of the boys' studying Botany merely by reading books and without touching a tree, the poet offered an alternative mode of learning by encouraging 'the personal experience of the growth from a sapling/plant to a tree … which is the result of nature's own instruction' (91). Hence, no kid was barred from climbing trees in school (Patha Bhavana) as the poet believed that it itself was a mode of learning about the tree. This experience enabled, wrote Tagore,

> the boys of [his] school [to acquire] instinctive knowledge of the physiognomy of the tree. By the least touch they know where they can find a foothold upon an apparently inhospitable trunk; they know how fare they can take liberty with the branches, how to distribute their bodies' weight so as to make themselves least burdensome to branches. [His] boys are able to make the best possible use of the tree in the matter of gathering fruits, taking rest and hiding from undesirable pursuers. (91)

Contrasting his upbringing in Calcutta where he hardly had an opportunity to grow in a natural environment like the life in Patha Bhavana, the poet was very particular in creating a milieu in which the learners were discouraged from rote learning, but were encouraged to acquire knowledge by being part of the environment. It was clearly articulated when he declared that 'I consider it as a part of education for my boys to let them fully realise that they are in a scheme of existence where trees are a substantial fact, not merely as generating chlorophyll and taking carbon from the air but as living trees' (92).

The above statement constitutes an integral part of his philosophy because the poet always prioritised personal experience over acquiring knowledge merely by reading books. His primary concern was to raise children as integral to the environment which was possible once they were taught to appreciate that balanced ecology was essential for human survival. By drawing attention to the fact that the environment was not discriminatory in its approach to humanity, the poet also established a profound truth. In other words, being opposed to a hierarchy of any kind, Rabindranath created a sociocultural context in which students were never differentiated in terms of wealth, religion or clan. According to him, wealth, religion and class-based segmentation were harmful to human existence because they contributed to the generation of artificial superiority. Therefore, in his school, 'much to the disgust of the people of expansive habits, [he] had to provide for this great teacher—this bareness of furniture and materials,—not because it is poverty, but because it leads to personal experiences of the world' (93).

Even at the cost of digressing from the principal concern of this chapter, the above point is made to show that Rabindranath's primary aim was to develop humanity as a close-knit unit of individuals who, despite being socioculturally disparate, remained one as their root was the same. This is a common thread underlying Rabindranath's creative texts in their multiple forms. Being a devout humanist, his primary concern was to evolve a mindset nurturing humanity as a well-knit unit. The British rule was indeed divisive, but it is equally true that Indians were separated socioculturally due to ethos and beliefs which were contrary to Rabindranath's idea of universal humanism. What was unique in the poet's understanding of humanity, as per Balai's realisation, was that nature also played a critical part in the survival of human beings as they were. The cutting of the silk-cotton tree symbolised the brutal desire of human beings who were blind to the fact that it was a stepping stone towards the destruction of Earth that allowed lives of many kinds to prosper. 'Balai' is thus both a narrative of warning and also a design of hope that unfolded with the story.

Muktadhara (The Waterfall): A Rebellious Voice for Human Survival

'Balai' has a powerful message against brutal industrialism that the Western civilisation pursued at the cost of humanity while *Muktadhara*, written in 1922, was Rabindranath's critique of colonial exploitation and also an attempt to articulate a voice against this. The play revolves around a dam that the king of Uttarakut, Ranjit, built to restrict the natural flow of water from the mountain spring. The purpose was to not allow the flow of water to Shiv Tarai, the village located below Uttarakut; this meant that they received no water for cultivation. So, it was a ploy for protecting the king's selfish interests for his kingdom and also to show his muscle power vis-à-vis those who depended on this waterfall for their survival. On another level, it was Rabindranath's own voice for social justice raised against science that was being used to subserve the vested interests at the cost of the hapless people. Seeking to obstruct the flow of a free rivulet (*muktadhara*), Ranjit, the Uttarakut king, imposed a design to adversely affect a specific section of humanity to satisfy his self-driven ego without recognising that in the creation of the mountain spring, he had no role to play, and he was wrongfully asserting his right simply to fulfil his partisan aims.

Muktadhara was a play in which the poet sharply critiqued those who resorted to scientific techniques as a mode of deprivation. Critics' theory that the play was also a critique against science per se does not seem to be persuasive since Rabindranath admired science as a means to generate logical thinking and invent medicines to save humanity from various dreadful diseases. In his essay in *Bharati* in 1898, when Calcutta was reeling under the plague epidemic, it was Rabindranath who campaigned for the plague vaccine when it was vehemently opposed by the people at large. The play depicts a special situation in which the king deliberately restrained the unbound stream for inflicting suffering on the people of Shiv Tarai which means that in this specific case, the scientific technique of building a dam was misused for personal gain. Second, the play presents a non-violent voice against atrocities meted out to humanity. Long before Gandhi appeared on the scene, it was Rabindranath who championed non-violence in his 1887 novel, *Rajarshi*, which was also transformed into a play, *Visarjan* (Sacrifice) in 1890. Both *Rajarshi* and *Visarjan* were about the banishment of goat sacrifice in Tripura by the king Govindamanikya in opposition to the royal priest, Raghupati, and also his brother, Prince Jay Singho. In *Muktadhara,* the minstrel Dhananjay represented the poet's concern for non-violence. Interestingly, by bringing back the same character from his earlier play, *Prayaschitta* (Atonement or Expiation), published in 1909, where Dhananjay spoke in an identical language, the poet can be said to have reaffirmed his faith in non-violence. Finally, it was a powerful comment on the nature of education that was being imparted during British rule. Of all the creative tracts, his approach to education was most hilariously articulated by Tagore in his satirical short story 'Tota Kahini' (1918) in which the king's effort to educate a parrot (*tota* in Bangla), a bird, ended with disaster; the king felt that by forcing the bird to swallow the written papers, the bird's education was to be complete; in the end, the bird died because of too much of papers that it had swallowed. There was a plot twist in this short story because of the king's desire to make the bird forget how to sing and, instead, learn how to read the scripture which needed to be done by application of force: 'Once upon a time, there was a bird. It was ignorant. It sang all right, but never recited scriptures. It hopped pretty frequently but lacked manners' (Das 1996: 272). The end of the training of the parrot was also very poignantly articulated when the poet wrote 'the bird was brought to [the king], guarded by the Kotwal and the sepoys and the sowars. The King poked its body with a finger. Only its inner stuffing of book leaves rustled' (274). Similarly, Indian kids evolved as *tota*s due to just rote learning.

The main theme of the play is the construction of a dam on a rivulet that originated in the mountain spring. As it was a gift of nature, any artificial obstruction of the flow of the stream was a sin towards the people of Shiv Tarai who would be victims once the dam was constructed. The dam was also a place where people congregated because the temple of Lord Bhairava was situated there. The height of the temple was awe-inspiring to the villagers of both Shiv Tarai and Uttarakut. However, the pilgrims were amazed to see the height of the dam, which was higher than that of the temple. Perplexed by the majestic appearance of the dam, they realised that 'the frightful object that was raised was a machine to halt the flow of *Muktadhara*'s water' (165). The dam is 'a monster [that] looks like a dragon skull with its fleshless jaws hanging down, [the villagers were scared because] the constant sight of it would make the life within you withered and dead' (166). For them, it was 'a monstrous obstruction in the sky', which had never been seen before; they thought of this endeavour as 'a sacrilege to allow to overtop the spire of the temple, [which] will also irritate the whole sky by its obstruction' (166). The king remained unmoved and Bibhuti who constructed the dam, with his support, attributed to himself the power to contain the roaring stream. On one level, it was an achievement because, with the dam in place, the village was not going to be washed out by the flood caused by incessant rain in the area; not only did the flood destroy crops but it also washed away lives. According to the engineer Bibhuti, his 'object was accomplished and the sacrifice of human lives has met with its fulfilment' (167). So, his efforts supported the view that human beings were capable of achieving anything even in opposition to providential intervention. On another level, the successful completion of the dam made him arrogant which was also a cause of concern to the villagers who thus, instead of appreciating his hard work, castigated him for having contributed to the suffering of the Shiv Tarai villagers for want of water necessary for cultivation. Bibhuti's arrogance was evident in his expression when he said that his 'object was to make Man triumphant over the sands and water and stones, which conspired against him. I had not the time to trouble my mind about what would happen to some wretched maize fields of some wretched cultivator in some place or other' (167). An arrogant Bibhuti was thus persuaded to believe that for his work, he could sacrifice even basic concern for those who would suffer from the obstruction of the flow of water. This was reinforced when he stated that even the death of the labourers who helped him construct the dam did not bother him because he had finally accomplished his goal. That his joy knew no bounds was evident when he stated that 'my machine has triumphed against the storm of mother's curses [and] he who fights God's own power, is not afraid of man's malediction' (167).

In *Muktadhara*, the bard expressed his views dialogically. There were voices within the kingdom which did not endorse the way Bibhuti defended his creation. One of them was the crown prince, Abhijit, who always criticised his father's decision to construct the dam. Once the dam raised its head, he, while appreciating the engineer for his endeavour, also requested to destroy the dam; he argued that the demolition of his creation that was harmful to the villagers would help him attain 'a greater glory' (168). Bibhuti defied the prince by responding in bureaucratic language: 'So long as [his] work remained unfinished, it was [his]. But now, it is finished, it belongs to all Uttarakut [and] I have no longer the right to demolish it' (168). The debate was concluded with Bibhuti's reluctance to revise his views: 'It is my mission to prove, by the force of the Machine, that God's throne is ours' (168), and he couched his reply arrogantly by reiterating that 'no road is left open to make the Machine slacken its grip' (168). Being persuaded to believe that it was morally wrong and a sinful act since the dam caused grief to the people, the messenger of the crown prince warned Bibhuti to not forget that 'the God who breaks, does not need the broad road for his passage; the smallest holes, which escape our notice, are enough for him' (168). Although Bibhuti is an obnoxiously self-acclaimed, proud individual, his deed was not appreciated by the villagers who felt that the dam, by stopping the flow of water, was likely to adversely affect the cultivation in Shiv Tarai. But the sane voice was muzzled, and the inhabitants of Uttrakut were happy at the sight of the dam which was, to them, an embodiment of their achievement. Here the poet presented a song to express sarcastically that due to being scared of their lives, the masses sang the song to please the king, Ranjit, for supporting the construction of the dam and also Bibhuti for having realised the unrealised potential of human beings:

> We salute the Machine, the machine!
> Loud with its rumbling of wheels,
> Quick with its thunder flame
> Fastening its fangs
> Into the breast of the world
> Hurling against obstructions
> Its fiery defiance
> That melts iron, crushes rocks. (169)

The song is an appreciation of the great marvel of science which allowed human beings to successfully bind the water flow from the mountains; it was a reflection of the ability of Bibhuti who, with his hard work, seemed to have attained a goal that had been considered impossible.

But, Bibhuti's successful endeavour made him disregard human needs; this disregard also empowered the king to execute his dictum, despite being aware of the consequences. It was a manifestation of how human values were sacrificed under the slightest pretext. In fact, it will not be an exaggeration to claim that the above song is the crux of the significant part of the play. The inhabitants of Uttarakut seemed to have been mesmerised by the dam, which was, thus, defiant as it was equipped to stop the gushing water. So forceful was the current of the flowing water that it was capable of crossing any hurdles that stopped its way.

Here Rabindranath displayed his anxiety and appreciation at the same time. As the available evidence suggests, he was the most rational of his contemporaries. The debate between Gandhi and Rabindranath over the 1934 Bihar earthquake which was, according to the Mahatma, god's caprice, shows that the poet was horrified with this kind of characterisation of a geological phenomenon. In a similar vein, he was persuaded to accept scientific undertakings so long as they helped humanity grow and prosper. *Muktadhara* was certainly a triumph of scientific endeavour and under normal circumstances, the poet would have supported it. But that was not the case, which confirms that Rabindranath always held human benefits above anything else. Here, the dam was discriminatory in so far as its utility was concerned: for Uttarakut, it was useful for (a) it demonstrated its capability of containing the mighty flow of water and (b) it was a source of adequate drinking water and also supportive of a good irrigation system with the supply of water throughout the year. But for those living in Shiv Tarai, the situation was just the opposite. With the obstruction of the flow of water, people there not only suffered due to a lack of adequate supply of drinking water but also water for cultivation—something most disturbing to the crown prince. The poet juxtaposed these two alternatives to argue that science was, by itself, not a useful tool; its usefulness was dependent on how it was utilised. Since the play was written immediately after the end of the First World War, Rabindranath had in mind the devastating impact of the war following the indiscriminate use of bombs and other lethal weapons for destroying human civilisation. In his critique of nationalism, he thus said that

> we can take anything else from the hands of science, but not this elixir of moral death [which was] imminent because we tend to not think for a moment that the hurts you inflict upon others will not infect you, or that the enmities you sow around your home will be a wall of protection to you for all time to come. To imbue the minds of the whole people with an abnormal vanity of its own superiority, to teach it to take pride in its moral callousness and ill-be-gotten wealth, to

> perpetuate humiliation of defeated nations by exhibiting trophies won from war, and using these in schools in order to breed in children's minds contempt for others, is imitating the West, where she has a festering sore, whose swelling is a swelling of disease eating into its vitality. (Tagore 1985: 48–49)

What is striking here is the fact that the poet made a profound statement on the basis of his understanding of a micro-situation in which science supported the construction of a dam in a fictitious kingdom, Uttarakut. So, *Muktadhara* was just a warning for humanity, given the devastating impact of the war, the brunt of which was borne by mankind, especially those hapless sections of people in British colonies deprived of even basic needs of daily existence. It was not a one-time suffering as Tagore elaborated above because it created a mindset, which drew its nourishment by nurturing hatred towards the weak and the vanquished. This was most dangerous since it allowed to sustain the divisive mindset which was anything but useful for humanity to blossom naturally. So, the dam was not just a physical manifestation of human desire; it represented a design of controlling one section of humanity by another. As it was a device to retain the superiority of the winner, it could never be a means for human betterment. Hence, the crown prince was a voice for empowering the disempowered though he was appreciative of the capability of the engineer. His statement—that by destroying his own creation, Bibhuti would contribute more to humanity—was based on his firm belief that the dam, by putting many in trouble, was likely to be a source of continuous discontent between the villagers of Uttarakut and Shiv Tarai. Here, the poet makes a larger point based on this micro-example. Disharmony was, under no circumstances, of any help to humanity. Hence, the poet expressed his wish to generate bonhomie among human beings regardless of their location or religious affiliation. This is the underlying idea that not only informed *Muktadhara* but all his creative texts. For instance, being opposed to machine civilisation, like Gandhi, the poet preferred to establish his alternative system of learning away from Calcutta in a village, that his father, Debendranath, christened as Santiniketan with a view to allowing the young minds to flourish in a natural environment. As shown earlier, 'Balai' epitomised his concern for the environment which was shown by the fascination of the main protagonist of the story for saplings and plants. *Muktadhara* is a reinforcement of an identical idea except that it was also a condemnation of unconditional appreciation for machines for establishing human superiority over nature which was, as the play shows at the end, ephemeral with the sudden collapse of the dam once the plan to pull it down succeeded.

The second important theme of the play revolves around the idea of non-violence as a mode of protest which the poet popularised long before Gandhi appeared on the Indian political scene. *Muktadhara* is an articulation of non-violent protest against authority. The main protagonist here is Dhananjay Bairagi, who evolved the non-violent campaign to champion the cause of Shiv Tarai, which was badly affected by the obstruction of the water flow from the mountain springs. As early as 1909, in his play *Prayaschitta* (Atonement/Expiation), he introduced a character with the same name and an identical task. Dhananjay was a voice of protest: In *Muktadhara*, he raised his voice against the king for his deliberate endeavour to subject the people of Shiv Tarai to terrible suffering; in *Prayaschitta*, he, by challenging the king when he enhanced rent from the cultivators, echoed the same language of protest despite adverse circumstances. Opposed to paying extra rent, Dhananjay explained that his decision was guided by his belief that service to humanity was service to God; he further stated that paying extra rent in famine conditions was extortion which would invariably lead to the lack of supply of food for survival. His confidence in non-violent methods of protest was evident when he asked the villagers to accept the torture with a smile because 'accepting defeat happily will not only add to their indomitable spirit … but will ultimately ensure their victory' (Tagore 2003: 228). What was striking is the fact that in this kind of opposition, the protestors needed to be too courageous to not be scared of death. Gandhi reverberated the idea when he underlined that a *satyagrahi* could never be subdued with the threat of death. The play, *Prayaschitta*, laid out a frame of thinking that gradually thrived. Here, Dhananjay was a representative of a new wave of conceptualising human protest, which was devoid of hatred or enmity. It was a model of protest based on love, care and empathy. This was evident as the play progressed. The king who was adamant about not reducing rent conceded the request once his son, the prince, having realised that their demand was genuine, joined hands with the protestors led by Dhananjay. Udayaditta, the prince, was readily accepted not as a king but as their brother who instantaneously became integral to Dhananjay and his team simply because he, being one of them, had the mindset to support their battle for survival. Long before non-violence became a creed for the mainstream nationalist, the poet conceptualised its importance in articulating a powerful voice for fulfilling basic human demands. For Dhananjay, it was a call for liberation, liberation from hunger and injustice. Dhananjay's non-violent struggle was directed for an immediate gain, namely, withdrawal of excessive rent; but, the campaign was also for emancipation from bondage: 'The togetherness for a genuine cause is a source of strength to realise what appeared to be unrealisable; it is a force which will help generate [the idea that] there was nothing above humanity' (253). There was a similarity, as will be shown below, between Dhananjay of *Prayaschitta* and Dhananjay of *Muktadhara* in the sense that in both these plays, once the objective was attained, he disappeared as if he was needed elsewhere to support the people fighting against injustice and humiliation.

There is therefore no denying the fact that the character Dhananjay that Rabindranath constructed in *Prayschitta* reappeared in *Muktadhara* because the circumstances were identical. As in *Prayaschitta*, the Shiv Tarai villagers in *Muktadhara* needed a voice which Dhananjay provided to organise themselves against the decision of the king. What had provoked the campaign in Jessore was the king's decree for extra rent; in a similar vein, in *Muktadhara*, the decision to obstruct the flow of water led the affected ones to challenge the king. Dhananjay was the missing link since as soon as he arrived on the scene, the situation underwent a sea-change; people gained confidence and finally, attained the goal. It will not be an exaggeration to argue that Dhananjay played the role of conscience-keeper since not only did he inspire the collectivity but his emotional appeal also had the strength to persuade the obstinate king.

As a priest of non-violence, it will not be out of place to suggest that Rabindranath jotted the contours of the non-violent struggle that Gandhi launched for political freedom. Published in 1888, *Rajarshi* (a novel), which was also transformed into a play, *Visarjan* (Sacrifice) in 1891, the poet unequivocally expressed his choice for non-violence. Being a historical novel that laid out the processes of transformation of a king into a saint, Rajarshi, who, by banning animal sacrifice in the royal temple, questioned the age-old belief of propitiating the gods with animal blood. It was a momentous decision since it was a departure from the past; the royal priest, who considered himself to be the custodian of rituals, dissented, but this barely deterred the king, Govindamanikya. The novel revolves around the battle between the king and the royal priest, Raghupati. Being a devout believer in non-violence, the king was surprised at the continuity of this brutal practice in his kingdom of Tripura. The dialogue between Raghupati and Govindamanikya is testimony to the poet's conceptualisation of non-violence. While stopping animal sacrifice on the temple premises, Govindamanikya defended his verdict by saying that he had realised that this barbarous custom could, under no circumstances, be an act to please the goddess—it was only through emotional attachment that the purpose of worship reached fruition. To counter this, the royal priest argued that since it had been going on for years, the goddess must have endorsed the practice, which meant that she liked offerings of blood; otherwise, she would have made her wish known in other ways. Opposed to this view, the king retorted by saying that the goddess turned her face when innocent animals were sacrificed before her. The discussion ended with Raghupati's threat that as king, Govindamanikya had the authority to administer his subject but in so far as the temple was concerned, it was Raghupati whose decree would prevail. Many of his subordinate staff, especially his main minister, also tried to persuade him to reduce the number of animals being sacrificed for decades. The rest of the novel was about the conspiracy that Raghupati hatched against the king to dislodge him from power.

On the surface, *Rajarshi* and the play, *Visarjan*, were about the banning of animal sacrifice. But these also reflected Rabindranath's firm belief in non-violence. By the decree, the king championed the claim that selfless devotion was the only means to express one's love for the almighty; animal sacrifice was symptomatic of man's savage mindset since animals were also part of the creation that the almighty nurtured. Hence, they had the same claim over the goddess as humans. Despite being only 17 years of age when he wrote this novel, Rabindranath was clear in his perception which we find articulated in his later novels. Non-violence was, to him, a creed which he never undermined as it became integral to his mindset. Dhananjay in *Prayaschitta* non-violently opposed the ruler, Pratapaditya of Jessore; but in *Rajarshi* and *Visarjan*, non-violence was established as integral to humanity, and Govindamanikya represented a powerful voice that was articulated when animal sacrifice was abolished despite vehement opposition from among those who thrived under his care. Given his distaste for animal sacrifice in the name of propitiating god, it was easier for him to draw on this when the poet wrote *Prayaschitta* in his late 30s. Here, non-violence was not just a matter of the inner self, but it became a weapon of protest against authority. As shown above, the goal, namely the slashing of rent, was achieved once the prince supported the claim to the chagrin of his father.

In *Muktadhara*, there are two protagonists of the non-violent mode of protest: one was the prince, Abhijit, who was persuaded to believe that nature needed to be protected from human intervention, and the other, the minstrel Dhananjay, who mobilised the protestors for non-violent opposition to the king. Despite being raised in the palace, Abhijit (who was found by the king near *Muktadhara*) hardly imbibed the ideas that his foster father, the king, appreciated; his appreciation of nature was thus barely appreciated. Nonetheless, he always admired nature which was so bountiful and a source of constant joy, which he expressed when he said that 'nature and the constituent objects, living and non-living are always beautiful [and] … have made my life sweet' (Das 1996: 179). His support for the campaign infuriated the king who immediately put him under constant vigil by the royal guards. This not only infuriated the villagers of Shiv Tarai but also created a milieu in which the protesters also realised that the only option left for them was to organise a non-violent campaign to achieve their goal. In such a situation, Dhananjay charted his course of action by laying out the conceptual parameters of the forthcoming struggle. In response to the suggestion that the villagers should hit the king back, the minstrel mentioned that the battle was guided by the principle of 'no blow … [because] … the aim is not for beating the waves, but for conquering them by keeping us steady' (183). While pursuing his argument for non-violent confrontation, he further stated that 'the true man within us is a flame of fire. He consumes all hurts in light. Only the brute beast is hurt. The brute beast is flesh, and it goes whining when it is struck—why do you stand with your mouths gaping wide open' (183).

Only by winning the heart of the enemy would the protesters successfully win the battle: because he did not 'want to hurt, and therefore he had no feat' (184). It was further elaborated in the following song, which represented an endeavour to encourage the villagers to participate in the non-violence as victory was inevitable:

> Victory to Him, whose voice thunders forth Truth
> Whose right arm smites unrighteous,
> Whose guidance leads mortals across death,
> Victory to Him! (197)

Dhananjay's confident claim for the success of the non-violent struggle was evident when he challenged Bibhuti, who had constructed the dam. Seeking to puncture his belief, Bibhuti challenged him that the destruction of the dam was impossible, given the technique and materials used for building it. Even the god Bhairava was not equipped to bring it down by using his divine power. 'You can't awaken the God … through sounding temple gongs and lighting temple lamps,' Bibhuti warned (202), to which Dhananjay replied that 'when you bind him with fetters, he will wake up to break them' (203). Provoked by Dhananjay, he further stated that 'our fetters are not so easy to break and … there are an infinite number of knots' (203). Dhananjay reaffirmed his faith when his associate started a song, exhorting that,

> Victory to him, the terrible,
> The Lord of Destruction,
> The Uttermost peace,
> The dissolver of doubts,
> The breaker of fetters,
> Who carried us beyond all conflicts. (203)

The above song was reflective of the mass zeal that was translated into action by the minstrel; this enthusiasm was clearly inconceivable to the king and his colleagues, including Bibhuti, who was confident that the dam was unbreakable. In face of the non-violent challenge, the opposition was not only feeble but also proved that an unjust battle could never be won. The confidence of Bibhuti was shattered when he found that 'the water of Muktadhara is freed'—which was unbelievable to him. How was it possible? It was explained by a friend of Abhijit who always opposed the obstruction of the free flow of Muktadhara from the mountain springs to Shiv Tarai. According to him, once Abhijit came to know, 'about a weakness in the structure, and at that point, he gave his blow to the monster Machine. The monster returned that blow against him. Then Muktadhara, like a mother, took up his stricken body into her arms and carried him away' (207).

Muktadhara was a play to highlight that human strength, despite its appearance of being fragile, prevailed over the technical superiority of machine-driven civilisation, and also, the brute force, endowed with the machines of destruction always remained handicapped given the awakening of the masses in opposition to an unjust system. The washing away of Abhijit reveals, on the other, the importance of sacrifice for a just cause; in non-violent struggle, one was required to pay a price to attain the aspired goal.

Muktadhara is Rabindranath's critique of colonial exploitation of nature for its well-being; it was also a play to show that colonialism was not invincible as it appeared on the surface. What was required was mass zeal to do away with an alien system that was contrary to humanity. As far as the mode of opposition was concerned, the poet can be said to have anticipated much of what the Mahatma conceptualised once he rose to prominence in India's freedom struggle. *Muktadhara*'s Dhananjay was the protagonist of non-violence or *ahimsa* as Gandhi preferred to call it. According to him, non-violence meant 'both passive and active love [with the aim of] ... refraining from causing harm and destruction of living beings as well as promoting their well-being' (Parekh 1999: 130). This suggests that by *ahimsa*, Gandhi did not entail merely 'non-injury' to others in a mere negative or passive connotation; instead, *ahimsa* had a positive or active meaning of love and charity. As the Mahatma clarified himself by declaring that,

> in its negative form, [*ahimsa*] means not injuring any living being whether by body or mind. I may not therefore, hurt the person of any wrong-doer or bear any ill-will to him and so cause him mental suffering. In its positive form, *ahimsa* means the largest love, the

> greatest charity. If I am a follower of *ahimsa*, I must love my enemy or a stranger to me, as I would my wrong-doing father or son. The active necessarily include truth and fearlessness.[4] (Iyer 1973: 179–180)

A careful analysis of the protagonist of non-violence, Dhananjay, reveals that he was guided by the precepts of *ahimsa* that Mahatma devised when he spearheaded the nationalist campaign. By instilling courage and fearlessness among the villagers of Shiv Tarai, he did what Gandhi expected to do to succeed in a non-violent struggle against brutal authority. In a letter on 3 February 1922, Rabindranath spoke about *ahimsa* in the same language which appeared first in this 1922 play. That *ahimsa* was a source of enormous strength was evident when he stated that

> I believe in the efficacy of *ahimsa* as the means of overcoming the congregated might of physical force on which political powers in all countries mainly rest, [and] … like every other moral principle, ahimsa has to spring from the depth of mind and it must not be forced upon man from some outside appeal of urgent need. (Das 1996: 775)

Long before Gandhi, Rabindranath was, therefore, a pioneer of non-violent protest, as his *Prayaschitta* (1909) and *Muktadhara* (1922) show. Conceptually, both of them upheld non-violence as a powerful mode of protest and an effective means of bringing socioculturally disparate people together. These two protagonists of non-violence also believed that unless one was emotionally inclined, it was not likely to succeed. For Dhananjay, in both *Prayaschitta* and *Muktadhara*, the non-violent campaign (against the authority for not being sensitive to what the ruled demanded) attained the goal because people spontaneously came together to address their concerns. It did not happen all of a sudden; Dhananjay endeavoured hard to develop a bonhomie among the people of Shiv Tarai. The idea that the bard propounded in these plays reverberated in his tribute to the Mahatma when he, while explaining the reason for Gandhi's success in his campaign, drew on how Dhananjay achieved an unachievable goal. It was evident when the poet said that

> when Mahatma Gandhi came and opened up the path of freedom for India, he had no obvious medium of power in his hand, no overwhelming authority of coercion. The influence which emanated from his personality was ineffable, like music, like beauty. Its claim upon others was great because of the revelation of a spontaneous self-giving. … The masses … dwelt upon the truth which shines through his character in lucid

4 Gandhi's letter to *Modern Review*, 21 October 1916, reproduced in Iyer (1973, 179–180).

> simplicity. … His … inspiration … transcends all varied manifestations of humanity, and makes the face of worldliness turn to the light that comes from the eternal source of wisdom. (846–847)

Nothing could be clearer than the above explanation highlighting how Gandhi developed oneness among the socioculturally disparate *satyagrahis* who devoted their heart and soul to the cause for which he was fighting selflessly. As the two plays demonstrate, whether in Jessore or Shiv Tarai, the villagers joined hands to accomplish objectives which served their exclusive purposes. It was Dhananjay who tied them together with reference to the goal that was a source of discomfort to them. In Rabindranath's perception, this was nothing unusual since human beings, since time immemorial, struggled together against odds, which were sometimes perpetrated by nature, sometimes by mortal beings. So, Dhananjay was a civilisational force that appeared in different historical ages to save humanity. Dhananjay also expressed that the desire to fight those forces which thrived by undermining humanity was instinctive—it was a zeal internal to human beings. Attacking bestiality that a section of humanity nurtured, the poet appreciated the endeavour that the Mahatma zealously pursued notwithstanding the adverse consequences. Here in Gandhi's political voice, Rabindranath saw the personification of Dhananjay who appeared in his mental universe long before the language of non-violence gained precedence in India's struggle for independence. In the face of the threat of incarceration or even death, Dhananjay remained an indomitable force which inspired the villagers in both Jessore and Shiv Tarai to the extent of even making the final sacrifice for attaining their legitimate goal. Gandhi too generated a deep-rooted concern among his supporters which made them suffer silently and face even 'the machine guns belching death' (847), which was possible because of their moral courage to battle against injustice, regardless of the consequences. 'As long as a people are afraid of physical suffering,' the poet believed,

> machinery for intimidating them will always be invented. Once we are able to say that we are no longer afraid of physical suffering or of death, arms and armaments lose their significance. If such a faith in put spiritual strength can be inculcated … then a whole people can be brought to accept such an idea, that, in itself, would be permanent freedom. (Ghosh 2008: 645–646)

One may argue that the non-violent struggle that Gandhi led to liberate India from the British yolk had its conceptual roots in Rabindranath's creative writings, especially those two plays, *Prayaschitta* and

Muktadhara. First, although he endorsed non-violence as a creed in one of the earliest novels, *Rajarshi*, when the king, Govindamanikya, banned animal sacrifice in the Bhuvaneshwari temple, he exemplified it as a mode of opposition when Dhananjay raised his voice against torture meted out to the hapless villagers in Jessore and Shiv Tarai. Also, through these two plays, the poet established the point that non-violence was an effective idea in awakening people because they were nurtured in a sociocultural milieu in which violence, being essentially divisive between the strong and weak, was despised; non-violence was a design of bringing people together on the basis of the sociocultural ideas that have flourished in India over centuries. Finally, it is now fair to argue that the theme of non-violence is foregrounded in Rabindranath's *Prayaschitta* and *Muktadhara*, many years before the Mahatma embarked on his historic liberation movement based on *ahimsa*. By reiterating the claim that 'Kingdom of God is within our reach and … any obstruction that may exist in our minds to the idea of its realisation is but flimsy and unreal' (646), the bard reaffirmed that non-violence was inherent in human minds, and what was required was to inculcate it as and when humanity was threatened to be devastated by selfishly championing sectional interests.

Muktadhara stands out as it is also a powerful commentary on education which should never be reduced to, the poet strongly felt, a passport for a comfortable job; it is a means of introduction to the rest of the world in its natural manifestation. When the play was published in 1922, Visva-Bharati had already come into existence; it was not only a centre for learning but represented a philosophy for preparing young minds to comprehend the world and also to take it forward in consonance with the basic aim of humanity. *Muktadhara* was also a caricature of students' behaviour that unfolded under duress since the atrocious king did not allow contrarian views to prosper. In the play, there is a small scene in which Rabindranath launches a satirical attack on the schooling system that flourished in Uttarakut. His view was based on the idea that school education was meant to indoctrinate young minds in accordance with the will of the ruler; school-going children and kids were taught to obey the political structure that rested on very specific power relationships. It was thus inevitable that certain specific modes of conceptualisation became prominent at the cost of those which were not merely contrarian but also a threat to the prevalent system of thoughts.

The scene begins with the dictatorial instruction of the schoolteacher to the students who were threatened with cane-beating in case they deviated from what they were asked to say to appreciate the gigantic dam which, they were told, was extremely useful for Uttarakut. So, during their journey to the dam site, the students, in one voice, hailed the king who was a mastermind for this unique idea; he was appreciated by the students since they were categorically told that it would not have been possible without the king's intervention; it was he who had extended all help to Bibhuti who built the dam to halt the free flow of the rivulet coming out of the mountain springs. As the young minds were taught to be enamoured by this unusual construction to stop the gushing of water from the mountains, they were kept completely blind to the devastating consequences of the obstruction of water on the villagers of Shiv Tarai. Here, the schoolteacher, being a representative of a specific mindset, expressed his unconditional loyalty to the king by deciding to take his students to the site. He justified his feat by saying, 'Your Majesty is about to confer special honour on the Royal Engineer, Bibhuti; and I am taking my boys to the festival, in order to share in the rejoicing. I do not want my boys to miss any opportunity of participating in the glory of Uttarakut' (Das 1996: 174). The boys' response did not seem to be unusual when they appreciated the endeavour by clapping and saying that by constructing the dam, the king 'has shut up the drinking water of the Shiu-tarai people' (174). Besides teaching a lesson to the neighbouring Uttarakut village, the aim was also to make the students in Shiv Tarai smart. The intervention was needed to make the boys of Shiv Tarai smart and capable in course of time which means that they were required to be transformed by the effort of Uttarakut's school kids. The story, as it unfolded so far, appeared to be an innocent narrative of rivalry between two kingdoms. But, beneath the surface, there existed a powerful message which Rabindranath conveyed unambiguously while elaborating his approach to education. The schoolmaster insisted that the boys of Shiv Tarai were bad because their religion was 'rotten' (174) and they did not have a 'high bridged nose' (174); this also reveals that the poet couched his critique as one against racism. It was further clarified in the play when the schoolmaster characterised the physical attribute, such as a high-bridged nose, as an important feature of 'the greatness of the race' (174). The statement that Uttarakut never lost a war was reflective of its greatness, argued the schoolmaster, who also believed that by this feat, the kingdom civilised the barbarians. He now came out with a perceptive view defending that these boys remained steadfastly committed to the kingdom since they were taught so. By assuring the king, the teacher thus justified his point by saying that

> these very boys will one day be a terror to all those who have the misfortune to be born outside our boundaries. I shall be false to my vocation as a schoolmaster if this does not happen. I never allow myself

> to forget for one moment the great responsibility which we teachers have. We build up men! Your statesmen merely use them. (175)

Implicit here is the poet's scathing critique against the physical might being considered to be an attribute of greatness. By being severely critical of the desire of a specific segment of the population, Rabindranath expressed his disenchantment with the idea of nationalism which was a politico-ideological design of espousing the interests of one section of the population against another. According to him,

> the idea of Nation is one of the most powerful anaesthetics that man has invented. Under the influence of its fumes the whole people can carry its systematic programme of the most virulent self-seeking without being in the least aware of its moral perversion—in fact, feeling very resentful if it is pointed out. (Tagore 1985: 25)

Unable to appreciate the self-seeking endeavour of a particular section of humanity, Rabindranath castigated nationalism as 'a great menace' (67), because it 'has thriven long upon mutilated humanity' (26). This was the message that he delivered in *Muktadhara*, the purpose of which was to dissuade the supporters of the British authority who appeared to have been awestruck by the pompous growth of industrial nations in Europe. His emotional discomfort was very clearly articulated when he questioned those in India who were persuaded to accept the lessons from the West as gospel truth contrary to the core principles of humanity: 'the narrowness of sympathy which makes it possible for us to impose upon a considerable portion of humanity the galling yoke of inferiority will assert itself in our politics in creating the tyranny of injustice' (74).

The point that emerges here is that the greatness of one nation could never be a source of satisfaction for humanity simply because it involved (a) segregation and (b) consolidation of barriers, detrimental to the growth of humanity as a whole. As shown by the poet, the schoolteacher epitomised a design of education to sustain a mindset supportive of separating one section of humanity from another. Opposed to this kind of divisive system of education, he provided a completely new discourse of thinking by drawing on Vedantic texts that unfolded a mode of learning based on concerns for humanity as well as an appreciation for the dialectical interconnection between human beings and their ecological milieu. Keen to develop an alternative, the poet prepared a blueprint by drawing upon his philosophical preferences; in his perception, education was not just a means to get employment; it was a well-defined mode for generating concern for human beings in general, the underprivileged in particular. The prevalent system of education that flourished under the aegis of colonialism was not because instead of being a device of enlightenment, English education was one of those means that consolidated foreign hegemony in India. It was a system to produce sets of loyalists for running the system of governance supportive of the alien design. In a very fierce but persuasive manner, the poet thus mentioned that

> since our education bears no relation to our life, the books we read paint no vivid picture of our homes, extol no ideals of our society. The daily pursuits of our lives find no place in those pages, nor do we meet there or anything we happily recognise as our friends and relatives, our sky and earth, our mornings and evenings, or our cornfields and rivers. Education and life can never become one in such circumstances, and we are bound to remain separated by a barrier. Our education may be compared to rainfall on a spot that is a long way from our roots. Not enough moisture seeps through the intervening barrier or earth to quench our thirst. (Tagore 1962: 45)

Education that was imparted under the aegis of the empire was futile since it hardly equipped us to comprehend the social, economic and political contexts in which we were born and raised. This was an instrumental design directed to fulfil the objectives for the furtherance of the colonisers' partisan interests. *Muktadhara*'s schoolteacher was a carrier of that system of education which did not allow the young minds to explore the unknown because that was likely to generate contrarian ideas. The children became the parrot of his 'Tota Kahini'. Convinced that the English education was mechanical, Tagore was persuaded to embark on this project to seek to create facilities for the development of the mind as well. Drawn on children's curiosity about knowing the unknown, his schemes were directed to put in place a system which was both innovative and enabling. While elaborating his views on 'my school', he thus mentioned that since

> children's minds are sensitive to the influence of the great world to which they have been born … [t]heir subconscious mind is active, always imbibing some lesson, and with it realizing the joy of knowing. This sensitive receptivity of the passive mind helps them, without their feeling any strain, to master language, that most complex and difficult instrument of expression, full of ideas that are undefinable and symbols that deal with abstractions. And, through their natural gift of guessing they learn the meaning of words which we cannot explain. (Ghosh 2008: 518)

What stands out in the above statement was his insistence on children being allowed to be free from restrictions that decided what they should learn. Instead, the poet felt that if they were allowed to move around like free birds, they acquired the training of nature which was always full of resources to quench their curiosity. As long as the system of rote learning prevailed, warned Rabindranath, the natural creativity of the human mind was certain to be muzzled, and this was neither self-fulfilling nor contained any excitement for learning. This was most scathingly stated when in the same essay, he further maintained that when the children's mind was most inquisitive, they were brought to

> the educational factory—lifeless, colourless, dissociated from the context of the universe, within bare white walls staring like eyeballs of the dead. We had the God-given gift of taking delight in the world, but such delightful activity was fettered and imprisoned, stilled by a force called discipline which kills the sensitivity of the child's mind, the mind which is always on the alert, restless and eager to receive first-hand knowledge from mother Nature. We had to sit inert, like dead specimens of some museum, whilst lessons were pelted at us from on high, like hailstones on flowers. (518–519)

The poet himself learnt from his experience that bookish knowledge was not at all a useful device for learning; instead, not only was it responsible for the rise of constricted minds but also led to sterile thinking since the children were bound by routinised sets of activities which gave them no joy but sadness. Because he himself realised this when he was sent to a conventional Bangla-medium school, he did not want to subject the children to the emotional torture that he underwent. What was most important was to create 'an environment' in which the development of children's mental faculty was not allowed to be undermined. With this, learning was to be a source of fulfilment and gratification which was not conceivable because colonialism was a strong determinant of human behaviour in India. The prevalent education system was a deterrent to the evolution of the natural self of the children. According to Tagore, by generating those values on which colonialism safely rested, the British rulers gradually developed a system which was nourished by the servile mindset that had emerged in colonised India. So, the behaviour of the schoolmaster, being nurtured in the atmosphere of servility, did not seem to be an aberration. It was manifested when it was found that the schoolmaster

> wants to mould the child's mind according to his ready-made doctrine and therefore wants to rid the child's world of everything that he thinks

> will go against his purpose. He [thus] excludes the whole world of colour, of movement, of life, from his education scheme and snatching the helpless creature from the mother heart of Nature, shuts it in his prison house, feeling sure that imprisonment is the surest method of improving the child mind. This happens only because … as a grown-up person he thinks that this is the time-tested method [and was thus] not willing to [accept that] the adult mind in many respects not only differs from but is contrary to the child mind. (Das 1996: 505)

By being so candid in his assessment of the situation in which teaching of children was pursued, Rabindranath firmly believed that the system was not only debased but was enough to completely kill the inquisitiveness that a child was privy to by being a child. The system that generated servility of mind had its roots in and drew its sustenance from colonialism. The poet found two serious constraints that acted as deterrents to the development of a child into a responsible adult. One constraint was linked to the environment in which freedom was denied to the child. As long as children were not allowed to fulfil what they wanted freely, education continued to be mechanical. According to him, 'only through freedom can man attain his fullness of growth and when we restrict that freedom it means that we have some purpose of our own which we impose on the children, and we have not in mind Nature's own purpose of giving children its fulness of growth' (508). Associated with this was the second constraint which was scathingly articulated by reference to how the schoolteachers behaved when they interacted with their students. Disappointed by those who perpetrated torture in the name of being strict disciplinarians, Rabindranath was far more caustic when he condemned them as 'tyrants'. These schoolmasters, to give 'outlet to their inherent lust for tyranny … make use of these helpless children and impose on them their own code of behaviour. They try to crush,' he further added,

> their minds with tasks which are lifeless, which are mechanical, which kill the intellectual mind, the fresh mind. They impose all kinds of torture because these tyrants take pleasure at the very sight of it, and such a great opportunity for such enjoyment they can never hope to attain outside their school premises. (508–509)

Perhaps his own brief experience of being in a school in Calcutta was so nightmarish, that it was possible that his painting of schoolmasters being tyrants can be said to have emerged out of this. However, one cannot ignore the wider concern for humanity which remained a critical influence in so far as his views on education were concerned. Tagore expressly stated that the tyrannical behavioural manifestation of schoolmasters 'causes the greatest mischief possible in the human world' since they expressed their professional commitment, not with 'imagination and sympathy and understanding' but with 'the machine-like behaviour of an executioner or a prison warden' (509). It did not come to the poet as a surprise because 'the tyrants, … of the educational administration … want the children to grow up according to the pattern that they have set for themselves [in accordance with] the government's administrative directions' (509). These views were complementary to what Tagore conceptualised as his form of education that eventually was articulated with the inauguration of Visva-Bharati in 1921.

Despite being aware that the scene did not seem to be very encouraging, Rabindranath was also confident that reversal was possible with the zeal and commitment of those who were persuaded to believe that they needed to be proactive in transforming the otherwise sterile system of education. What he emphasised was an ideational change to instil in the public mind that so long as the existent system of education was allowed to survive, Indians would remain slaves to the colonisers since in it lay the strength of the administration. In other words, as soon as independent thinking became part of education, loyalty to the British government and the Indians' political slavery to the British were likely to be seriously questioned.

Muktadhara has thus messages which are multidimensional in character. A surface reading of the play reveals that it revolved around an organised non-violent campaign that drew its sustenance from the spontaneous opposition of the Shiv Tarai villagers against the selfish motive of the Uttarakut king to allow them access to the water that nature provided for the people of that area. It was Dhananjay, with support from the crown prince, Abhijit, who mobilised the affected villagers against the king and which finally led to the collapse of the dam. This play is also one of those poet's creative texts that upheld many of his politico-ideological priorities. Prominent among them was his fierce critique of the system of education that developed at the behest of British colonialism. Like the boys in *Muktadhara*, those who received education in schools imparting English education were taught just to appreciate the alien rule as a source of enlightenment and empowerment largely because they hardly had a chance to explore the unknown which was always bulldozed by the teachers who were also taught to undermine this aspect of learning. Being indoctrinated in a planned manner, the boys of Uttarakut completely lost their capacity to think independently and realise that the dam was a source of suffering for their neighbours; instead, they rejoiced as, by stopping the flow of water, it subjected them to severe discomfort and agony.

Concluding Observations

'Balai' and *Muktadhara* are specific statements with wider implications. On a surface reading of these texts, one is persuaded to argue that it was Rabindranath's comments on the disconnect between environment and human beings, on the one hand, and the brutality of those wielding authority on the other. However, the message that one comes across is far more serious than it appears. These texts underline the poet's concern for the dialectical unity between the natural environment and the human beings that usually escape notice with the ruthless progress of industrial civilisation. The cutting of the silk-cotton tree by Balai's uncle was thus not a simple event but pregnant with the idea that for a proper ecological balance, which was essential for the quality survival of human beings, the environment needed to be nurtured with care and compassion. Balai's aunt represented the sentiment that the poet expressed in this short story. It was not just mere care for nature; through this statement, the poet made a profound statement that was integrally connected with the development of children as a responsible part of human society. It was a source of their mental nourishment which was manifested when he mentioned that 'children love the earth with its dust and its dirt, and they love the sun, the wind and the rain. They do not like to be dressed up, they enjoy themselves most when they are discovering the world with their senses, and they are not a bit ashamed to be their natural selves' (Tagore 1962: 80–81).

The poet believed that children should be allowed to develop naturally, which meant that they are encouraged to enjoy being intimate with the earth because 'the four elements of earth, water, air and fire form a whole and are instinct with the universal soul' (73). With the triumph of industrial civilisation, the opportunities for being acquainted with these four elements were dwindling fast. The outcome was likely to be disastrous since 'doubtless nature, for its own biological purposes, has created in us a strong faith in life, by keeping us unmindful of death, … which needs to be safeguarded, under all circumstances, for our well-being' (Das 1996: 494). The bard was aghast at the system of education that thrived at the behest of colonialism because, instead of highlighting the importance of the environment in human life, the schools ended up being 'factories'; he hilariously expressed how the schools functioned with machine-like precision by saying that

> at half-past ten in the morning, the factory opens with the ringing of the bell; then teachers start talking, the machines start working. The teachers stop talking at four in the afternoon when the factory closes, and the pupils then go home carrying with them a few pages of machine-made learning. Later this learning is tested at examinations and labelled. (Tagore 1962: 67)

Being aware that the British government was not expected to allow children to grow naturally, the poet, by critiquing the prevalent system of education, laid the foundation of an alternative. It did not seem odd to him because colonialism needed a system to support and also strengthen a mindset in its favour. Hence, it was most likely that the colonisers devoted a great deal of attention to consolidate 'the factory' of education because 'one advantage of a factory is that it can make goods exactly to order. Moreover, the goods are easy to label, because there is not much difference between what the different machines turn out' (67). Implicit here is both a critique and a heart-felt desire to evolve an alternative system of pedagogy in which the young learners had an opportunity to learn what gave them a human identity in the true connotation of the term. 'Balai' was an attempt to stipulate the bard's well-thought argument in defence of nature which was integrally linked with the growth of Balai along with the apparently useless silk-cotton tree. That he wanted a photograph of his 'friend, the silk-cotton tree' before his departure to England confirms the intimate emotional cord that he developed with the tree that he nurtured from when it was just a shoot. There is another aspect in Rabindranath's argument which exposed the limitation of the existent mode of imparting learning in British schools. Here the children were removed from their natural flair for learning since they were trained in a specific way which was supportive of the British rule. In *Muktadhara*, the boys of a school uncritically admired the dam notwithstanding being aware of the adverse consequences of the obstruction of water for the people of Shiu-tarai. And also, the role of the teacher was despised since the boys parroted the statements that he asked them to utter to please the king; this was also a source of irritation to the ruler, Ranjit, who was accompanied by his minister, during the inauguration of the dam. The teacher was condemned by the king as a sycophant which was explicitly stated by him when he said that 'inside the skull of this schoolmaster of yours, there is nothing but the butter made of cow's milk' (Das 1996: 175). In colloquial Bangla, rubbing somebody's feet with butter is tantamount to sycophancy. The response of the minister was very meaningful since he supported the act as valuable which he explained by saying that 'nevertheless, Sire, such people are useful [because] he loyally repeats the less, day after day, according to the instruction that he has received. If he had more brains, such a thing as this would not be possible' (175). This revelation also approximated *Animal Farm* which George Orwell wrote in 1945; it was a satire of how the entire Soviet administration was geared to create a set of brainless pigs to sustain Stalin's regime; there the sane voice got marginalised as the majoritarianism triumphed. Human selfishness was thus a source of concern to the bard who always condemned this by underlining that 'owing to this lack, we suffer from the lack of true freedom in our social life which comes from the general welfare and mutual sympathy and cooperation' (Tagore 2008: 'Sriniketan', 491). Given the fact that 'our knowledge, feelings and experiences are abstracted from life' (491), the hope about the growth of humanity was nipped in the bud. His concern was translated into responsibility for guarding the young minds associated with his brainchild, Visva-Bharati,

> against the least chance of learners carrying away the belief that Visva-Bharati bases its ideal upon any ulterior expectation, political or otherwise [because] ... it's one object is to help each of [the learners] to realise his personality, as an individual representing his people, in such a broad spirit, in such an unobstructed sunshine of spiritual expansion of consciousness, that he may know how it is the most important fact of his life for him to have born to the great world of man. (Tagore 1996: 'Notes and Comments', 494)

A devout believer in humanism, Rabindranath always linked individual contribution with the well-being of the people which further means that his primary concern was to build and consolidate a sense of togetherness; otherwise, one's birth as a human being was futile. So, what was required to be done was a evolve a consciousness leading to the emergence of a mindset that, while connecting the individual with his collective self, was meant to contribute to Rabindranath's concern for universal humanism. The message reverberated in *Muktadhara*, though it was political as well: political because the bard devised a scheme to alter the prevalent power equations that existed between the ruler and the ruled by resorting to non-violence. The very idea of constructing a dam for protecting Uttarakut's interests was guided to inflict pain and agony on the neighbouring human habitat in Shiv Tarai. The king was empowered since he had the royal engineer, Bibhuti, who found in his feat evidence to achieve an unachievable goal. There was hardly a contrary voice; the Shiv Tarai villagers were helpless before the brutality of the Uttarakut king though the crown prince, Abhijit, was with them. The scene had undergone a sea-change with the arrival of the minstrel, Dhananjay, who mobilised the villagers for a non-violent struggle against the powerful king. With Abhijit's intervention, the dam collapsed and washed him away. So, the play ended on a painful note although the villagers of Shiv Tarai won the battle.

By reading *Muktadhara* between lines, one clearly understands that Rabindranath metaphorically articulated a voice challenging the colonial authority that hardly took public agony into account while devising a design of governance. In the play, the dam represented the will of the colonial ruler that was respected by those thriving on colonial favour. Here, the poet attacked the heartless way in which science was utilised to cause harm to humanity, on the one hand, and also condemned those who wilfully ignored man-made difficulties just to please the ruler. By creating an environment where the voice of protest seemed to have completely died down, the ruler remained invincible. With the generation of a mindset that flourished since opposition was so feeble, the brutal rule continued uninterruptedly. The poet was disenchanted with the colonial government which hardly paid any attention to the well-being of the colonised; this was evident when he couched his resentment by condemning the construction of the dam as it was an obstruction to the flow of natural water. By 1922, when the play appeared in the public domain, Rabindranath realised that British rule could never be a panacea for a colony like India. Despite differences of opinion, he admired Gandhi as not only did he empower the hapless Indians against the British by giving them a powerful voice of protest but also devised non-violence as an equally powerful weapon. The success of Dhananjay in *Muktadhara* was testimony to the bard's confidence in non-violence as an effective means for attaining the goal. The second hypothesis that gained precedence in most of his later writings was his complete disillusionment with the British empire. In his last speech, entitled 'Crisis in Civilisation', which he delivered in 1941 on the occasion of his birthday, just two months before his death, he clearly expressed what he felt with the gradual debasement of the British rule when he said that

> the early period of my life ended in an agony of disenchantment. I started to discover more and more how those who professed the highest civilised values could be cast aside with the utmost ease, whenever their national interests were at stake. ... The sight of the terrible poverty of the Indian masses grew inescapable. I realised that perhaps in no other modern state was there such a complete denial of the basic needs of living: food and clothing, education and health services. And, yet it was the exploited resources of this country that had been adding, year on year, to the wealth of the British race. (Tagore 1962: 355)

If one reads the above text in combination with the core message in *Muktadhara*, one is persuaded to argue that the poet's disenchantment started long before he wrote this speech in 1941. That the colonial power was selfish to the core was an obvious truth since colonialism owed its emergence to the idea of exploitation of one section of humanity by another. This was very clearly articulated in his 'The Canker of European Civilization' when he mentioned that

> excessive enjoyment cannot be equally distributed amongst all: if the few are inordinately rich, the many must be deprived of their dues. At the root of the conflict … between the ruling nations and the ruled', he further added, 'lies the organised longing of … unrestrained enjoyment. Such extreme inequality is in conflict with the noble ideas of humanity. Destructive forces generate and gather, openly or in secret, whenever human unity is … threatened'. (Tagore 2008: 415)

Disappointed with the British civilisation that he admired for it rested on some of the core values of humanity, Rabindranath came to terms with the conceptual assumption that colonialism was detrimental to the progress of humanity. In other words, colonialism was a refinement of human exploitation at the cost of human unity. The poet was dismayed at the way British rule unfolded in India: Instead of becoming a harbinger of civilisation, it built a heartless machine to thrive by depriving the colonised of what was due to them. It was not merely an attack on the colonised masses of India but a threat to humanity as it also endorsed the claim of the powerful of unrestrained enjoyment by inflicting pain and agony on the weak and hapless section of humanity. Being a humanist to the core who always raised his voice against endeavours at demeaning humanity, Rabindranath minced no words while castigating the British rule by stating that

> lost in the glamourous aspects of the British culture, I had never thought that, out of it could come so cruel a distortion of long-cherished values; that distortion, I knew, at last, was the emblem of a civilised nation's contempt and callousness towards our vast masses. (Tagore 1962: 'Crisis in Civilization', 355)

To conclude, *Muktadhara* was not just a narrative of the denigration of a king who allowed his whimsical decision to be executed at the cost of many; it was a powerful voice against a coercive and exploitative authority. Here, in his poetic language, he forcefully argued a point that was easily intelligible to his readers rather easily. It was, therefore, in other words, not merely a play for popular entertainment but also conveyed a persuasive message to them to put across the point that the fierce battle against colonial rule was the only means to do away with the inhuman system of governance that flourished in the wake of colonialism. Dhananjay who appeared first in his play *Prayaschitta* (1909) reappeared in *Muktadhara* (1922). It was not a strange coincidence since the bard, being persuaded to believe in non-violence as an effective mode of challenge, favoured the character who trained the protesters to fight non-violently against the ruthless king of Jessore and later the king of Uttarakut. One is thus persuaded to argue that long before Gandhi arrived on the Indian political scene, it was Rabindranath who not only found in non-violence a powerful voice but also helped built human faith in the non-violent struggle against attempts at demeaning the core values of humanity.

References

Gandhi, M.K. 1934. 'Village Industries'. Harijan, 16 November. In *Collected Works of Mahatma Gandhi* 59: 356.

———. 2005 (rpt). *The Hindu Swaraj or Indian Home Rule*. Ahmedabad: Navjivan Publishing House.

Iyer, Raghavan. 1973. *The Moral and Political Thought of Mahatma Gandhi*. New Delhi: Oxford University Press.

Parekh, Bhikhu. 1999. *Colonialism, Traditions and Reform: An Analysis of Gandhi's Political Discourse*. New Delhi: Sage.

Tagore, Rabindranath. 1962 (rpt). 'Crisis in Civilization'. In *Towards Universal Man*. Bombay: Asia Publishing House.

———. 1962 (rpt). 'The Problem of Education'. In *Towards Universal Man*. Bombay: Asia Publishing House.

———. 1962 (rpt). 'The Vicissitudes of Education'. In *Towards Universal Man*. Bombay: Asia Publishing House.

———. 1985 (rpt). *Nationalism*. Madras: Macmillan.

———. 1996. 'Notes and Comments, 1924'. In *The English Writings of Rabindranath Tagore*, ed. Sisir Kumar Das, Vol. 2. New Delhi: Sahitya Akademi.

———. 1996. 'The Parrot's Training'. In *The English Writings of Rabindranath Tagore*, ed. Sisir Kumar Das, Vol. 2. New Delhi: Sahitya Akademi.

———. 1996. 'The School Master'. In *The English Writings of Rabindranath Tagore*, ed. Sisir Kumar Das, Vol. 3. New Delhi: Sahitya Akademi.

———. 1997. Rabindranath Tagore to CF Andrews, 24 January 1921. In *Selected Letters of Rabindranath Tagore*, ed. Krishna Dutta and Andrew Robinson. Cambridge: Cambridge University Press.

———. 2003 (1909). *Prayschitta*. In *Rabindra Rachanabali* (Collected Works of Rabindranath Tagore, hereafter *CWRG*), Vol. 5. Kolkata: Visva-Bharati.

———. 2008 (rpt). 'Gandhi's Ideal'. In *The English Writings of Rabindranath Tagore*, ed. Nityapriya Ghosh, Vol. 4. New Delhi: Sahitya Akademi.

———. 2008 (rpt). 'My School'. In *The English Writings of Rabindranath Tagore*, ed. Nityapriya Ghosh, Vol. 4. New Delhi: Sahitya Akademi.

———. 2008 (rpt). 'Sriniketan'. In *The English Writings of Rabindranath Tagore*, ed. Nityapriya Ghosh, Vol. 4. New Delhi: Sahitya Akademi.

———. 2008 (rpt). 'The Canker of European Civilization'. In *The English Writings of Rabindranath Tagore*, ed. Nityapriya Ghosh, Vol. 4. New Delhi: Sahitya Akademi.

———. 2009. 'Finding a New Education'. In *The Oxford India Tagore: Selected Writings on Education and Nationalism*, ed. Uma Dasgupta. New Delhi: Oxford University Press.

Part III

UNSETTLING THE CONVENTIONAL IDEATIONAL PARAMETERS

Rabindranath was against gender disparity. He imbibed this idea from his family where women were treated with respect and compassion. Furthermore, his grandfather, Dwarkanath, and his father, Debendranath, undertook severe constructive steps to pursue their concern for education among girls. They believed that their efforts were a stepping stone towards accomplishing their espoused goal of gender parity. They joined hands with Christian missionaries by providing them with financial support when they built schools for girls. Hence, the poet carried forward a tradition that had evolved in his family. However, not only did Rabindranath pursue the objectives laid down by his father and grandfather but he also viewed women's liberation as part of the greater concern of human emancipation. By challenging age-old constrictive practices, he addressed an issue which did not appear to have emerged so clearly in the efforts of Dwarkanath and Debendranath. In his essay, 'The Religion of Man', which he delivered as a Hibbert Lecture at Oxford University in 1930, he developed this point by stating that

> we Indians have had the sad experience in our own part of the world of timid orthodoxy, its irrational repressions and its accumulations of dead centuries dwarf man through its idolatry of the past. Seated rigid in the centres of stagnation, it firmly ties the human spirit to the evolving wheels of habit till faintness overwhelms her. This mechanical spirit of tradition is essentially materialistic, it is blindly pious but not spiritual, obsessed by phantoms of unreason that haunt feeble minds in the ghastly disguise of religion … This happens to … generations of insipid races that have lost all emphasis of significance in themselves, having missed their future. (Tagore 1996: 134–135)

Tagore offered to (a) provide a persuasive critique of why Indians developed the mindset that was not, at all, forward-looking, and by doing so, (b) he strove to unsettle the so-called established sociocultural ideas and practices. Being critical of gender division, he believed that without an inter-relationship between man and woman, no society could progress. He articulated his argument by drawing on the idea of freedom which, he strongly felt, remained elusive unless there emerged mutual love, care and concern for one another. It was very succinctly argued when he stated that

> freedom in the mere sense of independence has no content, and therefore no meaning. Perfect freedom lies in a perfect harmony of relationship, which we realize in this world not through our response to it in knowing, but in being. … [T]he further world of freedom awaits us there when we reach truth, not through feeling it by our senses of knowing it by our reason, but through the union of perfect sympathy. (156)

On the surface, the argument is just an attempt to establish the claim that empathy for one another was a source of inspiration; at a deeper level, it draws on Rabindranath's understanding of human civilisation which drew on selfless love and concern for others. In other words, this was not a sermon, but the poet's urge to rise above pettiness—to join hands with one another regardless of artificially created sociocultural differences. He was aware that it was easier said than done since,

> the present stage of the history of civilization has become primarily masculine, a civilization of power in which woman from captivity spends her surplus of wealth of emotions in merely decorative purposes of society. Therefore, the civilization has lost its balance. (676)

The above argument is complementary to the poet's belief that women 'brought to [his] life the inspiration love and beauty, invocation of power that lies dormant until touched by womanly grace' (676). In pursuance of this idea, he further argued that women were integral to human existence. He warned that unless this was respected, mere political freedom from colonial rule was futile. Hence, he argued that 'woman cannot be pushed back for good into the superficial region of the merely decorative by man's aggressive athleticism [for] … she is not less necessary in civilization than man, but possibly more so' (678). Having witnessed the growing resentment among women all over the world and also in India, he did not doubt that 'woman is [not just] seeking today her freedom of livelihood, struggling against man's monopoly of business, but [also] against man's monopoly of civilization' (678). There was, therefore, no other option but to accept women as equal partners in consolidating human civilisation which was possible once,

> the aggressive trespassers of today will have to remove their boundary pillars to make room for the apparently feeble creatures, and the union of man and woman will represent a perfect cooperation in building up of human history on equal terms in every department of life. (678)

Not only did the bard identify the deep-rooted causes of gender discrimination but also warned individuals with a misogynist mindset of adverse consequences. The ideas that he developed in many of his creative essays figured prominently in his literary creations as well. There is no doubt that his ideas were revolutionary, and he anticipated most of the claims future feminists were to make in the days to come. Nonetheless, the rebellious voice that he articulated in his creative texts did not seem to exactly correspond with what he stated in the texts, referred to before. *Yogayog* was, for instance, an endeavour to capture the helplessness of Kumud when: She was persuaded to marry Madhusudan because she was destined to do so due to an inexplicable providential intervention. In other words, the conjugal bond, according to Kumud's religious upbringing, was beyond the reach of human agency: This connection was predestined and written in the stars by a divine hand. However, as time went by and Madhusudan's cruelties mounted, Kumud was forced to give up her idealised notion of conjugal life and responsibilities. In a brave act of rebellion, she left him and returned to her brother's house, but her act of feminist agency was dashed by the systemic operation of misogyny. Similarly, 'Poila Nombor' and 'Strir Patra' are unique because they articulate feminist assertions through epistolary means. Along with *Yogayog*, these two short stories see the bard troubling the sanctity of the conjugal bond, especially as it is reified by Hindu dharmic texts and sociocultural practices. In contrast, Rabindranath steps out of the Bengali bhadralok sphere with his short story 'Laboratory', where the entry of the female figure into the public sphere is showcased through the character of Sohini, a Punjabi woman, whose defiance of patriarchal norms and customs is couched in terms of her devotion to her husband's professional mission. The poet's scathing critique of the highly restrictive bhadralok ideals of femininity is subtly planted in his choice of a female protagonist who hails from a region other than Bengal, perhaps in an effort to evade the opprobrium of his readership.

References

Tagore, Rabindranath. 1996. 'The Music Maker'. In 'The Religion of Man'. reproduced in *The English Writings of Rabindranath Tagore*, ed. Sisir Kumar Das, Vol. 3. New Delhi: Sahitya Akademi.

———. 1996. 'Women's Place in the World'. In *The English Writings of Rabindranath Tagore*, ed. Sisir Kumar Das, Vol. 3. New Delhi: Sahitya Akademi.

6

Rabindranath Tagore on Gender

Arguably, one of the most significant facets of Tagore's political thought is his fierce commitment to gender justice. This commitment manifests itself very prominently in almost all of his fictional writings and also influenced his public and private life. Tagore never failed to recognise the dynamism and subtle workings of the patriarchy or the fact that its insidious nature enabled it to pervade almost every aspect of society. Thus, his gender activism is inextricably entwined with his philosophical views on personal freedom, morality, love and spirituality on the one hand and his opinions on political freedom, self-determination and religion on the other.

Tagore's indictment of tradition as the custodian of oppression stands out as the dominant theme of his activism, and nowhere is this clearer than in his work on gender. With an upbringing shaped by the radical ideals of the Brahmo Samaj, it is not surprising that Tagore located the fight against sexist oppression not merely in the realm of policy but the personal—in childhood, filial duty, romantic love and marriage, childbirth and widowhood, in one's relationship with art and spirituality and even in death. Tagore was unique in illuminating the patriarchal foundations of these cornerstones of Hindu society by way of hyper-contextualised, exceedingly specific short stories, novels and plays about individual women, their inner worlds and outer lives. It is this specificity that ensures the wide relatability of his stories. Tagore situated himself in the humdrum nitty-gritty of everyday life as experienced by individual women, who, despite collectively being the subject matter of powerful men's burning debates on the nation and its people, nonetheless continued having to live in service of the patriarchy and were deemed too insignificant to merit non-fetishistic literary attention. Tagore bucked this trend of heroic male allyship by doggedly writing stories centred on the lives and personalities of women protagonists, who, in the face of misogynist cruelty, held fast to their moral codes and inner wellsprings of autonomy. By fixing his gaze on the less glamorous aspects of the fight against patriarchy, Tagore uncovered the political in the personal.

Tagore's gender activism extended beyond literature into his work as a pedagogue, a thespian and director and as an ideologue. Whether it's his gender-inclusive ashram and university in Santiniketan which prized the unfettered education of girl children, his relentless fight for the inclusion of women in theatre or his championing of widow remarriage, Tagore remains an indispensable ally to the women's liberation movement in India, and his insightful critiques of gender inequality continue to be relevant to students of feminism even today.

Historically speaking, the concern for gender equality had hardly swayed mainstream thinking in Bengal until Rammohun Roy (1772–1833) arrived on the scene. With his initiative, the cruel sati custom was abolished once the 1829 Bengal Sati Regulation was adopted during the reign of Lord William Bentick as India's Governor-General. Besides the rescinding of sati, Roy was also instrumental in mobilising opinion against caste rigidity, polygamy and child marriage. It is argued that Roy 'attributed social evils in Hindu religion and society to the poisonous effect of idolatrous notions' (Kopf 1988: 14) which were contrary to most of the Vedic beliefs. He appeared to have prepared the ground for Vidyasagar (1820–1891) who introduced the practice of widow remarriage notwithstanding the steep opposition of mainstream Hinduism. In view of Tagore's concern for gender equality, this chapter, by dwelling on the creative texts that he articulated to support his point of view, argues that his intervention not only strengthened the campaign for socioeconomic changes but also contributed immensely to the conceptualisation of women issues in a completely different theoretical format. As mentioned earlier, the ideas that the poet put forward were both drawn from what his predecessors in the Brahmo Samaj, including his father, stipulated but also an expansion of those ideas which they failed to pursue due to adverse social reactions. By focusing on his novel *Yogayog* (Nexus), this chapter focuses on the argument that the poet evolved in favour of gender equity despite being opposed by orthodox Hindus. It is an account of the mental torture that a married woman undergoes due to the nuptial bond she shared with her husband. The chapter is also an elaboration of the processes that contribute to a voice of protest amidst challenges. Rabindranath, similar to some of his nationalist colleagues, took up the cudgels for ending sexist oppression and exploitation of one section of the demography by another due to their gender identity.

Conceptual Pathways

By the time Tagore was a powerful voice, the Enlightenment values championing equality regardless of sex seem to have developed organic roots in Bengal. The idea of gender equality became part and parcel of the campaigns for social reform which was clearly an intellectual aid to the poet when he focused on issues relating to gender discrimination. For him, it was a social disease that needed to be treated firmly to create a society free from gender prejudices. There was hardly an escape because the social context supportive of gender discrimination was constructed deliberately. The idea was most persuasively argued by Simone De Beauvoir in her *The Second Sex* when she stated that 'feminine reality has been constituted [in which] they have been defined as the Other' with the consequence of being denied 'a legitimate space in the human *Mitsein* [communal existence]' (Beauvoir 2011: 17). This point was graphically illustrated by the author when she further added that

> men's economic privilege, their social value, the prestige of marriage, the usefulness of masculine support—all these encourage women to ardently want to please men. They are on the whole still in a state of serfdom. It follows that woman knows and chooses herself not as she exists for herself but as man defines her. She thus has to be described first as men dream of her since her being-for-men is one of the essential factors of her concrete existence. (159)

Critical here is the idea that women do not exist as an agency independent of men; their entire being is structured, governed and shaped as per the social context which is the male's creation. There are many authors such as Kate Millett (1970) and Carole Pateman (1988) among others, who pursued the point by touching on various aspects of gender issues in the contemporary context. The scene continues to remain the same unless 'men and women do not recognise each other as peers, that as long as femininity, [as it is conceptualised now] is perpetuated' (Beauvoir 2011: 771). What it means is that unless the prevalent mindset representing specific kinds of social, economic and politico-ideological preferences is transformed, 'the new woman cannot appear' (777). An analytical perusal of the principal texts on gender reveals that women remain discriminated against because of the existent socioeconomic circumstances that drew on the politico-ideological framework, supporting a set of preordained ideas which were required to change. The task is easier said than done since these ideas are not only socioeconomically well-entrenched but have also evolved as integral to one's social existence. There have been protests at the best of feminist scholars, who genuinely felt the need for change for the sake of building an egalitarian society in which discrimination around social, economic and political axes is an anathema.

The aforementioned admittedly unnuanced discussion is useful when arguing the point that Tagore's endeavour was an integral part of the concern that many authors who focused primarily on the theme of gender parity dealt with to persuasively conceptualise the theme. Being a creative writer, the poet put forward his views through the characters that appeared in many of his texts. It is not possible to deal with all of his characters who represented the thematic concern that he sought to articulate. By discursively analysing the nature of the character with reference to the socioeconomic context in which they emerged, the chapter provides useful inputs to graphically present Tagore's socio-economic and politico-ideological preferences as well. The aim here is to understand his approach to gender equity which was both contextual and transcendental: contextual because his views were an offshoot of the milieu in which he was raised and nurtured; transcendental because the ideas that he propounded remain relevant in similar socioeconomic and political circumstances.

Formulating the Gender Question

A universalist, Tagore was a crusader against any kind of discrimination, whether on the basis of religion or archaic mindsets. Drawn on the experiences of being raised in a family that welcomed the values of Enlightenment, his condemnation of anything artificially compartmentalising human beings was a natural response. Discriminatory practices, thus argued the poet, had their roots in deliberately created socioeconomic designs for segregation. In his opinion, 'it is a symptom of our egotism, this clinging with fanatical fervour to all that is accidental [to our civilisation], making it ... a source of discrimination [which] is the greatest calamity, in the present age, for peace and welfare of all' (Ghosh 2008: 747). Being persuaded to believe that the supremacist mindset was an impediment to universal humanism, the bard linked his concern for gender parity with his principal socioeconomic objective which remained distant as long as women were kept in chains:

> the history of man is the history of the building up of a human universe, as has been proved by the fact that everything great in human activity inevitably belongs to all humanity. And we may be sure that all our religious experiences and expressions are building up from the depth of the ages of one great continent of religions on which man's soul is to win its prosperity through universal commerce of spiritual life. (748)

According to Tagore, purely ritualistic religion was futile in so far as human welfare was concerned. Instead, religion, for him, represented a way of life directed to achieve universal well-being. Being disenchanted with the narrow vision that contemporary religion embodied, the poet raised his voice since it was responsible for generating and also consolidating varieties of socioeconomic discrimination. As a practitioner, he always devised a means to translate into reality his conceptual ideas. Based on his concern to build a universe drawing on concerns for one another, he built Visva-Bharati which was also a laboratory for executing some of his plans for universal well-being. The twin campus of Visva-Bharati, Santiniketan and Sriniketan, created an environment in which Tagore's concern for gender equity was translated into many designs which, he felt, was a stepping stone to bring about the desired change in the prevalent mindset among those associated with this place of learning. Finally, universal prosperity was possible only through cooperation, regardless of gender, class and ethnicity which means that goal-driven endeavours were to be undertaken to root out the deliberately designed socioeconomic milieu. Here too, the examples of Santiniketan and Sriniketan will suffice to prove the point. By allowing co-education, Tagore sought to create an atmosphere of bonhomie among the inmates of the two schools, Patha Bhavana and Siksha Satra, which he founded to put into practice what he felt so strongly to evolve togetherness among the students regardless of their gender identity.

A very insightful thinker, Tagore also analysed how the present socioeconomic priorities contributed to segregation around the gender axis. In his well-thought-out argument, he put forth a model which explains how views opposed to gender parity evolved historically because of the socioeconomic context in which they always received approbation. While seeking to explain why man-woman discriminatory segregation emerged in the first place, the bard attributed the biological difference between sexes 'to the inequalities fostered by circumstances' (Das 1996: 552). Women seem to be naturally constrained because of their inherent nature which did not allow them to be fit for all kinds of work. This was what gave man, argued Tagore, adequately justified reasons to draw the line:

> man is not handicapped by the same biological and psychological responsibilities as a woman, and therefore he has the liberty to give her the security of home. This liberty exacts payment when it offers its boon, because to give to withhold the gift is within its power. (552)

So, naturally endowed biological differences created an imbalance that instilled in women the idea of men being superior. This was the source of 'unfreedom', noted Tagore. According to him, 'it is the unequal freedom in their [man-woman] relationships which have made the weight of life's tragedies so painfully heavy for a woman to bear' (552). This is a profound conceptual statement that is illustrative of how women, by being instinctively receptive to this unequal freedom, accepted their socially degrading position as inescapable. Nonetheless, it was suffering for them which was likely to cause disruptions in inter-gender bonds, if any. Tagore explained the obvious outcome of such imbalances by saying that

> all great suffering indicates some wrong somewhere. In the present case, the wrong is in the woman's lack of freedom in her relationship with man, which compels her to turn her disabilities into attractions, and to use untruths as her allies in the battle of life, while she is suffering from the precariousness of her position. (553)

Thus, women continued to remain subjugated because of the socially defended restrictions that they upheld as given; or, in other words, it was pre-destined for the woman to endorse what she received as soon as she was born as a woman. There were occasions when they were seemingly treated at par with their male counterparts; but, that was a subtle way of sustaining the socioeconomic imbalances which Tagore articulated by saying that by being instinctively tuned 'to perform their services in such a manner that they … may be raised from the domain of slavery to the realm of grace [which denotes that] women have tried to prove that in the building up of social life they are artists and not artisans' (553). Condemning the paternalistic male attitude towards women, Tagore also drew our attention to the processes whereby women were reduced to an instrument for carrying forward the dictated instructions of their male counterparts. Tagore scathingly articulated his viewpoints by exhorting that

> when necessity drives women to fashion their lives to the taste of the insensitive or the sensual, then the whole thing becomes a tragedy of desecration. Society is full of such tragedies. Many of the laws and social regulations guiding the relationships of man and woman are the relics of a barbaric age when the brutal pride of an exclusive possession had its dominance in human relations, such as those of parents and children, husbands and wives, master and servants, teachers and disciples. The vulgarity of it still persists in the social bond between sexes because of the economic helplessness of woman. Nothing makes us so stupidly mean as the sense of superiority which the power of purse confers upon us. (533–534)

Between genders, there existed a clear demarcation in which women were clearly disadvantaged. Their role was socially determined which also reinforces the argument that they had hardly the freedom of action regarding what they deemed appropriate. For Tagore, one of the primary reasons needed to be located in the milieu in which women did not have independent sources of income or, were not allowed to work for generating income for themselves. This was certainly plausible though the lack of income was one of the many factors that impeded the rise of women as independent agencies. For instance, as recent research has shown, women are subject to various kinds of constraints due to various kinds of socially transmitted devices of segregation around multiple axes. On this basis stems the idea of intersectionality which is a framework for conceptualising a person, group of people or social problem as affected by a number of discriminations and disadvantages. This is a theoretical endeavour to account for people's overlapping identities and experiences to grasp the complexities of prejudices that they face. Conceptually persuasive, the theory of intersectionality iterates that people are often subject to multiple sources of oppression: their race, class, gender identity, sexual orientation, religion and other identity markers. Emphasising that identity markers (female or any socioeconomically disadvantaged groups) do not exist independently of each other, and each informs the other, often creating a complex convergence of oppression (Crenshaw 1989). It is true that one does not get an explicit reference to the idea of intersectionality in Tagore's conceptualisation of gender issues though one gets an idea that he was aware of this aspect if one contextualises his viewpoints by reference to the prevalent colonial context. Indians were socioeconomically and also politically marginalised with the onset of colonial rule; women, by being part of the same system, had hardly escaped the shackles of colonialism which was the backdrop in which the poet intervened to comprehend the complexities of gender discrimination. What is worth pointing out here is Tagore's courageous stance to create a milieu for women to break free from the chains of oppression. It was evident when he stated that

> the present age has sent its cry to women, asking her to come out from her segregation in order to restore the spiritual supremacy of all that is human in the world of humanity. She has been aroused to remember that womanliness is not chiefly decorative. It is like that vital health, which not only imparts the bloom of beauty to the body, but joy to the mind and perfection to life. (Das 1996: 555)

The above conceptual points help us comprehend the foundational theoretical ideas on which Tagore based his approach to gender and socio-economic discrimination that they were subject to in British colonialism. Whether it was Nandini in *Rakta Karabi*, Bimala in *Ghare Baire*, Ela in *Char Adhyay*, Damini in *Chaturanga* or Sucharita in *Gora*, the idea does not seem to be different; they represented an urge to break the social constraints justifying 'women-enslavement' in a male-dominated patriarchal society. By identifying the sources of intersectionality or multiple sources of society-driven oppression that women failed to escape, Tagore, like some of his colleagues, put forth, in the public domain, those issues which hardly received serious attention presumably because of the available socially validated constraints. He, however, did not stop by simply flagging the issues; by creating bold characters in his creative writings, the poet devised a design for socioeconomic metamorphosis which set out a tempo for significant attitudinal changes in course of time.

Tagore's argument remains incomplete unless one is drawn to the other aspect highlighting what he specified as 'self-introspection' by women themselves. As argued before, that women needed to be conceptualised differently was the outcome of wider socioeconomic changes across the globe. Despite being a deterrent, colonialism also introduced the Indians to the liberating Enlightenment values which set in motion processes of impactful socioeconomic changes in India. Ideas for gender equity were rooted in these values which came to India in the wake of colonialism. It was easier for Rammohun Roy or Vidyasagar to accomplish their objectives because of the support that they received from the rulers. Concerns for gender parity had their roots in the philosophy of Enlightenment which was a natural gift to the colonised. Tagore was, however, a little uncertain because the influences from outside might not be adequate to remove the internalised misogyny in women. Here, the poet had in mind the well-entrenched prejudices (which were justified as given) that women nurtured instinctively because of their socialisation in a socioeconomic and politico-ideological milieu and which were integral to their existence as women. In other words, that women were meant to fashion their socioeconomic preferences in accordance with the patriarchal priorities appeared to have been axiomatic. Hence there was no escape route. Given the deep-rooted mindset in support of large sets of debilitating social mores and economic designs, it was not easy for the women to get out of what they had been taught to follow since their birth. These ideas survive without much difficulty since they were transmitted from one generation to another. In *Ghare Baire*, Bimala's elder sister-in-law's condemnatory attitude towards Bimala's seemingly unfeminine behaviour is a perfect example of the kind of finger-wagging that the progressive-minded had to confront in their engagement with the old guard. Here, Tagore delineated the tortuous path towards feminist enlightenment that the Bimalas of the world must traverse. On this journey, 'radical and critical questioning serves as a roadmap, which one uses to examine one's own preconceived notions and prejudices, as well as the sociocultural forces that determine one's relation with the world'

(Tagore 1425 Bangabda: 365). Tagore readily admitted that this path was not free of obstacles, but he rejoiced in the power of questioning to overcome all such obstacles on the road to freedom. Despite the sorrows and dangers involved in this process of radically transforming attitudes, Tagore was confident in the inevitability of change for he believed that 'the tides of time cannot be reversed' (366). Unlike some of these orthodox nationalist colleagues whose politics hinged on a nostalgic yearning for the past, Tagore was aware of the oppressive underpinnings of such a stance. In modernity, he saw opportunities for progress, social justice and widespread enlightenment. It is this relentless optimism that forms the bedrock of his women characters' unshakable faith in modernity.

Voicing the Voice of Protest

As argued above, there is a correspondence between Tagore's concern for gender parity which he articulated in his critical essays and the characters that he developed in his novels, short stories and dance dramas. By selecting some of the major characters from his texts, this section is an elaboration of the views that the poet propounded to defend the politico-ideological priorities in favour of gender parity. In other words, what is most striking is the fact that the characters that Tagore designed spoke in an identical language championing his concern for a society free from gender discrimination. There is another aspect that also deserves sedulous attention, namely, in order to spread out the message, he did not merely talk about the middle-class woman but also dwelled on how the marginalised sections of society suffered due to gender prejudices. The main character, Prakriti, in the dance drama *Chandalika* (Untouchables), was a powerful voice that she raised against established social practices denying her a rightful place in society; being a Chandal (untouchable), she remained ostracised primarily due to constructed values and mores permanently segregating the lower castes from the rest simply because of the accident of birth. Basic here is the point that Tagore delved into gender issues at two levels: At the contextual level, he endeavoured to capture gender discrimination, which drew sustenance from the well-entrenched social and economic practices and complementary ideological priorities detrimental to the evolution of a level-playing field for all. At the conceptual level, he, being inspired by the ideas of Enlightenment philosophy, graphically explicated the tensions between the context-centric indigenous ideas and those derived from Western sources. On occasions, Tagore resolved the tension himself and on others, he left it unresolved. Bimala in *Ghare Baire* is illustrative here:

It was Nikhilesh who introduced her to Western liberating ideas, which helped her understand why caste segregation was a debilitating influence. Here she was a liberated woman, but the sudden death of her husband, Nikhilesh, radically altered her perception of life and she readily accepted that her apparently deviant behaviour provoked divine retribution; here, Bimala was not different from her elder sister-in-law who, being blind to the prevalent social restrictions for a widow, never appreciated the former for being zealously receptive to the transmitted Western values.

Unfolding of Ideas

Tagore held revolutionary views in so far as gender was concerned. His characters in novels, plays and short stories, where protagonists of ideas did not receive the approbation that the poet had expected confirms that despite being progressive, the well-entrenched socially justified prejudices were strong enough to easily dismiss them. Nonetheless, these characters epitomised a format of thinking which helped build persuasive arguments in favour of gender equity. The novel, *Yogayog* (Nexus), written in 1929, is an elaboration of how Tagore developed his point of view through those characters who spoke in a language that the poet evolved to set in motion processes leading to women's empowerment.

Initially entitled *Teen Purush* when the novel was serialised in the weekly journal, *Bichitra*, between 1927 and 1929, it was renamed *Yogayog* in its 1929 published form as a book. The novel is about a society in transition where 'a decaying aristocracy makes way for rising mercantile capitalists, causing a major upheaval in social relations' (Chakravarty 2013: 109). By dwelling on the plight of a woman, Kumudini, who was caught in the rivalry between her family—the old aristocratic Chatterjees—and her adopted family post her marriage to the Ghosal family, which belonged to the *nouveau riche* section of Calcutta's elite families that thrived out of collaboration with the East India Company. Unlike *Char Adhyay* or *Ghare Baire,* the politics of the novel was not of the nationalist variety since its historical context was the decline of the landed aristocracy in Bengal and the ascendancy of an entrepreneur class. As history shows, the poet's grandfather rose to prominence first as a *banian* (interpreter) and later as one of the most successful entrepreneurs in colonial Bengal with support from the British rulers, including the Governor-General, William Bentick. Many of his contemporaries followed the same path. It was a revolutionary change since involvement with trade and commerce was never considered to be a respectable profession. Nonetheless, that hardly deterred many

Bengalis who spontaneously joined business presumably because it was a source of quick money.

The rivalry between these families had a past which was manifested during the Durga Puja when the Ghosals, in order to establish their social esteem, 'made the image of their goddess two cubits higher than that of the Chatterjees, who retaliated by erecting arches along the route' to obstruct the movement of the idol (Tagore 2011: 803). The consequences were disastrous because 'the High-Imagers then set out to break the arches and the Low-Archers to break their rivals' heads' (803). Litigations followed which hardly gave a reprieve to the Ghosals given that they had neither money to defend their point in the court nor the social recognition to support their claim. It was obvious as the poet most categorically articulated that 'the defamers had a louder voice because their pockets were deeper. So, it was not difficult to find drummers for their false campaign from among their priestly scholars to support the charge that the Ghosals were fallen Brahmins' (803). The Ghosals had thus swallowed the insult because they lacked both wealth and strong evidence in their favour. There was a plot twist now: The wealthy Chatterjees lost their sheen in society with the decline of their income from the landed property for a variety of reasons, including the lack of interest in cultivation among the scions of the family while the Ghosals, especially the new generation found newer means to earn quick money with the arrival of the East India Company and its willingness to involve the native collaborators. It was an opportunity for the Ghosals to rise as a successful family given the opening of newer avenues for generating income. While pondering over the dwindling of the name and fame of the Chatterjees, the poet thus noted that

> such stories were rather cheques from the past on an insolvent present. The days of glory were gone; its history like an empty vessel made a lot of noise. Anyway, just as the lamp goes out when the oil is finished, so does the night end at daybreak. The fortune of the Ghosals dawned with the extraordinary luck of Madhusudan, the Ghosal scion. (804)

Two points need reiteration here to connect the novel's main theme with the prevalent socioeconomic background: First, the rise of mercantile capitalism in the wake of the consolidation of colonialism opened up many newer ways of making money. Having understood this, Madhusudan left no stone unturned to take advantage of the situation. Second, with the increase in their income, their social image was also enhanced which reconfirms the truth that money remained a primary decider of social esteem. Beginning her business career as a kerosene-dealer, by dint of hard work, Madhusudan expanded his business from

> the bylanes to the main street [and] ... large entries to his credit account served as a stepping stones in his rise from a retailer to a wholesaler [which was, as the poet illustrated] like our great epic starting from an introductory chapter and ending in the chapter on an ascent to paradise. (805)

The intelligent Madhusudan rose to prominence in the business world, and his fame as a successful businessman quickly spread, which took him to many social gatherings of Calcutta elites. His hard work enabled him to become rich in a short period; it also allowed him access to the class of elites who immediately accepted him as one of them presumably because of his wealth which was visible to the naked eye. Being the sole owner of the marketplace and his two-storied mansion, 'Madhuchakra', a name suggested by his teacher of Sanskrit whose affection for Madhusudan 'had suddenly become more pronounced than in the past' (806). The storyline would have been familiar had we not known what had happened in the aftermath. Madhusudan's determination helped him reach where he was, but his desire to take revenge as his family was humiliated by the Chatterjees in the past added new dimensions to the plot. His insistence to get his bride from the Chatterjees reveals that he nurtured his feelings of being insulted by them on many occasions, including during that infamous Durga Puja because they were not rich enough then. The narrator however prepared the reader for many twists in the plot with the statement that 'a family nursing wounded pride is rather like a wounded hyena—ferocious in the extreme' (807). It was easier for Madhusudan to accomplish his goal since the Chatterjees did not seem to oppose the proposal, given the fact that there could have been no better match. They were running out of choice because (a) they no longer remained as rich as they had been earlier since 'all their properties were slowly sinking in the quicksand of debt' (815), and (b) the issues of Kumudini's marriage raised many questions given the fact that she was also crossing the eligible age (815). Financially, the Chatterjees were on the brink of a severe crisis which led them to sell the mansion in the village and shift to a rented house in 'the Baghbazar area of Kolkata' (815). With the death of the head of the Chatterjee family, Mukundalal, the entire responsibility of running the family rested on his eldest son, Bipradas, whose marriage did not take place because 'bride-to-be dies of a malignant fever only a couple of days before the actual wedding' (817). Bipradas was also responsible for supporting his younger brother who was studying abroad. But later, the brother being extravagant made Kumud offer to sell her gold ornaments to help, Bipradas. The above details reveal the actual context in which other important decisions followed.

As already mentioned, Bipradas was keen to find an appropriate match for Kumudini who was an accomplished girl, trained in playing the esraj along with learning classical vocals by a trainer. He was in search of a match for his sister. With the arrival of a matchmaker, he was very happy; the matchmaker came with a proposal from Madhusudan which Bipradas immediately declined since Madhusudan was too old for Kumudini. The matchmaker tried to persuade him by saying that the bride-to-be would be queen since the British government was soon to bestow on him the title of Raja (king). Initially reluctant, even Kumudini agreed to the match presumably because she was indoctrinated to believe that a particular wedding happened as destined by providence. A specific mindset developed to justify the belief that marriage was governed by providential intervention. Here the poet elaborated on the processes of how it happened in Bengali families. Kumud thus believed that it was 'a godsend opportunity' which they should not lose (821). While seeking to conceptualise patriarchy, the poet explained how Kumud justified her decision though she was also opposed to the proposal because of the massive age gap between her and Madhusudan. As Rabindranath explained,

> the thought that marriage has also a complication by way of personal liking, never entered her head. From her childhood, she had seen her four sisters married one after the other. There was a *kuleen* [high caste] family and nothing mattered by the *kul*—the family lineage. They lived on, day in and day out, engrossed in their children and the rest of the family. When they were hurt, they did not protest, they could never imagine that things could be different. [Just like] a mother cannot choose her son, … it was the same with husbands. God had not opened a shop for people to choose what they wanted. No one could override Fate. (821)

This argument explains the growth of a servile mindset among women which helped the social restrictions to draw sustenance over centuries. Many contemporary feminist theoreticians evolve conceptual parameters to understand the phenomenon. Nonetheless, a careful reading of Rabindranath's text on women written in the early 1920s preceded all of them. It illustrated how women developed ways of thinking on the basis of a specific kind of socialisation imparted by the family. By suggesting that

> when a woman refuses to acknowledge the distinction between her life and that of a man, she does not convince us if its truth, but only proves to us that she is suffering. All great suffering indicates some wrong

> somewhere. In the present age, the wrong in woman's lack of freedom in his relationship with man, which compels her to turn her disabilities into attractions, and to use untruths as her allies in the battle of life, which she is suffering from the precariousness of her position. (Tagore 1996: 553)

Here is a broader point that illustrates the discrimination at home while raising a girl and a boy in Bengali families. Women were nurtured with the vision that they were appendages to their male counterparts. Hence, there was hardly a scope for revision of their social status. It was most forcefully argued by the poet when he says that

> many of the laws and social regulations guiding the relationships of man and woman are relics of a barbaric age, when the brutal pride of an exclusive possession had its dominance in human relations, such as those of parents and children, husbands and wives, master and servants, teachers and disciples. The vulgarity of it still persists in the social bond between sexes because of the economic helplessness of woman. Nothing makes us so stupidly mean as the sense of superiority which of the power of the purse confers upon us. (553–554)

Condemning the social imbalances because of the economic strength of man over woman, the poet found the logic vacuous since the demarcation was based on the prejudices born out of arrogantly justified power by the men at the cost of half of the total demography. The argument is faulty since it illustrated a design in which the segregating mindset appeared to have decisively acted in favour of discrimination based on the biological differences between sexes. A society justifying masculinity as a criterion for being recognised as a healthy society was likely to be doomed since 'the greed of power and possession, which can have no finality of completeness in itself, … lay a violent hand upon its own ponderousness of material' (412). Here, being a devotee of universal humanism, the poet referred to how he felt when such an attempt was made to separate man from woman:

> At the present stage of history, civilisation is almost exclusively masculine, a civilisation of power in which woman has been thrust aside in the shade. Therefore, it has lost its balance and it is moving from war to war. Its motive forces are the forces of destruction, and its ceremonials are carried through an appalling number of human sacrifices. This one-sided civilisation crashing along a series of catastrophes at a tremendous speed because of its one-sidedness. And, at last the time has arrived when woman must step in and impart her rhythm to this reckless movement of power. (412)

The poet believed that women represented the voice of peace since they were naturally endowed to absorb pain and agony. Given the fact that masculinity drew human civilisation to destruction, the poet also insisted that women should come forward to discharge their duty based on what they internalised; unless this was done, it was difficult, if not impossible, to halt the obliteration of humanity from the Earth. Hence, Rabindranath believed that 'woman cannot be pushed back for good into the mere region of man's decorative by man's aggressiveness of power [for] she is not less necessary in human civilisation than man, but possibly more so' (415). Being hopeful that woman ushered in a new dawn in human civilisation in view of their natural strength, the poet thus concluded that

> at last, the present age has sent its cry to woman, asking her to come out of segregation in order to restore the spiritual supremacy of all that is human in the world of humanity. She has been aroused to remember that womanliness is not chiefly decorative. It is like that vital health, which not only imparts the bloom of beauty to the body, but joy to the mind and perfection to life. (555)

Conceptually, Rabindranath was far ahead of his age which was evident in his critical essays though, in his creative writings, he did not seem to have shown that courage. Hence Bimala of *Ghare Baire* changed her behaviour only in response to what her husband suggested; Ela and Damini failed to go beyond the male dictation though they had built their own world. Similarly, here in *Yogayog*, Kumudini also endorsed the views which, despite not being accepted by her brother, Bipradas, agreed to go ahead with the marriage proposal with Madhusudan by saying that 'my match must have been already fixed with him of whom you speak' (Tagore 2011: 822). To Bipradas, it was a bolt from the blue that Kumu so happily endorsed the marriage despite knowing that it was not a good match for her; he made another last attempt by saying that 'this is a matter of your whole life [and] … do not commit anything on a whim' (822). To his surprise, Kumud replied that her decision was based on her choice which was manifested when she said that 'it is not a whim, not a whim at all [and] I swear to you [that] I cannot marry anyone else' (822). Women instinctively acquire certain beliefs given the way they are socialised within the family. Bipradas failed to comprehend this aspect of her thinking which the poet articulated by adumbrating that 'this one dark corner of [Kumud's] mind was altogether outside his sphere of his influence' (822). So, notwithstanding Bipradas' misgivings, the match was fixed and surprisingly, Kumud was 'ecstatic with the idea of her union with someone who existed only in her imagination' (823).

Still, Bipradas was uncertain as he apprehended that by taking Kumud, Madhusudan was likely to settle an old score because he remembered that the Ghosals had been humiliated by his family long ago over the immersion of the Durga idol; it was possible then because they were as wealthy as the latter. But, now, the Chatterjees were nowhere near their counterpart given the loss of their wealth which made Bipradas wonder 'if the proposed marriage was also the beginning of a sequel to the old feud' (823). Being convinced that her sister would face the brunt of the old rivalry, he made another attempt to restrain Kumud to not accept the proposal. Seeking to dissuade his sister, Bipradas revolted at her illogical mindset in support of the idea of marriage being fixed in heaven. As one who believed in the idea of marriage being nothing but a contract, he thus argued that

> marriage ties become real when both parties are honest to themselves. It is no use tuning an instrument if the player is tone-deaf. Look at our mythology—Sita was as great as Rama, Sati matched Mahadeva and so did Arundhati and Vashist. The gentlemen of today have no merit themselves, that is why this one-sided clamour of chastity on the part of the women. They cannot supply the oil but want to wick to give light. And, the wick—it simply burns itself to ashes. (826)

It did not work out since Kumud was adamant about marrying Madhusudan since she had internalised the idea that he was a godsend. The idea of Sati, the dedicated wife, remained ingrained in her, and she justified that despite being at fault, 'Madhusudan, her husband-to-be, is eternal and emotionless [and] ... she was born to accept him as she was destined to do so by the almighty' (826). It was a well-entrenched mental universe of patriarchy in which women were raised as an appendage, first, to their father and brother, then to their husband and finally to their son. Despite his revolutionary views on gender, the poet couldn't do away with the social boundaries in which women were treated differently from their male counterparts.

The storyline does not seem very unfamiliar since what Bipradas apprehended even before the match was finalised came true because the very first meeting between the groom and bride's sides 'produced a clangour of dissonance which drowned the festive tune of the wedding' (832). Kumu was helpless because she did not expect this at the first meeting with her in-laws but was unable to say anything since, she knew, it was her conscious choice to go to Madhusudan despite the opposition of her brother. Instead of questioning those from her in-law's family who created the ruckus, she firmly believed that 'her lord will never let her down' presumably to sustain her mental strength to sail through the crisis and also to not agonise her brother because of her suffering due to such unexpected misbehaviour of the members of her adopted family. The second shock of her being the wife of Madhusudan came when she found that Madhusudan, instead of travelling with his newly married wife, travelled to Calcutta in a different saloon car along with his English friends. She was further disturbed when Madhusadan's younger brother's wife, Nistarini, also known as Motir Ma (mother of Moti, the son of Nistarini) mentioned that Bipradas came to the station to receive those who accompanied the groom. She was not persuaded to believe the intention of Madhusudan which her brother kept on hammering. She held herself responsible for the humiliation that her brother suffered for her. Her mind thus, the poet explained 'went on torturing itself over all that which could not be undone [and, she] kept recalling [her brother's] sick and tired but calm face and his deep, gentle eyes full of compassion and blessing' (838). But there was no escape route for Kumud and the rudeness of [Madhusudan] in his behaviour pushed [her] away as well every time' (839). For Madhusudan, raised with a sexist mindset, it did not seem odd at all because

> he had expected that his wife would also be part of the banal world [in which] women's life, enveloped in trivial household chores, was indirectly governed by the whims of menfolk. It had never entered his calculating head that to relate to one's wife was also an art and that the husband-wife relationship was built on a foundation of understanding, trust and give and take. (839)

A man-woman relationship as husband and wife is based on the acceptance of equality between two individuals due to the nuptial bond. Nobody is superior or inferior in this kind of solemnised relationship. In another text of 1933, the poet reiterated his firm views by saying that 'most men forget that conjugal rights make one superior over the other partner [because] marriage is like a tender sapling that requires constant care' (Tagore 1959: 171). The idea was completely alien to Madhusudan who did not pay much attention to his wife even when she had fainted. Not only was he annoyed with this message but he also refused to take care of her when she needed attention: 'She will go into faint every day and I have to massage her with ayurvedic oil. Is that what I married her for' (Tagore 2011: 849). Angrily, he disapproved of Kumu being unwell and expressed his annoyance by saying that 'I am a busy man [and] I do not have the leisure to wait upon a hysterical woman' (849). Kumu's response was highly tempered; she thus said that even 'if you want to humiliate me, you will not succeed [because] I shall take your insults to heart' (849). Reminded of her brother's gentlemanliness, Kumu never dreamt of such ugly behaviour from his husband which was manifested when she further said that 'be as cruel as you like but do not demean yourself' (849). In Kumu's statement, the poet reaffirmed the belief that humanism remained the cornerstone of human civilisation, and could never be undermined. For Kumu, it was completely unknown since she was raised in a family that always upheld humanity over anything else. Being nurtured by her mother, who left her husband because he (Mukundalal) spent nights with the dancing girls, she also dared to stand up against the mental torture meted out to her by her husband. Here, one must not forget the immense influence of Bipradas on Kumu who was raised by him just like his daughter. To her values, Bipradas epitomised the core values of humanity; presumably because of her emotional training, it was not easy for her to accept Madhusudan though she accepted him as her husband because she believed their marriage was providentially determined. Thus, the novel segregated love from marriage; marriage meant the rights of a man over a woman's body which, in other words, became a site to establish a man's hegemony once he was married to a woman. Second, *Yogayog* is a powerful text for its exploration of sexuality within marriage. While Binodini in *Chokher Bali* and Bimala in *Ghare Baire* expressed their desire to fulfil their sexual needs, Kumu was different. She deflected her desire onto an absent deity because she was unable to respond to her husband who forced himself on her to claim victory—though Rabindranath questioned 'could this be called a victory?' (882). Contrarily, the instinctive female desire was represented by the character Shyamasundari, the widow of Madhusudan's younger brother. While Kumu characterised her submission to Madhusudan for satisfying his lust as 'an act of subversion' (Chakravarty 2013: 112), Shyamasundari happily expressed her desire for physical union with his brother-in-law. It was an expression of fulfilling her physical and emotional needs along with her determination to hold power and authority within the domestic establishment—she realised that only by keeping Madhusudan under her spell, she could easily have both. Still, given the social prejudices against the mistress of the patriarch, these goals remained elusive to Shyamasundari. So, it did not seem odd as she was cast aside once Madhusudan's purpose was served. By referring to the plight of Shyamasundari, the bard evolved a powerful critique against the institution of marriage which was merely a social seal of relationships without respecting the foundational values on which the institutionalised conjugal unity rested. It was also argued that marriage was therefore not a sanctified institution since married men and women tended to undermine it under the slightest pretext. Here, the poet criticised both Madhusudan and Shyamasundari because both of them, by deviating from the fundamental ethos of marriage, were entrapped in a social maze that was difficult to escape. The contrast is Kumu's approach to conjugal life. Despite being aware that Madhusudan had hardly loved her, she never objected when he forced himself on her. Instead of expressing her annoyance, she surrendered each time by saying that she was 'at his service [and always] awaits his call' (Tagore 2011: 881). She assured him that 'she was always there to respond to his order [because she was] incapable doing anything on [her] own' (881). Kumu surrendered because it was her duty to do so; yet, she was unable to absorb the shock because, for her, it was a surrender to the bestiality of Madhusudan with which she could never reconcile. Her reaction to this incident was marvellously captured by the poet when he said that 'she was sulking against her deity, in much the same way as an innocent child bears the chastisement of his father without protest, out of a deep hurt'. She raised the question, 'Was the call which she expected to be divine going to end in this debasement? In this unfaithfulness of the soul? Has my lord lured me as a prey to his desire for female sacrifice? Did he want his offering to be a mindless lump flesh?' (882)

Being a priest who always put human emotions over anything else, it was expected that the poet was certain to question the nature of the relationship in which women were just prey to fulfil the bestial desire of the menfolk especially once the relationship was institutionalised through marriage. With his sharp critique of Madhusudan's behaviour vis-à-vis Kumu, the bard reaffirmed the idea of marital rape. It was certainly not in vogue when he wrote *Yogayog* though Rabindranath did not hesitate to question the bestial interaction of Madhusudan with Kumu as it was devoid of love and empathy of the former for the latter. Sex was thus a weapon that was indiscriminately utilised by the menfolk to ascertain their authority over women. What is further unfortunate was the fact that this idea gained ground because the women did not seem to have raised their voices to the extent it was expected. Being a resource at the disposal of those with sexist views, sex is also 'a resource that men and the like-minded women control, ... a perception [that] ... reigned supreme [presumably because] it seems impossible to avoid the trap [drawn on] an appropriationist logic of domination built in the prevalent mindset' (Haraway 1988: 592). Nothing is more explicit than this description of Kumu's revulsion and Madhusudan's lust for asserting his conjugal rights. For Kumu, 'a cruel, dark, senile lust from outside devoured her, like the legendary monster, Rahu eclipsing the moon' (Tagore 2011: 883). What affected her most was the lack of dignity which was manifested in Madhusudan's 'unbridled lecherousness where love was akin to craving for material wealth' (883). The poet graphically described Kumu's helplessness by saying that Mdhusudan's

> clammy touch was what Kumu found revolting. She did not mind her husband's age but was pained that his age has no dignity left. To give oneself was more like the ripening of a fruit in free air and light, but one could not ripen a raw fruit by crushing it. That this precious time was denied was what she found so hurting and insulting. (883–884)

Kumu detested her husband's forcible sexual interaction and tried to escape the feeling of revulsion by shifting her attention to the baby of the house, Gopal, just to escape 'from the polluted air to the clean breeze of a flower garden' (884). Not only did Rabindranath broach the idea of marital rape because of sexual incompatibility but he also referred to 'the sanctioned violence accompanying many marital relationships' (Chakravarty 2013: 114). It was a revolutionary idea, especially in a context when women were considered to be an appendage to the family and, as a result, their claim to be equal to their male counterparts never received adequate attention as it was likely to generate social upheavals given the implicit adverse implications of social imbalances. That the novel provoked severe criticism was obvious since it contained within itself the inspiration for turning, to speak metaphorically, society upside down.

The poet was aware that whatever he was suggesting was difficult to achieve given the existent sociocultural milieu though women of his time realised that sexual incompatibility needed to be conclusively addressed. Given the social pressure, the idea remained almost hidden which Kumu explained by saying, 'I have no illusion left. My life is shamelessly exposed. There is no cover left to console me with. Don't women have any space to themselves till they die? God made their world so rigid?' (907).

This was a statement of a hapless woman who built a castle of hope before marriage since she always believed that God must have prepared her companion in accordance with her choice. Not only was she disillusioned but she was also humiliated at Madhusudan's bestiality to claim his conjugal rights. Under no circumstances, she could be taken out of her distress which Motir Ma illustrated by saying that 'no gardener would now be able to revive this sensitive creeper even with an outpouring of indulgence' (907). Being aware that, as her husband, Madhusudan had a right to have an intimate interaction with her, she thus agreed that her 'inability to give myself up honourably to my husband is a great sin on [her] part' (907). And this caused her great distress after the incident, and she was disturbed 'at the prospect of the degradation of surrender without respect' (907). Kumud was no exception in nurturing the views that were contrarian to the general rule in most families; women were taught to accept their husbands despite being not appreciative of what they stood for. In other words, they were expected to surrender even to the whims of their husbands because that was socioculturally endorsed over generations, leading to the consolidation of a mindset supportive of the values governing the man–woman relationship once it was institutionalised through marriage. Here, the confession that Motir Ma made is of significance; despite having understood the agony that Kumu had undergone because of Madhusudan's bestiality, she argued that

> it didn't matter whether the husband was good or bad, he was only a token to prove the glory of the devoted woman. I had not the slightest doubt that whomsoever the god of marriage, Prajapati, chose for me, I was bound to love him. From my childhood I had watched my mother read the Puranas, heard the commentators and concluded that it was easy indeed to conform to the holy scriptures. (909)

At one level, Kumu nurtured the same idea as that of Motir Ma since she also believed that in the selection of her husband, God had a role to play. In other words, she expressed the belief repeatedly when she was asked by Bipradas; and, her response was the same, namely, marriage was providentially settled and she was ready to accept whoever was chosen as her husband. Here is the end of the compatibility of the views, held by Kumu and Motir Ma. Being nurtured by her brother, Bipradas, she was, however, consulted before the decision was taken. So, unlike other women, she had had the privilege of being a part of the decision regarding her fate. What is being reinforced here is the poet's idea of modernity in which man and woman were treated equally; and, especially in marriage, the woman needed to be given a voice since it was, she, who had to leave her maternal home to be with someone who was generally unknown to her. Rabindranath here redefined the nature of freedom which was equal for all. Opposed to gender discrimination, in *Yogayog*, he ensured that Kumu's views were taken as seriously as those of other members of the family. As shown earlier, Bipradas was not keen for her marriage to Madhusudan since it was, according to him, a mismatch given the massive age difference between her and her husband-to-be. But due to Kumu's insistence, despite being reluctant, he had finally agreed:

> This marriage of mine, it is I who made it happen—but out of what a childish illusion! Whatever beguiled me then was entirely false. Yet with what utter conviction, what stubbornness I went into it: nobody could have stopped it. Her elder brother [Bipradas] knew that, so he did not stop me, but I was aware that he was extremely worried and apprehensive. Even then, I didn't curb myself. I was such a fool. From

> now on, not only do I suffer, but I make others suffer too, and curse myself as the curse of all this suffering. (909)

There are two integral parts to this argument: First, Kumu, despite having had the opportunity of rejecting the proposal, agreed to go ahead as she believed that this had providential approval. She was confident that her deity would ensure her a happy conjugal life which, on the other, made her accept Madhusudan despite being aware of the massive age differences and the old rivalry between the two families. Second, being aware of her brother's objection to the proposal, she defied Bipradas out of her firm belief that marriage was providential and that nothing could go wrong. As one who always took up cudgels against socioculturally discriminatory mindsets, especially regarding women, the poet evolved a model of gender parity, which was then inconceivable. At the same time, the poet's model was sensitive to the prevalent sociocultural ethos justifying gender discrimination. Rabindranath was ahead of his time though he could not always develop arguments in his creative texts in favour of his libertarian thoughts. In the process, he acquainted his readers with the reality that appeared to be fading out though not completely disappeared. Notwithstanding being coercive, these ideas were justified as integral to the maintenance of a social balance which resulted in their general acceptance; there was another aspect: through discriminatory processes of socialisation, girls were raised with ideas that remained an anathema for the boys. This was the foundation on which two different mindsets—one for the boys and another for girls—emerged in human society. To defend his point of view, the poet referred to 'the customary binding of the feet of the Chinese woman [was] not a torture degrading her individuality, ... but an affection of man for woman' (917). What it meant was that which was intrinsically natural would appear to be abnormal. *Yogayog* presents this concept with reference to the changing behavioural pattern of Motir Ma who, though initially supportive of Kumu, gradually changed as the novel progressed presumably because of the mindset that she internalised as a woman. Not only did she express her resentment towards Kumu, given her defiance of the established customary conjugal relations between husband and wife, she openly criticised her because she 'did not accept gracefully when fortune turned to offer her a gift', which referred to Mdhusudan's willingness to consummate the marriage by force, notwithstanding the humiliation that she suffered in the process (917). Unlike Motir Ma, who represented a divided self because she, despite being appreciative of the views in support of gender equality, finally surrendered to the age-old ideas of gender disparity, Shyamasundari, the widow of Madhusudan's younger brother, fulfilled her long-nurtured desire to prevail over Kumu by being womanly in the conventional sense. She was ready to face Madhusudan's abuse smilingly because she was taught to be so in order to retain her place in his heart. Although it was an illicit relationship, they hardly bothered and did not find it necessary to hide their 'care for each other in the public' (932). Even after being hit by Madhusudan, Shyamasudari never raised her voice because not only did she accept this as given but also by being close to him, she was likely to become the woman in control of the household activities. It was not possible since Motir Ma was more reliable to Madhusudan than Shyamasudari. Nonetheless, Shyama was hopeful and allowed Madhusudan to derive sexual pleasure from her. Besides his 'crude addiction to her', Madhusudan seemed to like her because she 'sincerely thought him superior in every respect and was prepared to do anything to soothe his pride which got a daily jolt during Kumu's stay' (932). As the situation became unbearable for Kumu, she left her marital home to stay with her brother. This was also a source of humiliation for Madhusudan especially when it was openly discussed that his illicit affair with Shyamasudnari forced his legally wed wife to desert him. Under these circumstances, Madhusudan went to Bipradas's house to bring her back, which Kumu vehemently opposed. Two factors created conditions for Kumu to return. Both of these were socioculturally conditioned. First, it was a matter of disrespect if a married sister, who was supposed to be in her marital home left the adopted home. So, Bipradas was subject to social pressure since her sister remained with him for a long period. It also confirms that sociocultural ethos, despite being exploitative, remained critical to human existence in then Bengal. Second, Kumud's pregnancy was also an important factor that compelled her to go back to her marital home for the sake of her unborn child. It was socially unacceptable for a pregnant woman to stay amidst her relatives when she was expected to be with her husband despite being abused by him.

The decision for Kumu to go back with Madhusudan was a foregone conclusion because of a specific kind of sociocultural vision that governed the man–woman/husband–wife relationships. The last part of the novel *Yogayog* is most poignant. Both brother and sister played Raag Bhairon which was 'sombre, quiet and plaintive'; it was a recalling of the mood of Mahadeva in the morning after he had reconciled the loss of Sati. By using a mythological metaphor, the poet explained the pain that both the brother and sister underwent when Kumu's departure was imminent. For Bipradas, it was a classical tune, in which 'deep sorrow and ecstasy mingle together': He was ecstatic because Kumu was going back to her marital home, which was a fulfilment of a social norm that he was unable to flout;

it was also a source of agony for him since he was not sure whether there would be any further meeting with Kumu who had been raised by him given the untimely death of their father. It was manifested when Bipradas expressed his pain by comparing his feeling of loss with that of Kanva, the father of Shakuntala, who left him to join her husband. By recounting the scene which Kalidas most poignantly depicted in his *Abhigynam Shakuntalam*, Bipradas reminded Kumu of the story:

> Remember when Shakuntala was staring out to join her husband Dushyanta, the sage Kanva travelled some distance with her. Much sorrow and humiliation lay on the way to the destination he was leading her to. But she did stop even there but crossed over to eternal peace. This morning's Raag Bhairon captures the same peace, and my heartfelt blessings may reach you towards entire fulfilment—a fulfilment which many inundate your inner and outer being and flush all your sorrow away. (954)

There are reasons to believe that the poet's revolutionary self was constrained as he appeared to have accepted the return of Kumu knowing well that the situation was not going to change radically. His reference to the rendition of Raag Bhairon, coupled with the reference to the *Abhigynam Shakuntalam*, was a source of his optimism justifying the decision that Bipradas took despite all odds. It was, in other words, a surrender to the age-old customary values in which women were always taken as appendages in the family and were to be tuned to the needs of the menfolk. At the same time, it was also an attempt to reverse the sociocultural ethos which was receptive to gender parity and opposed to those prejudicial practices supportive of gender discrimination. Primarily, it was a voice that gained momentum in the course of history. So, by initiating an endeavour that was articulated in protests against the archaic sociocultural values, the poet used in an era of modernity in which the idea of gender disparity was being questioned, though in muted form: This was evident when Kumud was asked to go back to her marital home by Bipradas although nothing was likely to change in her adopted home. In short, *Yogayog* was a narrative of protest and acquiescence at the same time: Kumud's voice against abuse and marital rape represented an attempt based on her understanding of the man-woman relationship as equal due to her social upbringing and it was, at the same time, an instance of succumbing to the well-entrenched sociocultural pressure, which finally forced her to accept what she had detested so strongly so far.

The novel also represents a battle between the decaying aristocracy that thrived on income from land and a mercantile class drawing on wealth built out of trade and commerce. So, with the arrival of the British in Bengal, two contradictory socioeconomic forces competed with each other which the rivalry between the Chatterjees and Ghosals epitomised. What is however most striking was the lack of compatibility between the new era of modernity and the concomitant sociocultural changes that should have happened. Madhusudan was a glaring example. Although he rose to prominence, earning enormously by being involved in business, he hardly gave up the archaic values of the bygone era which was manifested in his firm belief in a wife being a stooge for him as her husband. This was the contradiction of the age which witnessed a lag, a serious lag indeed because those who adopted newer ways of generating wealth hardly deviated from the social prejudices which figured prominently in a feudal set-up. In contrast, Bipradas was nurtured in an environment far away from Calcutta where the old sociocultural values remained predominant. In other words, Calcutta, being the host of the British mercantile classes who also brought with them Western liberalism, especially the Enlightenment principles, was a place for these values to strike roots. Nonetheless, it did not affect everybody equally as Madhusudan demonstrated. Contrarily, Bipradas, being raised in rural Bengal, readily accepted the liberal politico-ideological ethos and for him, male–female equality was a given characteristic of human society. He had limitations too. Despite having nurtured the view against gender discrimination, he was unable to effectively intervene to reverse the sociocultural processes that forced Kumu to return to her marital home. This further confirms that the voice that Rabindranath raised was not effective enough to transform the prevalent socio-historical processes. Nonetheless, it was a voice that had the potential to gradually emerge strong, as history demonstrated. Kumud was caught in the quagmire of conflicting world views: On the one hand, she was reluctant to return to her adopted home; she was, on the other, unable to stay back in her brother's house. She also had a divided self which the poet captured in a very persuasive manner. Her divided self was testimony to her acceptance and non-acceptance of the established norms at the same time. It is therefore to argue that Kumu's decision to go back with Madhusudan after she learnt about her pregnancy was reflective of 'a return to conventionality and surrendering of her personal freedom and identity' (Chakravarty 2013: 117). Instead, the decision represented a search for an alternative in the changing environment. It was true that she had no option, at least on the surface, but to abide by Madhusudan's dictates; however, the fact that she expressed her opinion frankly despite adverse consequences also showed that she epitomised some of the embryonic ideas that evolved in the wake of visible sociocultural changes in Bengal. One is therefore persuaded to argue that while surrendering to Madhusudan's lustful desire to have sex with her, she never capitulated as it meant her degradation as a human being; similarly, her agreement with her brother in so far as her return to her in-law's house was concerned did not mean her transformation as 'a complaint wife' (118). So, it will be wrong to surmise that her external behaviour was compatible with what she thought internally. By drawing attention to this constant battle between the external world and inner feelings, the poet presented a nuanced argument because the two hardly coalesce. This means that mere acceptance of a bestial husband never meant that Kumu was happy in doing what she did; in a similar vein, by deciding to return to her marital home, she perhaps held the same opinion. Her pregnancy was a watershed in her life because it was, on one level, a fulfilment of her womanhood, and, on another, an opportunity to see the world differently presumably because there was a definite possibility for her to raise the baby according to her priority. The poet was silent here since the name of the baby, Abinash, was mentioned at the very beginning of the novel which he did perhaps only to contextually situate Madhusudan who was introduced to the readers as the father of Abinash (Tagore 2011: 804). Was it intentional on the part of the poet? It is difficult to know since the novel that was entitled *Teen Purush* (Three Generations) when it was serialised in the Bengali periodical *Bichitra*, ended with no answer to this question. One can, however, surmise based on some specific inputs that the author left in the novel: Rabindranath would not have been happy with the ill-treatment that Kumu had to undergo by being married to a lustful Madhusudan, who had risen to social prominence by virtue of his wealth. There is no denying that Kumu's disinclination to surrender to marital rape was reflective of the poet's unalloyed belief that marriage was just a contract that did not bind the woman to her husband. This entails, following the liberal conceptual dispensation, that women also had the right to annul the wedlock in case it was reduced to a disempowering instrument for muzzling her voice. In his eyes, Madhusudan was a villain who spread his tentacles simply because of a conducive sociocultural environment from which he drew sustenance. So, the argument is couched by taking into account the prevalent sociocultural context where these repugnant ideas struck roots. The poet pitched his argument at the individual level, by linking specific behavioural traits with the contemporary sociocultural context: He explained the nature of Madhusudan's personality which was certainly distasteful but not, entirely, inexplicable given the importance of the context in shaping an individual being. At the social level, he also exposed the contrarian tendencies acting as a determinant of human behaviour. Here, one is automatically drawn to the contrasting natures of Bipradas, Kumu's brother, and Madhusudan, her husband.

Madhusudan was arrogant and ready to fulfil his goals even by adopting foul means. It was evident when, despite her reluctance, Madhusudan forced himself on her just to prove that he had conjugal rights. Bipradas, on the other hand, expressed his reservation when the proposal for Kumu's marriage with Madhusudan was placed for his approval; he finally agreed once his sister conceded. This is illustrative of the claim that the poet continuously made of a woman being equal to her male counterpart. The fact that Bipradas mentioned several times that it was not a perfect match given the massive age difference also shows the triumph of one of the ideas of liberalism questioning an age-old practice of marriage in which the age gap was never taken into account. Nonetheless, instead of forcing her sister to accept his opinion, Bipradas remained true to his belief while accepting Kumu's decision. At this level, Bipradas epitomised one of the core values of liberalism, namely man and woman were equals. However, by allowing Kumu to return to Madhusudan's house, he appeared to have been trapped in the maze which did not allow him to forcefully argue that it was a misconstrued decision because of his apprehension that this, under no circumstances, would ensure happiness for his sister. Regardless of what he felt, Bipradas was unable to restrain his sister who had then no option but to return. What caught the readers by surprise was that despite having known that Kumu was perhaps 'leaving for good' (954), Bipradas consoled her with reference to what Kanva felt when he permitted Dushyant to rightfully claim his wife who, till then, had stayed with her father. Was this the poet's surrender to the age-old customary practice that once married, the woman no longer claimed a legitimate space in her parents' house? This was a difficult question to conclusively respond to. There is another aspect that should not escape our notice. The narrative, *Yogayog*, began with Mukundalal, Bipradas and Kumu's father, who forced their mother to leave home for Brindabon—by continuously hobnobbing with the dancing girls, despite her disapproval, he evinced the same patriarchal prejudices that Madhusudan later upheld while dealing with his daughter, Kumu. Bipradas developed the utilitarian anti-patriarchal views perhaps as a reaction to what he saw while being raised by his mother, who had been a victim of his father's patriarchal bias. Following this logic, it does not seem odd to surmise that Abinash was likely to imbibe those ideas that his maternal uncle articulated because he too was a victim of patriarchy. So, *Yogayog* is a novel that, despite having captured the possibilities of momentous sociocultural transformations in Bengal, is also a powerful sociocultural design to explore sexuality within marriage; it is also an account of how the stressed poet saw the reality which was neither completely receptive to the values associated with the ascendant mercantile capitalism nor vehemently opposed to the well-entrenched segregating sociocultural values and mores. *Yogayog* thus raises many questions which did not have conclusive answers presumably because it was written in the context of massive socio-economic and politico-ideological metamorphoses, a situation in which answers were difficult to seek since it was also a period of significant transition in Bengal when many sociocultural ideas jostled with each other to establish relevance.

Concluding Observations

A thorough analytical scan of *Yogayog* reveals that his concern for gender equity was not derivative but was rather instinctive. Persuaded by the efforts that his predecessors, like Rammohun Roy, Vidyasagar and also his father, Debendranath Tagore, undertook, the poet took onto himself the responsibility to carry the tradition forward. Being critical of the prevalent social system drawing on patriarchal prejudices, Rabindranath remained committed to this cause till the last days of his life. To the poet, the social design that ignored half of the demography was required to be replaced to create conditions in which women were treated at par with their male counterparts. The poet who established his fame as an author in Bangla attributed his reputation to the spontaneous willingness of women readers to read the texts that he wrote in vernacular language. Being candid in his appreciation, he thus said that

> Bangla has become a respectable language of expression largely due to its massive female readership; even those male readers who bought Bengali novels [even written by him] were ashamed to say it publicly because it would bring them a bad name. Despite being neglected by the male readers, the books in Bangla language were fondly nurtured by their female counterparts which helped books written in Bangla gain respectability and wider acceptance in due course. (Tagore 1410 Bangabda: 685)

So, for Tagore, women were harbingers of a new era when Bangla was no longer as despised as in the past. With this preface, Tagore now embarked on a bigger project, namely, to express his views to radically alter the widely practised socioeconomic norms and politico-ideological predispositions, which were disposed against women. As shown above, by drawing on the selective set of his writings (novels and short stories), the chapter substantiated the point with reference to how the female protagonists raised their voices against being discriminated against merely due to an accident of birth and a socially justified patriarchal system. Based on his understanding of Upanishadic messages and also the absorption of the Enlightenment values, he initiated a new literary genre to view women as respectable members of society in opposition to the mainstream conservative outlook drawing on gender disparity. A pattern is visible—whether it is Bimala or Ela or Damini—where they all were attempts at establishing independent identities as women. Interestingly, this was the pattern if one draws attention to Binodini of *Chokher Bali* (1903) or Nandini of *Rakta Karabi* (1925). In *Rakta Karabi,* Nandini, the young girl, used her feminine charm and attraction to destroy the deep-rooted restrictions that the invisible king had so far maintained for fulfilling his partisan aim of becoming rich at the cost of those working in the gold mines. It was Nandini who helped the king and all those who were associated with the extraction of gold from the mine realise the charm of life. The message that Tagore conveyed was about women bringing about a radical change in their behaviour that resulted in an appreciation of human values which, so far, had remained an anathema. Binodini or Bali as she was fondly addressed by Asha, another character in the novel, raised certain other issues. At one level, she was a conventional woman who expressed her unconditional love for her beloved Behari by saying that 'my life is empty, my heart is empty, there is emptiness all around me—come unto this emptiness, even if, for an instant, you have to come. I won't let go of you' (107). Questioning the social norms depriving widows of worldly comforts and charms, Binodini was a voice, a powerful voice indeed, which was difficult to conceive in the context of the mainstream conservatism that flourished in the 19th and early 20th century. Here is another dimension of the gender question that we will deal with in Chapter 6 in which Tagore attributed gender freedom to education; being educated, it was easier for a woman to carve out an independent space amidst other female members in the family. Illustrative here are the letters that were referred to in the novel. While depicting Kumudini, Tagore juggled two contrasting views: one that is desirous of gender freedom and the other that deals with impediments towards being treated as equal to their male counterparts. When Kumudini left her husband's home when she found him being entangled with a prostitute, Shyamasundari, nobody appears to have appreciated the decision and she was accused of being 'an arrogant woman [because] she did what she was not expected to do' (935). By virtue of being a man, the argument was elaborated further, Kumudini's husband 'was naturally superior to her—a fact that was unarguable' (935). This was tantamount to

> slavery [though] there does not seem to be an escape route [because] the wife becomes a property in a sacramental marriage. The day you go around the sacred fire seven times with the groom, your body and mind are bound to him forever. There is no escape. It is worse than death. Once you are born a woman you may not reverse the course of a woman's fate. (935)

With marriage, women lost their independence and became stooge at the beck and call of their husbands and other members of their adopted family. At the same time, the poet draws our attention to the processes supportive of the patriarchal grip over women which they themselves supported and nurtured. Kumudini's decision to leave her husband's home was condemned by her aunt and others who were not persuaded by her argument: They had lost their independent thinking after having been nurtured in an environment in which patriarchal prejudices seemed to have clouded their vision, not allowing them to judge issues independently. Patriarchy survived and also thrived because

> women themselves valued women the least. They were not even aware that this was the reason why it was so easy for men to dishonour women in every home. The women themselves had put out their own light. And then they lived in perpetual fear and anxiety, oppressed by unworthy men, and accepted the highest attainment in a woman's life was to bear all of this silently, without protest. (935)

Here, Tagore talked about a wider social constraint that was primarily due to the unavoidable impact of societal values, nurtured over generations. Women, instead of being an independent agency for social metamorphosis, became entrapped in the maze. Contrary to what was naturally expected, they unknowingly became an agent for patriarchy to remain unaffected. In other words, that women tended to argue for defending patriarchal prejudices was thus a natural outcome of being born and raised in an environment in which the torture that women suffered did not seem to be unusual. Nonetheless, Tagore, being one who always remained an uncompromising crusader for gender justice, warned his compatriots championing gender-based social imbalances when Biprodas, Kumudini's brother and a protagonist for gender equity, declared that 'so much violation of human rights could not be allowed any longer. Those whom society had degraded so much were now pulling the society down with them' (936). This was the silver lining since this contains a powerful message that Tagore articulated to establish the point that incessant struggle for gender equity was certain to bring about radical social transformation leading to gender equality by considerably undermining the age-old patriarchal hegemony justifying various restrictive socioeconomic and politically restraining practices.

While it is true that Tagore confined himself to discussing the problems of women coming from a particular social location (upper-caste, middle class), it is equally evident that he was keenly aware of the vicissitudes caused by the different markers that made up one's social location. He focused heavily on class dynamics, for instance, the novel *Yogayog*, focuses on a long rivalry between two families—the Chatterjees, bhadralok aristocrats who lost their money and were living on the dregs of their legacy, and the Ghosals, who used to be at the receiving end of the Chatterjees' torture when they were poorer, but had now come into money and were turning the tables on the Chatterjees in the name of revenge for years of bullying. Madhusudan Ghosal set this plan in motion by marrying Kumudini Chatterjee, the beloved younger sister of the Chatterjee patriarch Bipradas. This marriage was nothing but a way to 'buy' a Chatterjee girl and shamed the declining aristocratic family with arrogant, gaudy displays of Madhusudan's wealth. Over the course of the novel, Madhusudan turns out to be a cruel, controlling husband, who used his money to scorn his in-laws and manipulate his wife into cutting ties with her brother, who was struggling with debt and ill health. Kumudini struggled valiantly at first to escape her husband, but then conceived his child after what was essentially rape. With her fear of being a burden to her financially struggling brother on the one hand and the stigma of being a single mother on the other, Kumudini had no choice but to return to her cruel husband. Thus, *Yogayog* could be also seen as Tagore grappling with questions of class and gender and the intersection of the two in the institution of marriage. Kumudini herself becomes the terrain on which three symbolic battles are fought: first, the age-old rivalry between the Chatterjees and the Ghoshals, second, the tensions between fading feudal grandeur and ascendant mercantile lifestyles, and third, the impossibility of retaining a humanist sense of self in the face of systemic oppression, specifically misogyny. It is this last point that deserves to be fleshed out. Ordinarily, when modern readers see traditional forms of misogyny play out in the writings of 'progressive' authors of yore, it is often seen as a most charitable and nuanced response to say that no matter how ahead of his time the author was, he was, after all, in some respects at least, a man of his time—harbouring at least some of the social ills that characterised his milieu. But a *more* nuanced interpretation of Tagore's feminist writings, it may be argued, lies in a more careful interpretation of Kumudini's character arc. Kumudini's liberal upbringing, her independent-mindedness, her self-righteousness and self-respect, and her deep, abiding sense of personal dignity ultimately turn out to be a poor bulwark against the heavy shackles of the marital tie. Upon discovering that her rape had resulted in her becoming pregnant with Madhusudan's child, Kumudini has no choice but to obey the misogynist injunctions that govern her life as a pregnant wife, and return to her abusive husband's home, thus rendering ineffectual her rebellious escape to her brother's. Here, by applying the distinction between individual cruelty (Madhusudan's abusive behaviour towards his wife) and systemic oppression (the misogyny inherent to the institution of marriage, and especially to the baldly economic exchange that Kumudini's marriage was), it becomes clear that by ending the novel with Kumudini's broken-down defences and helplessness in the face of her detested pregnancy, Tagore was poignantly pointing out the ultimate impotence of individual progressiveness in the face of the systemic cruelty that is meted out by hegemonic social structures. Ending *Yogayog* with Kumudini's successful escape and divorce would not only have been wildly out of keeping with the context of the novel but would also have failed to serve Tagore's purpose, which was to critically illuminate the society he lived in. *Yogayog* is a feminist classic because of its ending, which masterfully brings out the near-inexorable nature of sexist oppression, and subtly points out that lasting challenges to oppressive institutions can only come from collective revolution and radical change.

In a nutshell, Tagore's approach to the gender question draws on his concern for according proper recognition of women who, despite being half of the population, remained socioeconomically marginalised and denigrated. By critically reimagining both the inner lives and agential existences of his female protagonists, Rabindranath populated the literary landscape with the experiences and thoughts of figures marginalised by the 'silence of the archive'. To borrow a couple of phrases from critical race theorist Saidiya Hartman's work, Rabindranath could be said to have written feminist 'histories of the present' through the process of 'critical fabulation', which Hartman defines as 'straining against the limits of the archive to write a cultural history of the captive, and, at the same time, enacting the impossibility of representing the lives of the captives precisely through the process of narration' (Hartman 2008: 11). This is a significant part of the package of ideas that he developed while being engaged in the wider struggle for human emancipation. Unlike his nationalist colleagues, including Gandhi, he was not persuaded by the argument that political freedom was necessary for eradicating much of the social ills inhibiting the equality of sexes. In fact, Tagore's argument was, as the above discussion shows, just the reverse. According to him, unless one's social prejudices were eliminated, freedom of any kind was futile. In other words, so long as the artificial but socially engineered designs controlling human behaviour were allowed to survive, no endeavour for radical social transformation was likely to succeed. *Ghare Baire* was a testimony of his heartfelt concern for erasing the Hindu–Muslim social distance; *Chandalika* was a scathing critique of the caste system justifying social divisions between high-caste Hindus and their 'untouchable' counterparts; *Yogayog* is an elaboration of how the male–female social divide subjected Kumudini, one of the main protagonists in the novel, to severe emotional torture which she had to absorb since she was born as a woman. Kumu's silent revolt against the sufferings took the form of self-ostracism. Like Binodini in *Chokher Bali*, she rebelled, but differently: while Binodini raised her voice against the barbaric attitude towards widows, Kumu protested against her husband silently and took refuge in the small room adjoining the storeroom for storing oil lamps. By raising his voice against oppression around caste, class and gender axes which was, so far, considered to be axiomatic, the poet was thus ahead of his time. Furthermore, in his writings, gender and sexuality in various configurations become 'an expressive device in exploring certain aspects of a power relationship' (Banerji 2020: 244–245). His novels, in particular, are illustrative here. Bimala in *Ghare Baire* expressed her sexuality in both familial and political contexts; Ela, in *Char Adhyay*, expressed her desires in the arena of violent nationalist struggle; Kumudini of *Yogayog* represented a completely different kind of sexuality; and in *Chaturanga*, Damini was explicit in her statements for the fulfilment of her womanly desire which might have been immoral if it was conceived according to conventional thinking. In fact, the arguments that he offered in defending his specially textured point of view for gender equality contributed to a new genre of literature, both in India and abroad. In other words, the model that he built remains a source of inspiration for future writers regardless of national boundaries. Hence, the poet can be said to have ushered in a new era pregnant with possibilities for radical social metamorphosis. His creative texts on social issues thus continue to inspire generation after generation seeking to develop new conceptual tools for capturing the zeal and also urge for noticeable change within inter-personal/inter-group power dynamics.

References

Banerji, Himani. 2020. 'Women, Gender and the Family in Tagore'. In *The Cambridge Companion* to Rabindranath Tagore, ed. Sukanta Chaudhuri. Cambridge: Cambridge University Press.

Beauvoir, Simone De. 2011. *The Second Sex*. London: Vintage Book.

Chakravarty, Radha. 2013. *Novelist Tagore: Gender and Modernity in Selected Texts*. London: Routledge.

Crenshaw, Kimberle Williams. 1989. 'Mapping the Margins: Intersectionality, Identity Politics, and Violence against Women of Colour'. Available at https://www.racialequitytools.org/resourcefiles/mapping-margins.pdf (accessed on 25 May 2022).

Das, Sisir Kumar. ed. 1996. *The English Writings of Rabindranath Tagore*, Vol. 2. New Delhi: Sahitya Akademi.

Ghosh, Nityananda. 2008. *The English Writings of Rabindranath Tagore*, Vol. 4. New Delhi: Sahitya Akademi.

Haraway, Donna. 1988. 'Situated Knowledges: The Science Question in Feminism and the Privilege of Partial Perspective'. *Feminist Studies* 14 (3): 592.

Hartman, Saidiya. 2008. 'Venus in Two Acts'. *Small Axe* 12 (2): 11. Available at Project MUSE muse.jhu.edu/article/241115 (accessed on 25 May 2022).

Kopf, David. 1988. *The Brahmo Samaj and the Shaping of the Modern Indian Mind*. New Delhi: Archives Publishers Private Ltd.

Millett, Kate. 1970. *Sexual Politics*. New York: Doubleday.

Pateman, Carole. 1988. *The Sexual Contract*. Stanford: Stanford University Press.

Tagore, Rabindranath. 1425 Bangabda. *Nari* (Woman). In *Kalantar*. Kolkata: Visva-Bharati.

———. 1959. *The Stolen Treasure* (*Churir Dhan* in Bangla). In *The Runaway and Other Stories*. Kolkata: Visva-Bharati.

———. 1996. 'Woman and Home'. In *The English Writings of Rabindranath Tagore*, ed. Sisir Kumar Das, Vol. 2. New Delhi: Sahitya Akademi.

———. 2008 (rpt). 'Brahmo Samaj Centenary'. In *The English Writings of Rabindranath Tagore*, ed. Nityananda Ghosh, Vol. 4. New Delhi: Sahitya Akademi.

———. 2011. *Chokher Bali* (A Grain of Sand). In *Classic Rabindranath Tagore: Complete and Unabridged* (English translation of selected novels and short stories). New Delhi: Penguin.

———. 2011. *Yogayog*. In *Classic Rabindranath Tagore: Complete and Unabridged* (English translation of selected novels and short stories). New Delhi: Penguin.

7

Gender Issues in Short Stories

Rabindranath was consistent while articulating his views on gender. Like the views of the protagonists in his novels, the characters in his short stories unambiguously echoed similar sentiments. A common thread running through all his gender-based short stories is the need for gender parity as conceptualised by the Brahmo Samaj of which Tagore was one of the main proponents. Since the message is the same, it does not seem essential to deal with every short story. Hence, this chapter will explore the feminist underpinnings of three of the principal characters in Tagore's short stories: Mrinal of 'Strir Patra' (Wife's Letter), Anila of 'Poila Nombor' (Number One) and Sohini of 'Laboratory'.

Before dwelling on the characters to substantiate Tagore's principal argument relating to gender parity, there are three prefacing remarks to situate these short stories in his conceptual perspective. First, out of many short stories, the above texts are selected since they articulated the poet's views on the theme most succinctly. What the bard developed in the novel *Yogayog* can be said to have reverberated in these short stories. The characters too spoke in the same voice, of course, in a different context. In other words, in order to establish his point, the poet took into account various kinds of socio-ideological forces to argue that it was not an easy task to establish gender equality—the discriminatory prejudices were too well-entrenched in society to eradicate so quickly. Second, the poet must have thought that conveying his ideas against gender disparity in short stories was likely to have a wider audience as compared to those who preferred to see such ideas in the longer text of novels. The point is conceivable since his short stories had an extensive readership as they were not serialized like some of his famous novels and published in full form in popular Bengali magazines such as *Bharati*, *Prabashi*, *Sabuj Patra*, among others. Finally, there are reasons to believe that these short stories are the abridged versions of many novels if they are assessed as conceptual endeavours to strongly defend the poet's politico-ideological viewpoints on feminism. For instance, whether one talks about Bimala of *Ghare Baire* or Sucharita of *Gora* or Kumud of *Yogayog*, there are hardly any differences between them and the main protagonists of 'Strir Patra', 'Poila Nombor' and 'Laboratory'. These stories capture the zeal for women's liberation in their respective ways. In other words, what connects these three short stories is the underlying concern of Mrinal, Anila and Sohini for their independent space in society not just as women but as human beings. What is evident here is the fundamental belief that Tagore always held regarding the importance of treating human beings as they are. Gender is a constructed phenomenon based on many of the social shackles that draw sustenance from age-old sociocultural prejudices against women.

In the light of these prefacing remarks, one may be persuaded to advance the argument that Tagore wrote about women, primarily belonging to the educated middle classes of Bengal. The argument has substance given his upbringing in a middle-class environment and also in a Calcutta-based family which, by being baptised in Brahmo dharma, discarded most of the orthodox ideas of Hinduism. The tradition, which had begun with his grandfather Dwarkanath Tagore and had continued with his father Debendranath Tagore, was a source of inspiration to the poet who gave definite space to what he derived from his illustrious predecessors. Furthermore, one should not forget that many of the early Brahmo Samaj members laid a foundation for these ideas by being rebellious to the widely accepted socioculturally obscurantist ideas of Hinduism. Here, one is tempted to refer to Rammohun Roy, who was a pioneer in this campaign; it inspired many of his colleagues and, later, his disciples to undertake similar feats in adverse circumstances. The poet's elder brother, Satyendranath Tagore, was also appreciative of ideas for gender equity which was evident when he supported his wife, Jnanadanandini Devi, to accompany him in all his official engagements in unconventional attire, condemned as being defiant to the traditional Bengali dress code. Raised in a relatively liberal milieu, the poet imbibed many radical sociocultural views relating to humanity; he did not believe that due to biological differences between man and woman, the exploitation of the latter was justified. Other than this, the prevalent sociocultural circumstances also influenced the bard to a significant extent: He was appreciative of ideas supportive of gender parity despite opposition from orthodox Hindus. It will not be out of place here to mention that the Dharma Sabha of Radhakanto Deb, which vehemently opposed Rammohun and Dwarkanath when they started the reformatory Brahmo Samaj, continued to oppose Rabindranath and his compatriots by mobilising opinion against them. Being committed to the idea that gender parity was a stepping stone for human emancipation, the bard, through his creative texts, articulated a voice, a powerful voice indeed, in support of treating man and woman as socioculturally undifferentiated.

As shown in Chapter 4, the novel *Yogayog* is a long statement highlighting how Rabindranath dealt with the gender question by underlining the plight of Kumud who, instead of absorbing the abuse of patriarchy, protested, though silently, against the mindset that nurtured gender disparity. In this chapter, the focus is on how the poet, by resorting to a different type of story-telling, expressed his views on gender equity. He constructed three powerful female characters who unequivocally stressed the importance of accepting women as equal partners in society by highlighting the sufferings that they underwent by being biologically different. These stories were poignant statements of women's emotional woes; these were also transformative endeavours since the principal protagonists, Mrinal, Anila and Sohini, were hardly restrained while condemning the prevalent systemic aberrations sustaining gender disparity.

Mrinal of 'Strir Patra'

Published in *Sabuj Patra*, 'Strir Patra' is about Mrinal, a housewife, who held conventional views regarding family and other commitments that were expected of a typical daughter-in-law in then Bengal. When she joined a joint family after marriage, we have no inkling of the radical views that she articulated in her letter to her husband: These views were hard-hitting in so far as patriarchy was concerned and were an unambiguous articulation of her own identity as a woman. The storyline is simple: Mrinal left her adopted home and took refuge in a far-away place near the sea. The letter is a poignantly expressed piece of a note, pregnant with opinions, upholding a critique of the prevalent anti-feminist practices and views. In short, the letter dealt with the fundamental problem of patriarchal oppression in its different forms: dowry, denigration of women and denial of their rights as human beings, inhuman stance vis-à-vis providing accommodation to women, restraints on their education, virulent outbursts against endeavours for asserting independence, among others. Although the tone of the letter was not, at all, abusive or attacking, it helped us understand the agony that a married, but childless woman. Being born as a girl was a source of humiliation which she illustrated by drawing attention to what her neighbours, particularly women, expressed when her brother died. Mrinal was abused for her survival though, here, she had no role; the neighbours thought that had she been a male, she would have escaped death. Even, when her in-laws' family came for fixing her marriage with a man (who later became her husband), she was not consulted at all which means that whatever the senior decided was mandatory for her. She had not dared to challenge and accepted the decision as preordained or fated to be complied with. After she was brought in as a daughter-in-law, she was openly discriminated against vis-à-vis other male members which she had no alternative but to accept without being displeased. The situation underwent a sea change once Mrinal lost her daughter immediately after her birth. She lost a chance of being a mother which probably would have secured her 'a respectable place in the family because a childless woman was always despised since she was considered a bad omen for the family' (Tagore 1422 Bangabda: 331). Yet, she absorbed the taunts that others hurled at her simply because she was taught to be non-confrontational for the sake of marital peace. For Tagore, this was a kind of 'idealism' that Bengali women internalised by being raised in circumstances in which this was zealously pursued.

The second part of the letter dwells on a peculiar relationship that Mrinal had with Bindu, another woman with the same fate who took refuge in her in-law's house to avoid physical and emotional torture meted out to her by her cousin brother. She was allowed as she was related to Mrinal's elder sister-in-law. Initially, she was welcomed as an extra helping hand for which no payment was necessary. Later, sympathizing with the hapless Bindu, Mrinal came forward to extend a helping hand to her since she felt that it was her duty as 'a human being'. She became close to her since there was none to support her, including her elder sister-in-law who abdicated her responsibility once her husband withdrew his support. Bindu was in a serious predicament in view of her being an unwanted incursion into the family. With Mrinal's intervention, Bindu was allowed to stay. Here is another twist in the story. Tagore trod a difficult path in human relationships which was non-conventional and taboo. Bindu's excessive love for Mrinal was a source of happiness and also irritation at the same time: happiness because her love for Mrinal reinforced her faith in human values articulated in love, care and compassion; irritation because of Bindu's passion for physical proximity (though not clearly stated) scared Mrinal as it was socially stigmatized. Mrinal was unambivalent while expressing what she felt about Bindu when she became obsessed with her. As she noted,

> Bindu began to love me with such fervour that I was scared. I have not seen a comparable face of love. I have only read about it and that also between man and woman. … She would gaze upon my face as if she could not have enough of it. … The girl was obsessed with me. … At times, I was exasperated with her, I admit, but through her love, I could get a glimpse of my own self, of which I had not been aware. This is the unencumbered self. (332–333)

Here, Tagore dealt with a theme highlighting a relationship based on a romantic involvement of a woman with another woman—a relationship that was socially taboo and despised. Mrinal admitted that she was aware of this kind of relationship on the basis of her reading of books, but by analysing her immensely compassionate feelings for Bindu she was not persuaded to believe that it was not only conceivable but also possible. Tagore's courage to put the nature of this socially unusual relationship put him in a class by himself because he not only sought to articulate but also conceptualise lesbian interactions (though in a guarded manner) ahead of the feminist scholars who were to theoretically defend the theme in the early 1970s.[1] This was a reciprocal relationship, Tagore hinted, which helped Mrinal rediscover her individuality and assert her independence. In view of the well-entrenched prejudices against the same-sex relationship, Mrinal was reluctant to continue which was evident when she agreed with Bindu's marriage to an insane man. Here, Tagore made a very caustic remark by contrasting women with men in a society appreciative of patriarchal norms and values. Women were objects of entertainment and also exploitation, and the men, by being men, were allowed to enjoy a shackle-free existence. In other words, no voice was raised when Bindu was married to a mad man simply because this was not his disqualification while Bindu, being a woman, had no other alternative but to accept the dictates of the family. For Mrinal, it was unacceptable and a crime against humanity. Nonetheless, it was not easy for her to halt the juggernaut in a situation that was not exactly in her favour. What upset her most was the support that her elder sister-in-law extended when the proposal came because she justified Bindu's marriage to 'a mad man by saying that since she was born as a woman, she had to accept the decision because by agreeing she got what women aspired for' (Tagore 1422 Bangabda: 334–335). What does it imply? The poet, seeking to explain the predicament of the era, suggests that the response of Mrinal's elder sister-in-law was not unnatural in an environment in which patriarchal values were well-entrenched; what is implied here is also Tagore's warning that so long as women tended to think in this fashion, their liberation was a distant goal.

'Strir Patra' stands out in another respect: Tagore appears to have addressed the dilemma that women in Bengal underwent. Bindu escaped the torture by committing suicide; she set herself on fire which was very common for women of the era. Mrinal, however, was sceptical since it could have been a murder because this was 'a fashion', she sarcastically

1 Martha Shelly's seminal text entitled *Lovers and Mothers* (New York: Sefir, 1981) is one of the most cited intellectual interventions on the theme.

said, by saying that it hardly happened 'with Dhoti-clad men' in Bengal. No answer was expected because, she further added, it was a man's domain in which women, considered to be appendages (lifeless too), were meant to be utilised as per men's 'requirements' (337). The liberated Mrinal had the courage to break the socially engineered barriers and socially justified design of shackled life; she thus declared that 'she will never return to where she lived in Calcutta with the members of her adopted family because she saw, in her own eyes, how women were forced to accept those inhuman and tortuous means to survive despite being anguished and left out (337). 'Strir Patra' was an elaboration of how women were brutalised, given the well-entrenched patriarchal prejudices; it was also a clarion call for a radical societal transformation which empowered women as they were and allowed them to independently pursue the course of action which they deemed appropriate for their well-being. The last paragraph of 'Strir Patra' has most poignantly illustrated Tagore's optimism when Mrinal declared that

> she was not going to die since she, like the mythical Mira Bai [who spent her life worshipping Krishna knowing well that it was not going to give her what she wanted], would continue to live like a woman by being committed to what she preferred to do on her own. This is the mantra that she learnt on the basis of her experience. So, she will live life by imbibing the spirit of being alive despite the torture that she underwent. (338)

Therefore, despite being paternalistic on occasion, the poet did not allow his bias to cloud his opinion. Mrinal, representing the bard's views for women's emancipation, agreed to lead an independent life away from the familial environment. This was an articulation of a design in which women created and also defended the space without being aided by their male counterparts. In other words, it was not just a call for independence but also an attempt at institutionalising the space that was created, as a result. Mrinal also referred to the brutality that a woman underwent by being married which not only uprooted her from the familiar environment in which she was born and initially raised but also placed before her new sets of problems that she had to negotiate. The new life was, instead of becoming exciting, reduced to mere physical existence since the adopted family did not seem to be generally forthcoming in accepting the daughters-in-law; they were welcome only as they contributed to the family by their physical labour; they were usually subject to torture because of the well-entrenched patriarchal impediments. Husbands, the only persons who could be their saviours, were generally restrained because of the fear of justifying age-old ideas of servility of the newly married. Furthermore, women without children were easy prey due to the rootedness of superstitions that generated hatred for them. There were, of course, exceptions in some families which however does not invalidate the proposition based on experiences of women in general in then-Bengal. Mrinal of 'Strir Patra' was thus an eye-opener in the sense that she fearlessly articulated what she wanted despite being challenged. Being exposed to Enlightenment values and also the ideas of the Upanishad, Tagore was confident of what he preached in favour of gender parity despite being vehemently criticized by his compatriots.

There is another critical aspect that one should not miss while seeking to understand Rabindranath's distinctive approach to feminism: by virtue of being a woman, she was subject to suffering on many counts which were conceptualised as 'intersectionality'. For instance, as soon as one was born a woman, there were well-defined 'dos' and 'don'ts' which were gender-specific as they did not apply to males. Once a woman was married, she was again subject to various kinds of restrictions from her adopted families and society. If she remained childless, as Mrinal was, she was further subject to another kind of prejudicial sociocultural norms, happily nurtured by those sustaining them. Mrinal is an ideal instance; she was treated differently because she was a woman; she did not receive recognition, let alone respect, as a daughter-in-law since she was unable to bear a child. As long as she was with her in-laws, she had hardly an independent existence; she was considered a burden or, at best, a helping hand in running the household chores. Her interaction with Bindu shows another dimension of intersectionality because Mrinal was heavily criticized for her love for the former as it was socially blasphemous. In other words, here, the poet referred to the same-sex relationship as normal human expression though he was aware that it was a serious threat to the existent sociocultural equilibrium. There is no denying that it was a bold statement on his part though he restrained himself in taking the relationship to a logical conclusion when he allowed Bindu to commit suicide. This also confirms the argument that at the individual level, Rabindranath was a revolutionary and hardly lost an opportunity to highlight his point of view; but, when he confronted systemic opposition, he did not seem to be as revolutionary as he appeared in his textual creations. By sending Kumud to her adopted home once she realized that she had conceived, the poet evinced the same pattern; similarly, despite being aware that Kumud was again subject to patriarchal oppression in her in-law's house, Bipradas expressed his helplessness by comparting his plight with that of the sage Kanva who felt the same when he accepted the departure of his adopted daughter, Shakuntala, to join her husband. One witnesses a pattern in Rabindranath's creative texts in this regard. Although Bimala of *Ghare Baire* explored a relationship with Sandip, her husband's acquaintance, she was made to realise the constraints by the poet by highlighting the limitations that he had; the death of Nikhilesh, Bimala's husband, was probably illustrative of a divine punishment that the narrator accepted presumably because it was also an outcome of the systemic mindset that governed a man–woman relationship outside marriage. The idea epitomised in *Ghare Baire* was just a reiteration of what he propounded in his 1901 novel, *Nastaneer* (The Broken Nest). Set in 1879, the novel, is also about a relationship between Charulata and her husband's cousin, Amal, in a context when the renaissance in Bengal was at its peak. Western thoughts of freedom and individuality were about to ruffle the calm feathers of a feudal society. Women's liberation was being talked about, but not beyond a few cases of widow-remarriage and some education. Intelligent, sensitive, graceful and serene, Charu was a traditional woman, whose mindset slowly and steadily absorbed waves from the world beyond. Encouraged by Amal, she was introduced to the world of literature to which her husband, Bhupati, did not seem to pay much attention. A relationship developed between Charu and Amal though it remained short-lived as the latter left them; this illustrated how the poet, despite his endorsement, was constrained by the systemic viewpoints. Nonetheless, what the poet strongly argued for was a space for an alternative voice that women articulated, sometimes in words and sometimes by being silent. It was a space which, in other words, always remained outside the domain of the conventional thinking relating to man–woman relationships. Hence, Mrinal had to leave home and place herself in an unknown sociocultural terrain which appeared to have given her an independent space to articulate what she genuinely felt for herself and other members of the family. It is true that, on many occasions, she was unable to say what she wanted presumably because of the systemic constraints which continued to act decisively in her thought processes; her liking for Bindu was not stated in a language which would have been socioculturally prejudicial though it was clear that the nature of liking did not seem to be the usual. So, 'Strir Patra' was the poet's novel endeavour to champion a viewpoint which was revolutionary in the sense that not only did it establish his concern for gender equality but also made a persuasive case for this cause.

Anila of 'Poila Nombor'

'Poila Nombor' (Number One), published in 1920, was another short story in which Tagore pursued his thoughts on gender issues. The storyline revolves around Anila and her husband and later in the story,

Sitangshu, who shifts to house number 1 or *poila* in Bengali. 'Poila Nombor' is primarily an elaboration of how Tagore negotiated with prevalent socioeconomic circumstances in which gender equality was an anathema. Unlike 'Strir Patra', where Mrinal expressed her views categorically, the main protagonist of 'Poila Nombor', Anila, approached the concern completely differently. As a married woman, she was a voice, a powerful voice indeed, against gender exploitation. She was also a good wife since she discharged her responsibilities towards the family in an impeccable manner, and everybody was happy. However, unlike Mrinal, Anila articulated her response differently; Mrinal expressed her views in strong language while being away from home. Anila was silent in her protest and left the family without any clue about her whereabouts. Here, Tagore conceptualised his approach, rather heuristically, by drawing on the arguments that her male companions offered on the basis of their interaction with her.

We must add a caveat here because 'Poila Nombor' is not just a statement on gender parity but also a scathing critique of the system of education that flourished under the aegis of British rule. The main protagonist is undoubtedly Anila, though her husband, by providing critical inputs on the prevalent mode of education, laid out some of the ideas that the poet espoused in this regard. In order to show that mere bookish education was futile, the bard presented Anila's husband as one who never went to university because he remained ineligible by not completing his school education. Not at all bothered by his failure, he considered it a source of empowerment since it gave him a chance to explore knowledge according to his priorities. Instead of being enthralled by rote learning, he concentrated on creative texts in French, German and Italian by learning the languages; he derived immense pleasure by being inundated with books written in these foreign languages. Gradually, he drew many of his compatriots belonging to the area in which he lived to begin a study circle. Although he was occasionally castigated as 'a debate master', his study circle became a centre for attraction from many across class and caste which made him happy as it allowed him to share his derivative ideas with participants in the study circle.

Fundamental in the preceding paragraph is the idea that the institutionalisation that the colonial government introduced in India was of no use except to fulfil Macaulay's dream of creating a corp of clerks to run the government and the British-controlled business houses. By insisting on education outside the formalised arena of education, the bard argued for an education which allowed human beings to be inquisitive and innovative. Now, the plot of the story begins once Anila, the female protagonist, was introduced in 'Poila Nombor'. The narrator brought

Anila into the plot by making her listen to her husband's explanation of what he learnt from these books written in foreign languages. She was a quiet listener. As soon as the study circle became popular, Anila was forced to take care of the participants by offering them tea and snacks, to which she never complained; she accepted it as a responsibility of being the wife though she was never asked whether she wanted to continue to be a participant. Here, the bard introduced an important dimension of how a woman lived as per the will of her husband; or, in other words, she hardly had an independent identity once she became somebody's wife. Some women readily endorsed this role as destiny and pretended to enjoy it; this became natural to them as they had no alternative but to internalise them in due course. Anila was of a different mould, and she opted for a course in her life that represented a concern for gender equality; her opposition was not vocal, but silently articulated in a fashion which the bard unfolded as the story progressed.

In the story, Anila was introduced to the reader by her husband as a very mature and intelligent person. That her father-in-law trusted her more than his son who was Anila's husband, was referred to by her husband to prove that she was honest and reliable. The dying father of Anila's husband gave her a portion of his savings for bringing up Saroj, the son of his first wife, fearing that his second wife might not look after her stepson after his demise. He thus said, 'Please take care of my son, Saroj who is likely to suffer since my second wife may not be as concerned for his well-being as she will naturally be for her children' (Tagore 1422 Bangabda: 377). Although her husband was annoyed with the decision, he, however, later understood that by choosing Anila for this task, he had shown how prudent he was (377). Anila took an independent decision when she engaged a private tutor for Saroj which made her husband angry though he immediately realised that since he was academically unfit, what his wife did in this regard was perhaps the best deed.

The narrative adds a new dimension when Anila has a neighbour, Sitangshu, who occupied the first building with the 'Poila Nombor' or number one in English. The family was rich and opulent and caused a sense of anger in Anila's husband. Not only was Sitangshu well-off but he was also a connoisseur of music and games which attracted many of the neighbours to him. Anila appeared to have been disturbed by the sudden spurt of activities in the neighbourhood though her husband believed that she was swayed by Sitangshu's opulence and multifaceted personality. This was made clear by the author when Anila's husband expressed relief when she asked him to change residence; this was, however, delayed because of Saroj's impeding school tests. His joy knew no bounds when he came to know that Sitangshu was going out of the city for two weeks for an excursion in south India. His sense of relief came out very clearly when Tagore stated that 'with his imminent departure for south India, the threat [sic] that disturbed him disappeared completely' (381). The proposed delayed shift to a new place became a source of agony when Anila left home without informing any of the members of the family. It was a bolt from the blue when her husband discovered a letter under the pillow which stated that 'I am going away; don't try to search for me and even if you do, I won't be found' (382). Because of his suspicion that Anila was perhaps emotionally involved with Sitangshu, he immediately concluded that she had eloped with Sitangsu since the latter had also left the city in the morning of the same day. He also realised that whatever the authors wrote about extramarital relationships was true now that it had happened to him. It also dawned on him that he had 'his contribution too because he neglected her to a great extent which created an emotional vacuum leading to search for her fulfilment of emotions' (383). The wife at home was considered to be 'an appendage and was expected to discharge her responsibilities as efficiently as possible and as her husband, he was to enjoy the comfort without extending any help whatsoever' (383). The story took a sudden turn when Anila's husband discovered 25 letters from Sitangshu to his wife, expressing his admiration for her. Sitangshu was so enamoured by Anila that he characterised her as 'a paragon of beauty and epitome of knowledge and wisdom though he did not want her as partner in the conventional way' (383). Being respectful to her, he further wrote that 'Don't misunderstand me; I am your admirer and my admiration for you is based on my appreciation of your devotion to the family despite being denied a rightful place there' (383) which was justified, her husband felt, since she was never allowed to be part of the gatherings that often took place in his residence at his behest. Nonetheless, by accusing his wife of infidelity, Anila's husband followed a familiar path of thinking. Here, the storyline conforms to the explanations based on a patriarchal understanding of women; this, however, underwent a sea-change when Sitangshu, who had supposedly stolen his wife, mentioned that he received a letter with the same message that her husband had received when she left him. The message was the same: 'I am going away; don't try to search for me and even if you do, I won't be found' (384). Through this skillfully rendered plot twist, the poet presented his views on gender in a remarkably creative manner.

'Poila Nombor' is a uniquely textured response that Tagore articulated to pursue his concern for gender equity. The text stands out in three complementary ways: First, here the poet leaves many things unsaid but gives enough indications to comprehend the urge to destabilise the available social format by defending gender discrimination in a persuasive manner. The narrative is an endeavour to grasp how the existing social mores created a vacuum in women which manifested itself in different forms. Being left out even in her adopted family, Anila underwent suffering without ever raising her voice. Second, this short story is also a graphic rendering of how silence can be a powerful weapon to vent one's grievances. This is, in other words, an exploration of an area of human endeavour seeking to chart out a meaningful course of action without stating anything to that effect. In this respect, Mrinal of 'Strir Patra' and Sohini of 'Laboratory' are different for, by articulating their views in black-and-white, they expressed unambiguously what they felt. Contrarily, Anila, by being silent, articulated a voice which was as powerful as the ones that the other protagonists of gender equality had raised with an identical objective. Finally, 'Poila Nombor' introduces a new literary style in which the unsaid became a powerful medium of equally powerful messages addressing the primary concern that the poet had. Being dutiful to everybody in the family, Anila built her image as 'an ideal daughter-in-law who devoted all her energies and time for the benefit of the members of her adopted family' (382). While she was hailed as an ideal daughter-in-law or wife, nobody seems to have bothered to find out whether she was contented or not by being sincere in her assigned role. Anila's husband was overjoyed when he found out that his wife prepared his friends' favourite food items though he never enquired whether that made her happy. She was considered to be the one who was always to give without expecting anything in return. With her one expression, 'I won't be found', Tagore said many things which probably would not have come out so poignantly had he explained the emotional turmoil that Anila was undergoing for performing the socially endorsed roles of wives and daughters-in-law. The poet is thus not merely a storyteller but an innovative thinker who endeavoured hard to put across the message for gender parity which deviated from the mainstream thinking on this theme.

As argued before, 'Poila Nombor' may have adopted a different literary style, but the message that it conveyed is of a similar texture because (a) it is about Tagore's concern for parity regardless of sex and gender, and (b) the narrative delineates a space in which 'the unsaid' became a powerful device to convey and establish his views for the cause of gender equality. In other words, by drawing our attention to 'the silent zones' of human behaviour, the bard can be said to have evolved new yardsticks to understand human emotions which one can feel provided one has compassion for the same. 'Poila Nombor' stands out for it is illustrative of a new literary design with which Tagore experimented to articulate the familiar voice against gender disparity that he raised here in a different fashion.

The message that the bard articulated in 'Poila Nombor' is directed against the system of patriarchy and emotional torture that women underwent in Hindu families. By being women, they lacked an independent voice. Anila prepared snacks for those attending the study circle despite the suicide of Saroj, whom she had raised as her son; she was hurt by her husband's indifference towards the incident. On the contrary, Sitangshu of *poila nombor* arranged the cremation of Saroj, which her husband did not resent although he appeared a trifle annoyed. That Anila silently absorbed the shock does not mean that she happily accepted her husband's behaviour; instead, it was a powerful message, which she conveyed by not neglecting her duties to please her husband—regardless of their pain and agony, women were expected to behave in a particular fashion. Being appreciative of the Suffragette movement of the first decade of the 20th century,[2] the bard wrote extensively in his travelogues (Tagore 2008: 56–61). Despite being impressed by the courage of British women, he remained restrained in articulating his views in that fashion. The reason probably lies in the contemporary sociocultural reality when women tended to suffer silently because they were emotionally moulded to be so. As shown in Chapter 1, Bimala of *Ghare Baire*, notwithstanding her bold step in expressing her love for Sandip, cursed herself by thinking that by being deviant from being a 'true wife', she was responsible for the death of Nikhilesh, her husband. That Anila protested, though silently, against the discriminatory mindset, was evident in those 25 letters that she wrote after she disappeared from her adopted home. Here the bard stands out because Anila's husband realised that Anila left home primarily because she never received the recognition that she deserved; she was part of the study circle as long as it did not attract many of her husband's friends; as soon as they came, she was reminded of her 'feminine duties' of preparing snacks for the participants as per her husband's instruction. That she was ill-treated by him was evident when, at the end of the story, he admitted that 'by being a good host to his friends, he paid no attention to find out what Anila felt when she was forcibly ousted from the study circle which she was enjoying being present as it enabled her to know what she would not have known otherwise' (Tagore 1422 Bangabda: 384).

2 Derivative of the term 'suffragist' which means 'belittling the women advocating women's franchise', the Suffragette campaign led to the promulgation of the Representation of the Peoples Act in 1918 by the British Parliament, which guaranteed voting rights to women over the age of 30 with certain property qualifications. With the adoption of Representation of the People (equal franchise) Act of 1928, women above 21 years of age were granted voting rights.

It reverberated in Anila's thinking because she knew that it was difficult, if not impossible, to eradicate the juggernaut of archaic beliefs from the prevalent sociocultural milieu. Hence, she probably understood her husband's predicament, which was manifested in his helplessness in taking steps to reverse the established practices. In other words, he did not seem to have adequate courage to even challenge the prevalent sociocultural practices despite having realised that they were exploitative of women. Here, the poet expressed his emancipatory views through Sitangshu. In his letter to Anila, Sitangshu also realised that the socioculturally-endorsed systemic constraints were too strong to be eradicated so easily. Nonetheless, he conveyed his willingness 'to liberate her from being exploited by the age-old sociocultural shackles' (384), which shows the bard's constantly-nurtured concerns for gender equality. By ending the story rather abruptly, because nobody knew where Anila went, though she was represented in the story by her letters, the bard raised a powerful voice in the public domain against those sociocultural prejudices that were allowed to continue to keep a significant half of the demography away from the public discourses. The voice gained momentum as the nationalist movement progressed. As history shows, many women participated in the campaign for freedom which however did not radically change the prevalent perception of women in general. Nonetheless, the views that the bard propounded in 'Poila Nombor' reconceptualised the gender question by arguing that silence was also a powerful medium for articulating protest, and Anila, being the main protagonist here, established the point unambiguously.

Sohini of 'Laboratory'

'Laboratory' belongs to a completely different genre of thought which did not seem usual in the context in which it was brought to the public domain. This is the story of Sohini, a Punjabi woman, who defied social shackles by deciding to have a baby out of wedlock. This is also the story of the determination of a woman, who was steadfastly committed to sustaining the laboratory that reflected her husband's vision for serving humanity since it became one of the most reliable pathological laboratories in Calcutta. Being deeply in love with her husband Nandakishore, Sohini efficiently discharged her role as a supervisor which sustained the laboratory even after her husband's demise. By seriously opposing her daughter's endeavour at selling the land on which the laboratory stood, she further proved that her devotion to the laboratory was testimony to Nandakishore's concern for extending pathological services to people at a reasonable rate.

Conforming to the poet's principal concern, namely, service to humanity, the story does not appear to be exceptional although the idea of having a child and raising her was not an easy one to defend in the contemporary sociocultural context. Here, the bard was a rebel who, through this short story, raised a voice against systemic design since childbearing for a woman without being married was not socially acceptable. It was certainly a rebellious stance; that the bard was constrained by systemic prejudices was evident when he constructed Sohini as a Punjabi woman, instead of a Bengali one. We must also add that the story unfolded in Calcutta, and not in Punjab, which was attributed to the fact that the idea would not have been accepted there as well. Given Calcutta's exposure to Enlightenment principles, Rabindranath was perhaps persuaded to shift Sohini with her daughter to Calcutta, where criticism was likely to remain considerably muted. By introducing Sohini as having been born, raised and conceived in Punjab, the poet appeared to have couched the story in this format because he was not sure whether the orthodox Hindus in Bengal would have appreciated the idea had it happened to a Bengali Hindu woman.

Being fundamentally creative, Tagore always conveyed a unique message with clear socioeconomic and political meaning through his innovative literary outputs. 'Strir Patra' and 'Poila Nombor' were imprints of a system of relationships in which gender issues were debated; the main protagonists raised their voices against discrimination around gender axes amidst well-entrenched contrarian social, economic and political forces. The poet aimed to evolve a mindset which was to be positively tilted in favour of gender parity. 'Sohini', published in 1940, is dissimilar from other creative texts on many counts: first, it is a story in which the main character was a Punjabi woman who represented a different kind of mindset presumably because of being a non-Bengali, raised in a milieu which was hardly similar to that of Bengal. Second, Sohini was ready to accept any challenge for defending what she deemed justified. In other words, she expressed her commitment to fulfilling the objective that she accepted as complementary to her goal. Finally, she hardly wavered in stating the 'unpleasant truth' regardless of the social consequences—that she had a baby out of wedlock notwithstanding the fear of being ostracised. In a nutshell, with his focus on an unusually uncommon situation especially from the point of the Bengali psyche, Tagore here introduced the readers to themes, relationships and mindsets which were not exactly familiar. Hence, 'Sohini', treading a completely unknown path, was an endeavour to capture a reality in which male–female interaction was conceptualised differently; nonetheless, there was a common thread of thinking that characterised women in general; Sohini, despite being a

Punjabi, wanted to carry forward the tradition that her Bengali husband bequeathed to her simply because that was the only way to express her unconditional love for him who, unlike other males, never treated her as 'a doormat' but a companion for fulfilling the jointly desired mission.

The storyline is unconventional. Tagore dealt with one's zeal for being self-independent and was also keen to show that women were equally competent to be able partners if they were convinced of their role in fulfilling the mission. Sohini met Nandakishore, her future husband, when the latter went to Punjab in connection with his professional needs. The marriage between Sohini and Nandakishore, though unusual in the conventional sense, was based on the common desire to do something good for society. Nandakishore had the intellectual prowess while Sohini had complemented him when he had begun his laboratory as a business venture. Drawn on his desire to be self-dependent, Sohini's husband nurtured the concern of making India scientifically independent; he was confident that it was not difficult since 'Indians have the brain though they lacked the initiatives [presumably because] of the alien regime that, by being severely restrictive, inhibits Indians' natural desires' (Tagore 1410 Bangabda: 270). Furthermore, his intelligence allowed him not to be misled or cheated, which impressed Sohini when she observed how 'the well-established businessmen of Punjab failed to deceive which they usually do with a non-Punjabi' (271). This was one of the reasons that endeared Sohini to Nandakishore to the extent being in deeply love with him that finally led to their marriage. In other words, being swayed by Nandakishore's intelligent ways of handling those who were cunning and deceitful, Sohini admitted to having found the right kind of person for herself.

'Laboratory' is a story in which the urge to become economically self-independent is explicit. This was a concern that Tagore had clearly articulated in the 1904 text, *Swadeshi Samaj*; Nikhilesh of *Ghare Baire* epitomised the concern which ran contrary to the nationalist design, justifying the application of force in case the nationalist dictates for both discarding foreign clothes and burning them in bonfire were violated. As shown in Chapter 1, it boomeranged during the 1905–1908 anti-Partition campaign in Bengal. With the sole purpose of creating indigenous facilities for developing scientific knowledge, Nandakishore represented a heart-felt desire that Tagore had epitomised as one who held views, different from his nationalist colleagues, for self-independence. This is also a story which drew on the poet's concern for gender equality. By being candid even in expressing her choice of Nandakishore as her husband, Sohini presented herself as an independent agency who did not seem to have bothered what others would say because of her decision to marry a person from a different kind of sociocultural milieu. Sohini was different from both Anila of 'Poila Nombor' and Mrinal of 'Strir Patra' in the sense that unlike them, she was engaged in an endeavour that was complementary to the mission that her husband had.

Sohini was involved in the work not because she was forced to but because she wanted to, which means recognition of Sohini, a woman, as an independent agency who became so in those socioeconomic circumstances which were not favourably disposed towards gender parity. The role of Nandakishore was not insignificant here since he devoted his energy to prepare the ground for Sohini to be independent and capable of thinking on her own. In his words,

> incompatibility is likely to arise if an engineer husband keeps his wife confined to the kitchen which is normally the case in most households; the implication is disastrous because unless both husband and wife are united with the desire to realize identical objectives, the married life will be everything but self-fulfilling; so, what is required to be done is to create a milieu in which husband and wife meet each other as compatriots which will make wife responsible to her husband and vice versa. (272)

Here Tagore not only elaborates but also defends the argument supporting why the interdependent man–woman relationship was critical for social well-being. So long as the inter-personal relationship is clouded by gender equations, the man–woman bond is likely to be fragile; but, if it is based on recognising each other as being integral to the relationship, it is immune from being adversarial. What is important for any relationship, as Tagore felt, is respect for each other because hierarchy is anything but conducive to a healthy understanding between individuals. This is more in wedlock because a woman joins the adopted family by being completely uprooted from the environment in which she was born and raised. Here, Nandakishore talked in Tagore's language, supporting that no conjugal bond survives, let alone flourishes, unless it is cemented by being respectful to each other. So, Sohini was not an exception since she corresponded with the characters that the poet created to pursue his concern for gender equity.

Nandakishore's sudden death came as a plot twist. Many sought to take advantage of her widowhood by attempting to coerce her into selling the laboratory. However, this is where Sohini came into her own by dishing out emphatic refusals to such manipulative proposals. Her fight to save the laboratory led her to a young scientist, Rebati Bhattacharjee, who she thought would be of assistance. This decision was governed by Sohini's firm belief that ensuring the continued existence of the laboratory that was the result of her late husband's hard work was the only way for her to express her love and gratitude for him. That she owed her transformation to her dead husband was a constant refrain which also reminds us of Bimala of *Ghare Baire*; like Bimala, who became what she became largely due to Nikhilesh's initiatives, Sohini kept remembering that it was possible for her to be a different person had Nandakishore not encouraged her to be immersed in studying books and texts for scientific knowledge along with him. She was always protective of the laboratory, so much so that she refused to hand it over to anyone, including her daughter who had, she was persuaded to believe, no emotional attachment to its continuity; hence, even if the laboratory was folded up, it would hardly have had any impact on her. So firm was her belief that she even disclosed that her daughter was born out of wedlock (297) which completely ruled out her claim of being a legal heir to Nandakishore. This is also illustrative of how protective Sohini was of the laboratory that evolved out of the hard work that she and her husband had jointly put into a cause. Besides her unconditional love for her deceased husband which did not seem unusual, that she was a different kind of human, who was compassionate towards living beings was also evident when she was found to be particularly caring for 'a stray dog which was almost dying due to malnourishment' 'that symbolizes her idea of devotion to god', as the author stated, 'in contrast to the ritualistic Hindu tradition of sacrificing animals at the altar for providential blessings' (276). Here, Sohini was Tagore's voice questioning the established rituals which were, he felt, deceptive since they, instead of being socially conducive, bred superstitious beliefs and prohibitive mindsets.

Sohini is an articulation of Tagore's concern for (a) self-reliance, (b) women empowerment and (c) universal humanism. As far as self-reliance is concerned, there is a historical continuity because what he argued in the 1904 text, *Swadeshi Samaj*, and articulated in *Ghare Baire* was also manifested in Sohini. In other words, it was a reiteration of the concern that the poet held so dear throughout his life. As regards universal humanism, Sohini represents a new woman who was so devoted to her husband not because of being just but because of his contribution to making her capable and free from prejudices, supportive of the social hierarchy. Linked with this was also his firm belief that unless women were adequately empowered to fight their battle on their own, this remained vacuous. What is also required to be highlighted here was Tagore being paternalistic in his attitude towards women presumably because this was the tradition that was handed over to him since the days of Rammohun Roy. Hence, it was not surprising that Sohini who was grateful to her husband for being so confident about her thus declared that

> in relation to the qualities that he [her husband, Nandakishore] found in me, he regarded my shortcomings as insignificant. He reposed his complete trust in a non-descript woman like me, as I have never betrayed his trust. My being incapable did not stand between him and me [because] … my smallness he always ignored but gave me unstinted support where he found that I was worthy. Who knows to what level I would have sunk, had he not valued my good qualities which remained hidden when he met me for the first time. (287)

This was an unqualified confession that Sohini made to unambiguously express her gratitude to the deceased Nandakishore. What shines through here was the poet's belief in humanity which was a casualty because human beings privileged mere material gain over this civilisational ethos supportive of basic human values. Thus, the message that Sohini delivered was not uncommon and a reinforcement of what Tagore strongly felt and sincerely propagated. There is another aspect which appears to be revolutionary in the then context, namely, the open declaration of being involved in physical intimacy leading to the birth of a baby out of wedlock. This was candidly admitted by Sohini when she said,

> I feel ashamed to confess that I had been involved in relationships which were socially unjustified. The very thought that I have been close to a number of men still ruffles me. … Our temptations lie hidden under our flesh and bones, but flare up at the slightest provocation. It does not inhibit me to [disclose] that very early in my life I went to the bed with many men. We, women, are not chaste all our life though we pretend to be so. … Let me tell … that I had no clear perception of what was right and what was wrong [and] there was nobody to guide me. So, I plunged into evil ways [sic] as I have been able to come out of it. Yes, my body was tainted, but not my soul. (278)

Here Tagore treaded into an unconventional terrain since Sohini's forthright disclosure of infidelity was indeed unthinkable in a context in which Victorian morality was always upheld. For the poet to put this in black and white was clearly an endeavour to not only challenge but also to boldly say that a woman's body was her domain and nobody else had any right over this. In a sense, Tagore foresaw the conceptualisation of the idea that Carol Hanisch developed in her pathbreaking essay, 'The Personal Is Political', published in 1969.[3] The idea that Hanisch conveys is about women being independent agencies for doing what they deem

3 Carol Hanisch, 'The Personal Is Political,' 2006, available at https://webhome.cs.uvic.ca/~mserra/AttachedFiles/PersonalPolitical.pdf

appropriate. Challenging the claim that women needed to be guided, she further maintains that the so-called exhortation that men, through their revolutionary struggles, brought about radical changes in the plight of women, was far from being true. This is not the place to argue either for or against the contention. What is striking in Tagore's Sohini was the bold confession of the main protagonist, Sohini, that she, by being involved in 'an illicit relationship' had had a baby: this was inconceivable then. Tagore was forthright in stating a socially unrecognised relationship and outcome which was, in his opinion, perfectly possible. By accepting Sohini's baby as his, her husband, Nandakishore also demonstrated that he was not at all guided by the archaic Victorian morality championing the hardcore Catholic predispositions. So, the short story is both a pathfinder and a harbinger of a new era of conceptualising gender relations afresh.

Given the complex unfolding of the story, 'Laboratory' can be conceptualised at many levels: At a rather mundane level, it was a presentation of the story of a hapless woman who was subject to social hatred since she had a baby without getting married. It was socially unacceptable given the hegemonic grip of Victorian morality in colonial India. At a far more perceptive level, the story is one of a rebel who, despite the social risks, allowed the baby to be born: it was an endorsement of the argument that the right over one's body was exclusive and social interference was thus not conceivable. The idea is now widely accepted though, in the 20th century, it hardly had social recognition. For the poet, it was an attempt to initiate a debate on this socially unacceptable phenomenon which also reinforces the point that it was a challenge to what was considered to be an axiomatic truth born out of deep-rooted systemic constraints. This is a pattern that one comes across in most of his creative literary texts. For instance, that the author allowed Kumud of *Yogayog* to return to her parents' house symbolised his concern for gender rights while the complacency of Motir Ma represented the woman's inbuilt desire to remain with her husband regardless of the torture that she underwent. The novel is thus a powerful statement of the bard's rebellious attitude against atrocities crippling half of the population due to the accident of birth. But the return of Kumud to her torturous husband, Madhusudan, once she realised that she was pregnant also shows that the poet did not appear to have had the mindset to violate the well-established social code. Probably, this idea came to him naturally and hence, Kumud was sent back to her husband to avoid Bipradas, her brother, being socially blamed and also as it was socially despicable for a married woman to remain in her parents' house. One thus notices a tension in Tagore's thinking because on the one hand, being committed to human emancipation, he scathingly critiqued the systemic lapses; on the other hand, he was unable to pursue his ideas to their logical conclusion which suggests that he was extremely cautious while setting his views vis-à-vis sensitive social issues.

Despite being a contentious short story, 'Laboratory' stood out since it had shown Rabindranath's unique mindset as an offshoot of myriad sociocultural influences. It is obvious that by being raised in a rather liberal environment at home, he imbibed some of the distinctive Enlightenment values that his grandfather, Dwarkanath, and his father, Debendranath, nurtured; he had access to those fundamental texts in the Western philosophical discourses which shaped his young mind to a significant extent. Similarly, his introduction to the Vedas and Vedantic texts also allowed him to be well-versed with the ideas that they epitomised; furthermore, his extensive travel in India and abroad were also sources of his conceptualisation of humanity. 'Laboratory' was an outcome of these influences which contributed immensely to the poet's equally nuanced ideas about humanity, especially man–woman relationships. Keeping in mind, the complex sociocultural milieu in which the story evolved, it is rather simplistic to simply say that 'Laboratory' was a deviant text since the principal protagonist was an unwed mother, which was socially condemnable. At a deeper level, the story also underlines how the poet challenged a well-established mindset in support of women being just an appendage to their male counterparts. Neither Sohini nor Kumud were silent observers; they raised a voice, though relatively muted, for gender parity by challenging discrimination against women simply because they were biologically differently textured by birth.

Concluding Observations

In one respect, it can be confidently argued that the bard's message in the novel *Yogayog* and what he conveyed in 'Strir Patra', 'Poila Nombor' and 'Laboratory' was identical though the literary style was obviously different. The principal protagonists, Kumud, Mrinal, Anila and Sohini upheld the views for gender equality by challenging the existing socioculturally restraining practices which were clearly prejudicial to women. Here is a conceptual point that needs reiteration: None of the protagonists actually argued for gender parity; instead, by questioning the archaic norms and mores governing women within the domestic environment, they challenged them, which was a stepping stone towards reconceptualising the gender question in a colonial context. In other words, notwithstanding the free flow of ideas from the West supportive of gender parity, it hardly brought about a noticeable metamorphosis in the prevalent sociocultural practices, vis-à-vis women. Those supporting the subaltern approach to history provide a plausible explanation of why it did not happen. It is thus argued that the Enlightenment ideas defending gender equality were not allowed to enter the domestic arena in colonial India. Hence, it remained untouched though, in other areas, these ideas brought about a radical metamorphosis in thought processes governing politico-ideological issues. The argument made by Partha Chatterjee is instructive here. According to Chatterjee,

> anti-colonial nationalism in India creates its own domain of sovereignty within colonial society well before it begins its political battle with the imperial power. It does this by dividing the world of social institutions and practices into two domains—the material and the spiritual. The material is the domain of the 'outside', of the economy and of statecraft, of science and technology, a domain where the West proved its superiority and the East had succumbed. … The spiritual, on the other hand, is an 'inner' domain bearing the mark of essential marks of cultural identity. (Chatterjee 1994: 6)

The argument can easily be exemplified by many instances: Beginning with Rammohun Roy who raised his voice against the custom of sati, followed by Vidyasagar who insisted on widow remarriage and later in 1891, when Bal Gangadhar Tilak campaigned against the Age of Consent bill. One may refer to the fact that when Rammohun mobilised adequate support for banning the sati custom, his mother and elder brother challenged him by filing a suit against him in the court of law since what he was pursuing was blasphemous to Hinduism. Besides stopping the brutal killing of widows along with their deceased husbands, the underlying spirit of Rammohun's initiatives was to do away with those 'customs, traditions and usages [that caused and sustained divisions among sections of the people] … and new social morality based on social equality and a recognition that the welfare of man is the objective of religion as well as politics had to be established' (Ghosh 1971: 89–90). His Brahmo Samaj colleagues, Dwarkanath Tagore, Babu Rajendra Lal Gupta and Keshab Sen were also implicated by the conservative Hindus for having allowed the British rulers to intervene in an area of their social existence which was exclusively a private domain. In a similar vein, Vidyasagar was vehemently opposed by the orthodox Hindus of Calcutta since widow remarriage was contrary to the well-entrenched sociocultural practices. The most formidable petition against Vidyasagar's reform was sent at the initiative of the veteran leader of the orthodox Hindu community in Calcutta, Raja Radhakanto Deb, with 36,763 signatures on 17 March 1856. The petitioners defended their argument by stating that 'the followers of Vidyasagar constituted a very small minority, and that it would not be prudent and just to enact a law in the interest of this negligible minority and thereby interfere with the rights of the majority' (Ghose 1971: 69). The most interesting petition in support of widow remarriage was the one sent by the leading Derozians of Bengal, Rasik Krishna Mullick, Radhanath Sikdar, Pearychand Mitra, among others. They insisted on the bill because they felt, it was 'a steppingstone towards establishing the equality of status of men and women in modern times' (69–70). Bal Gangadhar Tilak opposed the 1891 Age of Consent bill which raised the age of consent for sexual intercourse for all girls, married or unmarried, from 10 to 12 years in all jurisdictions, the violation of which was 'a criminal offence as it was to be described as rape' (Sinha 2019: 138). Despite being politico-ideologically very radical, Bal Gangadhar Tilak opposed the Bill because he believed that it was interference with the religiously justified Hindu sociocultural practices which was evident when he stated that 'we would not like that the government should have anything to do with regulating our social customs or ways of living, even supposing that the act of government will be a very beneficial and suitable measure' (Kosambi 1991: 1870).

The above examples are illustrative of a well-established trend that evolved in the wake of the nationalist movement in India. Ideationally, whatever belonged to the so-called domestic domain remained exclusive and no interference from the government, despite being beneficial, was allowed. This was an attempt to sustain the sovereignty of the colonised, as Tilak most clearly argued. Hence, the steps that Rammohun, Vidyasagar and their Derozian colleagues undertook, were considered endeavours towards demeaning Hinduism. Rabindranath's novel *Yogayog* and the aforementioned short stories need to be understood from this perspective. By tempering his views, the poet seemed to have been governed by domineering sociocultural practices. Hence, Kumud was sent back to her in-law's house, Mrinal and Anila remained invisible when they expressed their agony and pain and only through a Punjabi girl, the bard articulated what, to him, did not seem to be unusual. In pursuance of this argument, it can also be reinforced that Rabindranath was implicitly radical and remained so as it appeared to him to be strategically effective to convey what he so strongly felt for gender equality. So, both Bipradas of *Yogayog* nor Sitangsu of 'Poila Nombor' expressed their resentment in a muted way because they were mentally conditioned by the prevalent sociocultural milieu.

Nevertheless, Rabindranath's short stories have a didactic component in a number of ways. Prominent among them was his insistence on the idea that the man–woman division was socially constructed to fulfil the partisan aims of a section of the people. The above selective short stories were a testimony to the bard's claim that gender equality was critical to social progress. By championing the points that Rammohun and Vidyasagar, among others, raised in rather adverse circumstances, the poet continued a tradition that he inherited by being raised in a liberal family where gender distinction did not appear to be a constraint. While his predecessors, Rammohun and Vidyasagar, participated in an ideological struggle against the orthodox Hindus, the poet, by extensively writing on issues on gender equity in widely circulated magazines and journals, popularised the views cutting across social boundaries. His efforts were complemented by the Gandhi-led nationalist campaign that created a legitimate space for women in the freedom struggle. Women no longer remained mute observers but were participants in various nationalist programmes that Gandhi spearheaded under the aegis of the Indian National Congress. Although these short stories hardly had a political message, they proposed a powerful design of significant sociocultural metamorphosis which laid the foundation of an equally powerful voice in the public domain. The characters, Mrinal, Anila and Sohini, were constructed accordingly; they conveyed an important ideational idea in a narrative form which, besides dwelling on the plight of women in Hindu households also devised a mechanism to ventilate gender grievances. By articulating their views in letters, not only did Anila and Mrinal express their helplessness as women under the present circumstances but they also attacked the prevalent mindset supportive of gender discrimination. That their intervention brought about a change in the established patriarchal mindset was evident when Anila's husband admitted that he was equally responsible for Anila being reduced to an individual who was expected to work hard to please the male participants in her husband's study circle by preparing snacks for them. Anila was quite upset though she remained quiet since the task of preparing snacks denied her time to join the discussion in which she had been welcomed by her husband when he started the study circle. Contrarily, Sohini was bold enough to decide independently the course of action to retain the laboratory that her deceased husband, Nandakishore, had built to provide effective pathological assistance to the people of Calcutta at a reasonable rate. Here Nandakishore was no less radical because by accepting Sohini's daughter who was born out of wedlock, he also defied the established sociocultural norms. 'Laboratory' is therefore not only a voice of protest against the well-entrenched sociocultural ideas but it also represented a new social vision which was immune from the prevalent prejudicial mindset.

The above detailed enunciation of ideas that the poet developed in many of his creative texts, including these short stories, reinforces the point that his ideational interventions 'unsettles many conventional theoretical models, forcing a paradigm shift in the ways of conceptualizing' gender issues (Chakravarty 2013: 2). Suffice it to refer to his speech which he made in the 1894 condolence meeting following the death of litterateur Bankim Chandra Chatterjee. Here, he asserted that given the intimate interaction with Western cultural life and the growing importance of Western intellectual discourses, the idea of 'public' needed to be understood differently since it no longer remained an exclusively male domain. Being a champion of gender equality, the bard further argued that so long as gender disparity remained, it was not only a myopic perception but also an obstruction to the realisation of human emancipation. As women 'are denied their legitimate space in society, our social life is seriously incomplete' (Chatterjee 2000: 38), argued the poet in defending his concern for gender equality. Nevertheless, one also witnesses a tension in the arguments that he evolved because at one level, he, being persuaded by rationality, accepted the points the main protagonists offered; at another level, by tempering his responses, he also had shown how the existing social reality conditioned his thinking. Accordingly, the voice of protest that Anila, Mrinal and Sohini had articulated remained substantially muted because society was not yet ready to recognize them as independent selves despite being different gender-wise. Still, it was a radical ideational transformation in the sense that the bard's forceful arguments for gender parity led to reconceptualising the phenomenon in the changed sociocultural context of Bengal during colonialism. Hence, despite not having attained the goal, Anila, Mrinal and Sohini ushered in a new era of man–woman relationships in which the latter was not just an appendage to the former, but complementary to each other.

References

Chakravarty, Radha. 2013. *Novelist Tagore: Gender and Modernity in Selected Texts*. New Delhi: Routledge.

Chatterjee, Partha. 1994. *The Nation and Its Fragments: Colonial and Postcolonial Histories*. Delhi: Oxford University Press.

———. 2000. 'Two Poets and Death: On Civil and Political Society in the Non-Christian World'. *In Questions of Modernity,* ed. Timothy Mitchel. Minnesota: University of Minnesota Press.

Ghose, Benoy. 1971. *Iswar Chandra Vidyasagar*. New Delhi: Publication Division, Ministry of Information and Broadcasting, Government of India.

Ghosh, Sachindra Lal. 1970. *Raja Rammohun Roy: Pathmaker of Modern India*. New Delhi: National Council of Educational Research and Training.

Kosambi, Meera. 1991. 'Girl-Brides and Socio-Legal Change: Age of Consent Bill (1891)'. *Economic and Political Weekly* (3–10 August): 1870.

Sinha, Dikshit. 2019. *A Poet's Experiment in Rebuilding Samaj and Nation: Sriniketan's Rural Reconstruction Work, 1922–1960*. West Bengal: Birupjatio Sahitya Sammiloni.

Tagore, Rabindranath. 1422 Bangabda. 'Laboratory'. In *Rabindra Rachanabali* (Bengali), Vol. 13. Kolkata: Visva-Bharati.

———. 1422 Bangabda. 'Poila Nombor'. In *Rabindra Rachanabali* (Bengali), Vol. 12. Kolkata: Visva-Bharati.

———. 1422 Bangabda. 'Strir Patra'. In *Rabindra Rachanabali* (Bengali), Vol. 12. Kolkata: Visva-Bharati.

———. 2008. 'The Fifth Letter'. In *Letters from a Sojourner in Europe*. Kolkata: Visva-Bharati.

Conclusion

I

Rabindranath's thoughts evolved from a dialogical interaction with existential influences. Born in a context in which Hindu orthodoxy generally gained precedence, he was fortunate to have been raised in a milieu which was liberal and appreciative of the principles of Enlightenment. As history shows, contemporary Bengal underwent radical sociocultural metamorphosis with the foundation of Brahmo Samaj at the behest of Rammohun Roy and Dwarkanath Tagore among others (Kopf 1988). In his essay 'The Religion of Man', the poet did not seem eager to adopt the 'monotheistic religion based upon the philosophy of the Upanishad [which] his family adhered to' (Tagore 1996: 120). He was not persuaded to surrender to the family's faith since his 'mind at first remained coldly aloof, absolutely uninfluenced by any religion whatever' (120). He attributed his reluctance to 'an idiosyncrasy of [his] temperament that [he] refused to accept any religious teaching merely because people in [his] surroundings believed it to be true' (120). A priest of rationalism, the bard detested ideas that were imposed on him. Here too, he rebelled since it was assumed that, being part of a Brahmo family, he had to adopt a religious faith without being convinced of its utility; this was evident when he further argued that 'I could not persuade myself to imagine that I had a religion because everybody whom I might trust believed its value' (120). Without any imposition by his family, Tagore chose his path on his own: 'my mind was brought up in an atmosphere of freedom—freedom from the dominance of any creed that had its sanction in the definite authority of some scripture, or in the teaching of some organised body of worshippers' (120). This was advantageous to the bard because it allowed him to explore the world in terms of his own priority: He was neither constrained by 'the authority of some particular book' (120) nor a specific creed based on the acceptance of interpretations of holy books by a specific set of individuals, considered perceptive in their thinking. In other words, his agnosticism led him to, as he explained, 'unconsciously follow the path of [his] Vedic ancestors, [and was] inspired by the tropical sky with its suggestion of uttermost Beyond' (121). Being one who was not a victim of the prevalent religious and sociocultural claims and counter-claims, the bard internalised a vision which was critical to human existence over generations. His views were an articulation of a path of life that was immune from being governed by scriptural restrictions. It was thus easier for him to castigate orthodox practices which were extremely myopic in so far as human civilisation was concerned: 'he who has the healthy vigour of humanity in him has a strong instinctive faith that ideally he is limitless ... [and] our true worship lies in our indomitable courage to be great and thus represent the human-divine and ever to keep open the path of freedom towards the unattained' (134). Rabindranath, thus, expressed his complete faith in humanity which was, to him, a source of limitless energy and determination; at the same time, it was also an attempt to encourage those with their self-generated fear of not being able to reach the goal to independently express themselves. The bard's purpose was to instil courage and also confidence among those seeking to bring about changes in one's approach to humanity. The task did not seem to be easier given, as the poet saw, the fact that

> we Indians have had the sad experience in our own part of the world how timid orthodoxy, its irrational repressions and its articulation of dead centuries, dwarfs man through its idolatry of the past. Seated rigid in the centre of stagnation, it firmly ties the human spirit to the revolving wheels of habit till faintness overwhelms her. Like a sluggish stream choked by rotting weeds, it is divided into shallow slimy pools that shroud their dumbness in a narcotic mist of stupor. The mechanical spirit of tradition is essentially materialistic, it is blindly pious but not spiritual, obsessed by phantoms of unreason that haunt feeble minds in the ghastly disguise of religion. For our soul is shrunken when we allow foolish minds to weave repeated patterns of unmeaning meshes around all departments of life. ... This happens only ... to the generations of insipid races that have lost emphasis of significance in themselves, having missed their future. (134–135)

What we see here is Rabindranath's scathing critique to explain the decay of civilisation confronting India. The poet argued strongly against the well-nurtured mindset in favour of sustaining age-old sociocultural practices, religiously justified to segregate one section of human beings from another. Characterising them as dead wood, he questioned the continuity of such customary practices as nothing but an attempt to not allow human beings to realise their actual potential. Based on 'the phantom of unreason', these human habits, drawing sustenance from centuries-old values and mores, were sources of the ruination of society. Rabindranath identified the social ills which were, in his perception, the principal causes of the decline of human vitality. Although the argument has substance, it does not seem to be entirely valid, given the complete absence of discussions regarding the adverse impact of British rule in sustaining these archaic social rules and regulations—one of the main reasons for its sustenance. There is no denying that there were forces to nurture these archaic social mores and ethos, and the Enlightenment philosophy that inspired the social reformers in India laid the foundation of a voice against them. One may also argue that the Brahmo Samaj was an offshoot of the urge that drew its sustenance from Enlightenment ideas; the British-sponsored Asiatic Society also played a critical role in this regard. The urge for reform that the British rulers had at the outset of the unfolding of the Empire appeared to have lost its momentum when they focused their attention on how to exploit India's natural wealth to serve the industries in Britain. As is now well-established, the *divide-et-impera* policy helped the colonisers not only to sustain but also to consolidate the empire. That India's vivisection in 1947 was rooted in this policy of divide and rule does not require any further explanation, as contemporary evidence firmly establishes (Chakrabarty 2004). Nonetheless, what is unique in the bard's assessment of the situation is a concern for being self-conscious of the issues that were both crippling and debilitating. Under these circumstances, what was required was the generation of a voice from within against the primordial restrictive rules and regulations, which were also dehumanising since they were directed at justifying a permanent fissure among human beings. Tagore may not have paid adequate attention to the prejudicial effect of British rule because of his firm belief that social stagnation was far more venomous than imposed governance. Perhaps, this was why he disagreed with the revolutionary nationalists of Gandhi who believed that once political freedom was wrested, stagnating social habits could easily be tackled to their satisfaction. Here there is a similarity between B.R. Ambedkar and Rabindranath because the former always argued for state intervention for eradicating socially debilitating practices and habits. One should also note that there were differences between the poet and Ambedkar because, unlike Babasaheb, the poet was opposed to intervention from outside; he always favoured the regeneration of forces from within to combat these evil practices, as his 1904 tract *Swadeshi Samaj* persuasively argued. According to him, what is required to be done was

> to awaken the power within us and give it a direction ... [and] the attempt to emulate the English and trying to survive in disguise is also self-delusion [because] we can never be genuine Englishmen, nor can we successfully combat them by being imitative of their lifestyle. (Tagore 1908: 31)

Fundamental here is the urge to become self-reliant which was possible once one was confident about their capability. In the poet's perception, this was self-awakening which was attainable not by imitating the derivative sociocultural mould of the British civilisation; it remained so since by being true to the English sociocultural ethos, the Indians could neither be British nor had a chance to become so under any circumstances. In the process, the Indians ceased to become Indians as well: By forgetting one's sociocultural roots, one became both rootless and dissociated with one's milieu. On the basis of this argument, Rabindranath made a wider point by highlighting that by being born as a human being one did not become human because it entailed certain qualities that one did not find among, for instance, animals. Hence, he argued that

> the realism in Man is the animal in him whose life is a mere duration of life; the human in him is his reality which has life everlasting for its background. Rocks and crystals being complete in what they are, … while human facts grow unseemly and diseased, breeding germs of death, which divested of their creative ideal—the ideal of Man the divine. (Tagore 1996: 'The Vision', 137)

Thus, the bard separated man from those, who despite being born as a man, lacked the quality of being a man. According to him, one's birth as a man did not qualify him as a man since the duration of life was not at all a criterion of being a man. What was most important in his opinion was the potential of creativity that always remained hidden in every man; unless that was brought out in the open, the claim of being a man was one without substance. In order to persuasively establish his point, he further argued by contrasting the unfolding of man with that of music. According to him,

> the difference between the notes as mere facts of sound and music as a truth of expression is immense. For music, though it comprehends a limited number of notes, yet represents the infinite. It is for man to produce the music of the spirit with all the notes which has in his psychology and which, through inattention or perversity, can easily be translated into a frightful noise. In music, man is revealed and not in noise. (137)

What is articulated here is most insightful indeed. Here too, the poet defended his point by insisting on the immense capability that human beings possessed; hence unless human potential was fully realised, it was difficult, if not impossible, to fulfil the mission. *Char Adhay*'s Indranath talked in the same language, which was appreciated by the bard because it reflected his determination to wrest political freedom from colonialism. At the same time, he was also criticised by the poet because he did not pay attention to the core values of humanism; he mechanically implemented his ideas even at the cost of humane values which was manifested in his planned strategy to permanently separate Ela from Atin by ordering the latter to kill the former. In other words, to Rabindranath, humanism reigned supreme, and attempts towards undermining its foundational pillars were always a source of his consternation. That the idea was integral to his intellectual universe was evident in his many creative texts. For him, human beings remained as they were because they could recreate the sociocultural ethos in accordance with what they deemed appropriate for human well-being. Being inspired by the Upanishads, Tagore drew an analogy in which two birds sitting on the same branch of the tree enjoyed looking at each other despite being simultaneously engaged in different activities: While one fed the babies, the other looked at her. This was what was explained as

> an image of the mutual relationship of the infinite being and the finite self. The delight of the bird which looks on is great, for it is a pure and free delight. There are both the birds in Man himself, the objective one with its business of life, the subjective one with its disinterested joy of vision. (141)

What is evident here is that the bard, not being appreciative of an ascetic life since he enjoyed worldly existence, made a very perceptive comment about the parable that he found in the Upanishads. In his view, man was capable of meaningfully amalgamating apparently incompatible desires: worldly comforts along with the longing for the infinite. According to him, what was most critical was the awareness that there hardly existed contradictions between the two; what was needed was therefore the inculcation of a mindset in which both these desires coexisted—something that did not happen under normal circumstances since one prevailed over the other. Implicit here was his scathing critique of British colonialism which, in order to fulfil finite goals, ignored its infinite counterparts. What upset him most was the blind emulation of the British sociocultural ethos and values by a section of Indians, who found it an easy way to flourish at the cost of others. So, the idea that the bard articulated here was not entirely spiritual in character—it also had a temporal meaning.

A careful analytical dissection of Rabindranath's sociopolitical ideas also reveals that behind his storytelling mould, he wanted to create and sustain an ambience in which his countrymen realised their capabilities and potentials and could also effectively combat the British sociocultural ethos along with what prevented the evolution and consolidation of a well-knit collectivity. Rabindranath's model of man was thus based on appreciation for both the finite and the infinite; he also urged the Indians to unitedly fight the British. This was not an easy option because unity remained elusive as long as Indians were divided internally around the axis of caste, class and ethnicity. Nonetheless, he was hopeful as the history of human civilisation demonstrated that circumstances would soon bring all men together. Given his perceptive mind, he referred to the bees' behaviour to persuasively argue his point:

> [C]ivilised man has come far away from the orbit of his normal life. He has gradually formed and intensified some habits that are like those of the bees for adapting himself to his hive world. ... Social revolutions are constantly ushered in with suicidal violence that has its origin in our dissatisfaction with our hive-wall arrangement—the too exclusive enclosure that deprives us of the perspective which is so much needed to give us the proper proportion in our art of living. (155)

The views expressed by the poet are critical to comprehending his approach to human civilisation. As demonstrated in history, it is clear that dissatisfaction led to discontent and social revolution. On a surface reading, one may end up suggesting that Rabindranath, by questioning contemporary civilisation, was one of the protagonists who attributed the advancement of human civilisation to the decline of humanity. A serious reading of his thoughts however reveals that the imposed industrial civilisation in India created inconceivable sociocultural disbalance which, instead of being contributory to human existence, was a source of decadence. Challenging the heartless industrial civilisation, the bard raised his voice, saying that 'by producing an artificially cultivated hunger of worldly things [it] generates and feeds the energy that drives civilisation upon his endless journey' (Tagore 1996: 'The Teacher', 156). Pursuing his critique, he further said that 'personally I do not believe that this had ever been the principal driving force that has led to eminence any great civilisation of which we know in history' (156). What we witness here is not only the poet's distaste for industrial civilisation but also a pain that emanated from the devilish impact of the ascendancy of a mindset in its favour. In other words, his agony was not for the growth of the industrial civilisation, but for the mechanical mindset that drew its sustenance from the greed for personal gain even if that required the deprivileging of a section of humanity. It was an expression of loss which he articulated by saying,

> often I had listened to my eldest brother describing with the poignancy of a hopeless regret a society hospitable, sweet with the old-world aroma of natural kindliness, full of simple faith and the ceremonial poetry of

> life. But all this was a vanishing shadow behind me in the dusky golden haze of a twilight horizon—the all-pervading fact around my boyhood being the modern city built by a company of Western traders and the spirit of modern time seeking its unaccustomed entrance into our life, stumbling against countless anomalies. (Tagore 1996: 156)

Although the bard expressed his appreciation for a simple life that was a matter of history to him when he was growing up in Calcutta, he also explained the reason for the decimation of the simple life in which humanity prospered naturally as it was an espoused ideal for all social beings. Attributing the decline of such 'a sweet life' to a civilisation that thrived on dehumanising the industrial growth of a select group of nations, which allowed them to be nasty, inhuman and ruthless to those who had not had the fortune of becoming industrialised at the same time. So, industrialism was a divisive design since it created conditions in which one set of nationalities prospered at the cost of the other. Pursuant to this point, the bard laid the foundation of his idea of freedom which was not based on satisfactorily gratified human needs but 'a harmony of perfect relationship' (157), which further connotes that 'freedom in the sense of independence has no content' (157). Interestingly, with regard to the idea of freedom, Gandhi held similar views that the bard espoused. In *Hind Swaraj*, the Mahatma, while characterising the 'tendency of the Indian civilisation … to elevate the moral being that of the Western civilisation [as the propagation of] immorality [because] the latter is godless, the former is based on a belief in God' (2005: 55). Reinforcing the point, he further argued that 'so understanding and so believing, it behoves every lover of India to cling to old Indian civilisations even as a child clings to the mother's breast' (Tagore 1996: 'The Teacher', 156). Explicit here is Gandhi's (a) sharp critique of blindless imitation and (b) urge to be proud of India's civilisational roots. There is hardly any difference between the poet and the nationalist, Gandhi, who also insisted on the importance of India's sociocultural ethos in building a well-knit collectivity which, despite being diverse on many counts, generated a wave of unity cutting across socioeconomic barriers as well.

II

The selected novels and short stories in this book represent a distinct voice in favour of an explicit politico-ideological message. Keeping this in view, each chapter is an articulation of the views that Rabindranath espoused while contributing to the ushering in of a new vision based on his perception of many of the well-entrenched sociocultural values. More than being mere literary creations, these innovative texts championed cutting-edge politico-ideological ideas and also sustained a campaign to weed out those paralytic customs and mores which gained precedence as a result of the hegemony of the orthodox Hindus.

A careful reading of these specific creative texts reveals that Rabindranath, while tacitly attacking British rule as it drew on the *divide-et-impera* strategy, focused primarily on the prevalent sociocultural matrix, being justified as integral to Hinduism. The protagonists in the novels and short stories raised cudgels against the artificially constructed sociocultural boundaries to permanently segregate, inter alia, a man from woman and untouchables or Sudras from upper-caste Hindus. In *Gora*, Sucharita and her father, Paresh Babu, introduced Gora to a serious critique of Hinduism in their regular discussion with him while his mother, Anandomoyee had shown, in practice, that she was immune from caste prejudices despite her husband being an orthodox Hindu, which was manifested in accepting a Christian, Lachhmia, as a cook. There is no denying that these influences remained significant as Gora underwent a dramatic metamorphosis in reconceptualising humanity when he had had an opportunity to interact with the villagers away from Calcutta. The decision of the Hindu barber couple to adopt a Muslim child, Tamiz, following the arrest of his father, Faru Sardar since he allegedly attacked a white Indigo planter, was an eye-opener. Disturbed by this segregation between the Muslims and Hindus, the bard always felt that

> if Hindus and Muslims united in real friendship, a long stride towards the attainment of swaraj would have been taken. The trouble is that they do not unite. In the event of their union, each and every day in the calendar would be auspicious enough for swaraj to begin. (Tagore 1962: 275)

Furthermore, the hatred that orthodox Hindus nurtured even against the Christians did not escape the poet's attention, which was evident when it was revealed to Gora that despite being a Christian, Aanandomoyee was hardly constrained to adopt him once he became an orphan with the death of his Irish parents in the 1857 Sepoy outbreak against the British. The novel thus offered a powerful critique of conservative Hinduism at one level; it was also, at another level, a significant assessment of the nationalist intervention which, by being highly Hinduised, failed to appreciate the bard's espousal for universal humanism. Acquiescing with the bard, Gandhi also felt that the schism between the caste Hindus and the so-called untouchables was 'a bigger problem than that of gaining independence [because] it is not impossible that India may free herself from English domination before India has become free from the course of untouchability' (Tagore 1921 in Dasgupta 2018: 376).

Similarly, the prevalent gender disparity was attacked in *Ghare Baire* which was a scathing critique of socioculturally-constructed gender segregation. Bimala of *Ghare Baire*, Sucharita of *Gora*, Damini of *Chaturanga*, Ela of *Char Adhyay* and Kumud of *Yogayog* couched their argument for gender justice in an identical voice in opposition to the well-entrenched patriarchal prejudices. The efforts of the principal female protagonists—Sohini, Mrinal and Anila—in the short stories were also directed to champion the same goal in a contrarian sociocultural milieu. Rabindranath's concern for gender equality, therefore, helped build an oppositional voice against gender discrimination. Despite being aware of the adverse consequences, the poet did not hesitate to speak out about what he so sincerely felt for gender parity. In other words, by constructing characters who were opposed to sociocultural discrimination due to the accident of birth, Tagore carried forward a conceptual tradition that gradually engulfed the Bengali educated middle classes. So, simultaneously with perceptual transformation, these creative texts paved the way for a new era of thinking in which the issue of gender figured prominently.

Another important aspect of this text is its focus on the bard's idea of nationalism which is generally explained with reference to his 1916 lectures in Japan and the USA. Except for *Yogayog*, other novels that have received attention here dwell on how the poet conceptualised nationalism as a mode of politico-ideological mobilisation. His three lectures are often cited to argue that Rabindranath was opposed to nationalism—which is not entirely true—and that it is plausible to argue that he was critical of the idea that was rooted in the European sociocultural matrix; it was obvious given the fact that nationalism is a definite endeavour towards essentialising one's identity ignoring the point that it was unlikely to happen in India, given her disparate sociocultural texture. The novels, barring *Yogayog*, have a clear political message: opposition to revolutionary nationalism, espoused by the early Congress activities in the context of the swadeshi campaign of 1905–1908 since it was a Hinduised endeavour, felt Tagore, which was responsible for permanently segregating the Muslims from mainstream nationalist offensive, as history shows. For instance, Sandip of *Ghare Baire*, Indranath or even Atin of *Char Adhyay*, being believers of this conceptualisation of nationalism, resorted to acts which never received the poet's approbation because he never had faith in any divisive political campaign regardless of its so-called noble aim. Surprisingly, Rabindranath was reluctant to take these texts as representative of his politico-ideological priorities.

It was evident when he responded to the attempts to characterise *Char Adhyay* as one that contained his nationalistic devotion to the cause of freedom. According to him,

> much of the controversy over my *Four Chapters* [*Char Adhyay*] falls outside the province of literary criticism. This is only natural, for the background to the story is vividly coloured by the passions aroused by the political struggle and turmoil in modern Bengal. Not only are we close to that scene; there is, still, a constant radiation of its heart through our minds. It is for this reason that to many readers the setting of the story appears more important than the story itself. I can only hope that when the present agitation of spirit recedes into the distant past and becomes merely the subject of dispassionate historical research, the imagination of the reader will be free to accept the story in a spirit of detachment. In other words, it will be possible, then, to look at it solely as literature.[1]

In response to criticism of *Char Adhyay* in the public domain, Tagore reiterated that the novel did not convey a political message:

> [I]t is unnecessary in any literary appraisal of *Four Chapters* to discuss whether it propagates a particular creed or moral. It is obvious that its main interest centres around the story of two modern lovers. The revolutionary movement in Bengal has provided their love with its special dramatic setting. Descriptions of the movement are of secondary importance: what matters as literature is the portrayal of the poignance and pain of their love against the stormy background of the revolution. (363)

Nonetheless, the novel is about a context which cannot be completely divorced from the unfolding of the story. As the poet himself admitted,

> in the course of the story, the different characters have voiced their views about the revolutionary movement [and] ... if these comments on the movement had been entirely absent, the context would have lost all meaning. It must be assumed that the opinions expressed serve only to support and confirm the characterisation of the speakers. (362–363)

Indeed, the novel did not deal with the revolutionary movement per se because 'the end of the story is solely concerned with the love of Atindra and Ela' (362). So what the poet claimed has substance. Nonetheless, the

---

1 Rabindranath Tagore's reply to the criticism published in *Prabashi*, April–May 1935, reproduced in Uma Dasgupta (ed.), *The Oxford India Tagore: Selected Writings in Education and Nationalism*, New Delhi: Oxford University Press, 2009, 361.

context in which Atin and Ela's love flourished cannot be completely ignored. By dwelling on the difficulty faced by those committed to the revolutionary campaign in Bengal, the poet, rather inadvertently, commented on the specific nature of the revolution that galvanised the Bengali youths. Furthermore, the fact that Indranath's politico-ideological mission brought Ela closer to the group in general, and Atin in particular, also substantiates the claim that in view of their emotional compatibility for a common cause, they could easily form a group. The love between Ela and Atin was of primary significance in the story though it was equally significant to underline that they came together since they held identical politico-ideological commitments. Of course, there is no denying that ultimately, the context appeared to have lost its critical salience and their love gained precedence. Hence, the poet was partly correct when he suggested that what remained significant was the attempt by Ela and Atin to develop an emotional bond despite being committed to the oath that they took to not get married before India's political freedom before joining Indranath. That was certainly a comment made by the poet on the nature of the revolutionary campaign in Bengal: He expressed his disenchantment with the revolutionaries' endeavour since it impeded the realisation of one of the finest forms of human bond based on love. Nonetheless, by devoting enough space in the novel to the revolutionary activities in then-Bengal, the poet provided us with enough input to gather his opinion on contemporary nationalistic activities.

III

Rabindranath's widely circulated 1916 lectures on nationalism are frequently cited to show that he was not a 'nationalist' per se. Tagore, like Gandhi, was never persuaded by the Western conceptualisation of nationalism being a cerebral tool for essentialising human identities; for obvious reasons, it did not apply to India given her disparate sociocultural tapestry being highly diverse. Instead, what both Tagore and Gandhi preferred was a concept of collectivity based on the communal existence of humanity with its distinctive sociocultural diversity. Their choice boiled down to devotion to a multitude as it evolved over the generations by nurturing their distinct sociocultural traits. Illustrated here is their emphasis on village life as a unit of collectivity cutting across sociocultural divisions. The point of convergence of their views is based on their commitment to protecting the spatial sociocultural peculiarity. Also, for want of a better expression, they appear to have appreciated the expression 'nation' to denote a collectivity or multitude of people. It is thus not surprising that despite the word, 'nation' being 'illegitimate', *Gora* (1910), *Ghare Baire* (1916) and *Char Adhyay* (1934), among others, articulated a nationalistic voice, of course, not in the conventional conceptual sense. Of these novels, *Gora* is perhaps one of the most poignant statements of how sociocultural prejudices caused and consolidated divisions among the people. Hence, 'the deeper [Gora] penetrated the [life outside Calcutta] a more certain thought began to trouble his mind' (Tagore 2011: 575). The villagers, he realised, were torn between what they wanted to do for the country and the segregating social restrictions causing a serious impediment to develop a bonhomie among the people sharing the same sociocultural space. Gora thus 'could not help noticing that humans were using [these restrictive practices] as weapons to suck the blood of other human beings, brutally robbing them of their selfhood' (575). Being dismayed, he further held that

> because a section of his own countrymen was hostile to the country, because they viewed all aspects of their country in a negative light, a strong sense of patriotism had prompted Gora to protect his land from the humiliation of this self-detached view by trying day and night to cover his country's entire image with a dazzling emotional aura [which led him to take a vow that] he first renews his countrymen's respect for their own land before he took on any other task. (577)

In clear terms, the bard referred to his concern for patriotism which did not percolate down to the people at large presumably because of the socioculturally divisive practices. The same message is conveyed in *Ghare Baire* which was, on one level, a sharp critique of 'narrow nationalism' that the campaigners of the Swadeshi Movement (1905–1908) upheld; on another level, it was also a comment on the prevalent sociocultural prejudices that permanently separated the Muslims because of the failure of the Swadeshi leadership to bring them into their fold. By nurturing the view that Muslims 'would have to be subdued and shown who was the boss in no uncertain terms' (Tagore 2011: 747), the Swadeshi nationalists were determined to force them to toe their line of thinking because they believed that 'today they bare their fangs at us; but one day we'll make them dance to our tune' (747). Being opposed to this approach, the bard also underlined the fact that 'if India is a true entity, then Muslims are a part of it' (747). Rabindranath was critical of the nationalist hatred for the Muslims, but he also identified the limitations of the nationalist project in which no attempt was made to eradicate the prevalent sociocultural chasm among the Hindus. It was evident when he argued in *Ghare Baire* that 'the country is not just this land and soil, it is also the people' (734); the decision of the swadeshi activists to determine 'what they would eat and what they'd wear' (734) rightly provoked the people to say 'why should they tolerate and why should [those opposed to the swadeshi political campaign] let them tolerate that?' (734). Nonetheless, the then nationalists were hardly restrained, as the poet elaborated in *Ghare Baire*, when he defended his point by drawing on the expressed belief of Sandip, the leader of the swadeshi activists, of enjoying life because he, as claimed, was 'materialistic. … [His] joy stalks every footstep [because] whatever [he] desire[s] come very close to [him]' (699). He also believed that 'after this life and death, good and bad, joy and sorrow, all in vain, mere trifles' (699). What is clear here is the claim that, to the bard, nationalism entailed selfless devotion to the people irrespective of religion and sociocultural location. Rabindranath's approach to the political struggle for freedom can be said to have drawn on the (a) common concern for all and, consequently (b) devotion to the cause. Finally, *Char Adhyay* is another illustration of how the poet evolved his model in circumstances when togetherness was most important in fulfilling the goal of collectivity. It is true, as the poet himself underlined, that it was a story of love although the context was about the triumph of the nationalist voice, which Indranath, Atin and even Ela espoused. Although the poet did not appreciate the politico-ideological predilections of those committed souls, he gave us enough input to understand that he was vehemently opposed to nationalist endeavour in support of violence.

IV

In this final section, an attempt shall be made to dissect the poet's idea of freedom or swaraj. Being critical of Gandhi's hope of winning swaraj by generating sources of inspiration by involving people in spinning their own thread on charkha, the bard endeavoured to comprehend the concept in his own way. According to Rabindranath, one of the serious impediments of swaraj was the failure to unite Hindus and Muslims which was not possible through an institutional pact between the communities, as the non-cooperators believed. He attributed this to an age-old mindset which he explained by stating that

> the habit of mind which religious injunctions have built within us is the age-old citadel of communal feelings, not to be demolished by an outward unity on the basis of either the Khilafat movement [which united the Muslims with the Hindus since the former, with this unity, strengthened their battle against the abolition of Caliph by the British] or pacts based on opportunism. (Tagore 1962: 278)

A genuine Hindu–Muslim unity was thus impossible to attain by a mere institutional pact unless there existed a mindset in its favour. Furthermore, in opposition to Gandhi's insistence on spinning as a mode of attaining swaraj, the poet insisted that

> swaraj … was not as a matter of homespun yarn alone [because] people's welfare is an amalgam of several ingredients. To take one of them by itself cannot do much good. Health, recreation, the activities of the body and mind—thrown together in one combination, they make the picture complete. We want to hold that complete picture of welfare before our eyes; … Otherwise, simply by turning charkha, weaving homespun yarn and holding grave discourses, we shall not be able to project the realisation of what swaraj means. (282)

Here too the poet provided a scathing critique of Gandhi's claim that swaraj was possible only if Indians were engaged in producing home-spun clothes and delivering verbose speeches. For swaraj to succeed, one needed to be involved in activities relating to the production of enough food and adequate healthcare. It was an achievable goal once Indians were united regardless of class, clan and colour for the cause of the country's development. According to the poet, 'if the people of even one Indian village make their village their own creation, the first long step towards the solving of the problem would have been taken' (282). The goal was easy to attain with

> the spread of cooperative self-determination, … with it resultant inward experience of glory and pride. … Its absence, within and without, is the root cause of all our denials: denials of food and health, education and wisdom and joy. To think that swaraj could become a reality in spite of this poverty of spirit is absurd. (283)

What is highlighted here is the spirit of cooperative self-determination which was at the root of human success in ventures contributing to common well-being. Built on the notion that communal well-being was linked with individual well-being, Rabindranath developed a strong defence for his model of cooperative existence for human betterment as a whole. In other words, the feeling that with the socioeconomic development of the community in its entirety, the individual realised that 'through his work of common benefit, he realises the entire village in himself. His is a joyous and creative mission,' argued Rabindranath, 'in which the striving for swaraj has its true beginning [and] when others join him, it means that the village is set on the path of revival and fulfilment' (283). Tagore, therefore, always prioritised self-generated enthusiasm for one's benefit because it percolated down to common benefit; he also believed that the socioeconomic development of one village had a spiralling effect as a model on others which paved the way for all-round socioeconomic gains across the country. In a succinct way, he thus explained that

> Swaraj for the whole of India would begin in the village where the people have formed themselves into a united community set on improving its health and education, its economic life, and its amusements no less. The swaraj would then advance by its own power, its propulsion inherent in the organic process of its own living growth, and not in the mechanical rotation of the spinning wheel. (284)

Ideationally, it was a unique theoretical conceptualisation because neither khadi nor mere dependence on the charkha was adequate to conclusively address India's age-old problem of poverty along with the segregationist mindset creating divisions among the people. In *Ghare Baire* and *Gora*, Tagore dwells on the mechanism of self-development and also on the mode of evolving a mindset free from sociocultural prejudices. By challenging the Hinduised nationalist discourse that Sandip clung to in *Ghare Baire*, Nikhilesh carved out a distinct space for a completely different kind of nationalist discourse. Similarly, once Gora came out of Calcutta and mixed with those in rural Bengal, he realised that one of the main impediments for India to grow as a well-knit collectivity was the Hindu–Muslim schism and division of the people around the caste axis. In contrast, *Yogayog* shows how the unity among the people allowed them to organise a successful campaign against the dam to stop *mukta dhara* or the free flow of water. Dhananjoy Bairagi in *Muktadhara* (1922) was a voice against the divisive mindset, clamouring for the coming together of the people of Shiv Tarai regardless of caste and religion. Although, as per the poet, love was his predominant concern, a critical reading of the novel *Char Adhyay* reveals that Indranath's politico-ideological objective, despite his selfless dedication, remained unrealised largely due to his failure to knit the group as one because individual priority prevailed over love, which the bard always privileged over anything else.

V

Rabindranath Tagore's Ideational Challenges is an analytical attempt to show that Rabindranath Tagore in his own unique style raised some troublesome sociocultural issues which, he strongly held, were serious constraints towards attaining politico-ideological objectives that the nationalists espoused both during the Gandhian period and its preceding years. His creative texts were thus not merely literary articulation of the issues but were powerful responses to the prevalent conceptual parameters on which humanity rested. Although the poet did not appear to have made such a claim, his creative writings were full of politico-ideologically innovative ideas about human diversity that naturally flourished in the Indian subcontinent. By approaching the pertinent sociocultural and politico-ideological issues from a literary perspective, the poet can be said to have refashioned the contemporary views on humanity. A visionary Rabindranath Tagore evolved a new genre of critical thinking to challenge some of those contemporary ideational inputs, responsible for sustaining artificially created fissures among human beings, either due to their separate religious affiliations or sociocultural differences around certain constructed segmentary devices. He was a transcendental thinker as well given the validity, even today, of the conceptual framework that he developed to understand the sociocultural underpinning of the period in which he was born and raised. In fact, it will be not an exaggeration to claim that the poet's viewpoints have acquired tremendous salience in the 21st century when collective human existence is being continuously threatened by fissiparous campaigns drawing sustenance from forces engaged in dividing humanity. The bard was a source of self-determination when he was alive, and he continues to remain an inspirational figure even in his absence in the contemporary era.

References

Chakrabarty, Bidyut. 2004. *The Partition of Bengal and Assam, 1932–1947: The Contour of Freedom*. London: Routledge.

Gandhi, M.K. 2005 (rpt). *Hind Swaraj or Indian Home Rule*. Ahmedabad: Navajivan Publishing House.

Kopf, David. 1988. *The Brahmo Samaj and the Shaping of the Modern Indian Mind*. New Delhi: Archives Publishers Pvt. Ltd.

Tagore, Rabindranath. 1908 (rpt). *Swadeshi Samaj*. Kolkata: Visva-Bharati.

———. 1962 (rpt). 'The Striving for Swaraj'. In *Towards Universal Man*. Bombay: Asia Publishing House.

———. 1996. 'The Vision'. In 'The Religion of Man', reproduced in *The English Writings of Rabindranath Tagore*, ed. Sisir Kumar Das, Vol. 3, New Delhi: Sahitya Akademi.

———. 1996. 'The Teacher'. In 'The Religion of Man', reproduced in *The English Writings of Rabindranath Tagore*, ed. Sisir Kumar Das, Vol. 3. New Delhi: Sahitya Akademi.

———. 2011. 'Ghare Baire'. In *Classic Rabindranath Tagore*. New Delhi: Penguin.

———. 2011. 'Gora'. In *Classic Rabindranath Tagore*. New Delhi: Penguin.

———. 2018 (1921). Gandhi to CF Andrews, 29 January. In *Friendships of Largeness and Freedom: Andrews, Tagore and Gandhi, an Epistolary Account, 1912–1940*, ed. and compiled, Uma Dasgupta. New Delhi: Oxford University Press.

Bibliographical Notes

To provide an exhaustive bibliography on the sociopolitical make-up of Rabindranath Tagore is almost impossible—given not only his prolificity but also the quantum of research that has been done on his ideas. Nonetheless, no book is complete without a bibliography: (a) a bibliography contains books on the author's (here, Rabindranath Tagore's) sociopolitical ideas and (b) a bibliography is also directional to future researchers on this aspect of intellectual query.

Before I put forward the list of academic works that shaped this project, I would like to make some preliminary remarks. First, the book is drawn on the texts that Rabindranath Tagore himself wrote on various themes. There is a note of caution here: Since the written texts of the bard are context-driven, one is required to pay attention to the contemporary socioeconomic and political milieu. What is however striking is the strange relevance of the ideas that he evolved in the colonial context even in the 21st century. It is thus fair to argue that his views are transcendental. His conceptualisations regarding contemporary sociocultural issues are of great help to understand some of the pressing human problems of today. For instance, his approach to inter-community relations, especially between Hindus and Muslims, and his voice against untouchability remain relevant in today's context. Second, it is rather unfortunate that there have been attempts to confine him to the literary world just to project him as a litterateur par excellence. Hence there is no dearth of researched monographs on his literary creations. What is missing is the effort also to understand his texts as a manifestation of specific politico-ideological views. The proposed book is an attempt to initiate a new thought process seeking to grasp Rabindranath Tagore as a politically informed individual, who made a substantial contribution to the unfolding of ideas which did not always correspond with the mainstream approach to nationalism. As the bard believed, mere political freedom from British rule was not adequate to do away with the well-entrenched sociocultural prejudices that determined human behaviour, to a significant extent. Third, one of the serious limitations of universalising the bard's innovative politico-ideological views was the non-availability of most of his written discourses in other languages, besides his mother tongue, Bangla. Now, with a sustained endeavour, many of his texts are available in English and other foreign languages which perhaps was an important reason for the spurt of work on

Rabindranath's creative sociocultural and politico-ideological insights. Fourthly, there is hardly any work to link the ideas that he articulated in his novels with those he developed in his creative essays. On the face of it, *Ghare Baire*, *Char Adhyay*, *Chaturanga*, *Yogayog*, among others, are, for instance, narratives in the form of novels though a deeper reading of these novels reveals that they also contained specific politico-ideological visons. There is no denying that *Ghare Baire* illustrates the bard's concern for the deterioration of Hindu–Muslim bonhomie and also the failure of the then-nationalists to conclusively address this. That it was a lack of foresight is evident from this particular novel which was also a sharp comment on the divisive sociocultural habits that the orthodox Hindus happily nurtured despite being a source of alienation of one section of Hindus from the rest. By rereading the creative texts from a different perspective, the book has focused on the processes that contributed to the evolution of his unique ideas and views. Finally, I must add that the study is just a beginning of a new type of research in which an attempt is made to explore a rather untrodden aspect of the bard's intellectual universe with reference to a set of selective novels and short stories. Undoubtedly, there also exist many of his innovative texts which also contain inputs to comprehend his creative mindset. Given the paucity of space, it is difficult to deal with each and every creative text of Rabindranath to develop a conclusive opinion. Hence, the effort is directed here to dwell on those novels and short stories in which the poet evolved a specific conceptual mode of thinking to pursue the goal that he nurtured so assiduously so long as he remained on the scene.

There are three types of sources which are critical so far as this book is concerned. First, the poet's novels and short stories are, of course, the first important source since they help us understand both the ideas and the perspective in which they were conceptualised. Second, there are commentaries which are equally useful to conceive of the principal approaches that the commentators have adopted to un-fathom Rabindranath's sociocultural and politico-ideological views. Finally, the book has drawn on texts on literary criticism to grasp the intricate ways in which the bard generated newer ideas to understand better the prevalent socioeconomic and political circumstances which also indicates his distrust of derivative discourses.

As the book is a commentary on some of the major ideas of the bard, the discussion is couched accordingly. For instance, there is a general misconception that the poet was against nationalism which appears persuasive if one simply focuses one's attention on the three lectures that he provided in 1916 in Japan and the US. If, however, one rereads these lectures with reference to *Ghare Baire* or *Char*

Adhyay, for instance, one is likely to arrive at a different conclusion, namely, that the bard understood the idea of nationalism completely differently since, to him, devotion to one's motherland which can also be described as patriotism also denotes a kind of nationalism, conceptually different from that of the Western conceptualisation insisting on the homogenisation of sociocultural diversity as critical to the rise of a nation. Both *Ghare Baire* and *Char Adhyay* exemplify the bard's conceptual universe which led him to redefine nationalism as an ideational attachment to one's country regardless of differences around caste, class or clan axes. Hence, it is not conceptually valid to argue that Rabindranath was vehemently opposed to nationalism per se; his opposition was based on the effort to essentialise one's sociocultural identity disregarding the diversity that remained integral to the Indians given the disparate sociocultural milieu in which they were born and raised.

Select Bibliography

Anderson, Benedict. 1991. *Imagined Communities: Reflections on the Origin and Spread of Nationalism*. London and New York: Verso.

Balagangadhara, S.N. 2012. *Reconceptualizing India Studies*. New Delhi: Oxford University Press.

Banerjee, Prathama. 2014. 'Between the Political and Non-political: The Vivekananda Moment and a Critique of the Social in Colonial Bengal, 1890s–1910s'. *Social History* 39 (3).

Banerjee, Sreenath. 1914. *The Life of Dwarkanath Tagore*. Calcutta: Manomohan Press.

Bera, Sadananda and Narayanchandra Sau. 2013. *Rabindranath O Rajniti: Eekhan O Thakhan* (in Bangla). Kolkata: Kallol.

Berlin, Isaiah. 1996. *The Sense of Reality: Studies in Ideas and Their History*. New York: Farrar, Straus and Giroux.

Bhabha, Homi K. 2020. *The Location of Culture*. London and New York: Routledge.

Bhattacharya, Raja. 2020. *Dwarkanath: A Prince in a Colonized Nation* (Bangla). Kolkata: Patrabharati.

Bhattacharya, Sabyasachi. 2016. 'Antinomies of Nationalism and Rabindranath Tagore'. *Economic and Political Weekly* 51 (6), February.

———. 1997. *The Mahatma and the Poet: Letter and Debates between Gandhi and Tagore, 1915–1941*. New Delhi: National Book Trust.

Chakrabarty, Bidyut. 2020. *Social and Political Thought of Rabindranath Tagore*. New Delhi: Sage.

Chakrabarty, Dipesh. 2014. 'Friendships in the Shadow of Empire: Tagore's Reception in Chicago, circa, 1913–1932'. *Modern Asian Studies* 48 (5).

Chakraborti, Ranjit. 1983. *Dwarkanath Tagore: A Historical Evaluation* (Bangla). Kolkata: Granthabitan.

Chatterjee Kalyan. 2005. 'Gora: Tagore's Paradoxical Self'. *Indian Literature* 49 (3), May–June.

Chatterjee, Partha. 1997. 'The Fruits of Macaulay's Poison Tree'. In *The Present History of West Bengal*. New Delhi: Oxford University Press.

———. 1994. *The Nation and Its Fragments: Colonial and Post-colonial Histories*. New Delhi: Oxford University Press.

Chaudhuri, Rosinka. 2005. 'Hemchandra's Bharat Sangeet (1870) and the Politics of Poetry: A Pre-history of Hindu Nationalism in Bengal?' *Indian Economic and Social History Review* 42 (2).

———. 2004. 'The Flute, Gerontion, and Subalternist Misreadings of Tagore'. *Social Text 78* 22 (1).

Chaudhuri, Sukanta, ed. 2020. *The Cambridge Companion to Rabindranath Tagore*. Cambridge: Cambridge University Press.

Collins, Michael. 2013. *Empire, Nationalism and the Post-colonial World: Rabindranath Tagore's Writings on History, Politics and Society*. Oxford: Routledge.

Dasgupta, Subrata. 2007. *The Bengal Renaissance: Identity and Creativity—from Rammohun Roy to Rabindranath Tagore*. Ranikhet: Permanent Black.

Dasgupta, Uma. 2004. *Rabindranath Tagore: A Biography*. New Delhi: Oxford University Press.

Dutta, Krishna and Andrew Robinson. 1995. *Rabindranath Tagore: The Myriad-minded Man*. New York: St. Martin's Press.

Dutta, Pradip Kumar. 2004. *Rabindranath Tagore's 'the Home and the World': A Critical Companion*. London: Anthem Press.

Elmhirst, Leonard K. 2008 (rpt). *Poet and Plowman*. Kolkata: Visva-Bharati.

———. 1960. *Rabindranath Tagore: Pioneers in Education*. London: John Murray.

Fraser, Bashabi. 2020. *Rabindranath*. London: Reakiton Books Ltd.

Furrell, James W. 2004. *The Tagore Family: A Memoir*. New Delhi: Rupa.

Ghose, Benoy. 1971. *Iswar Chandra Vidyasagar*. New Delhi: Publication Division, Ministry of Information and Broadcasting, Government of India.

Ghosh, Murari. 2000. *Dwarkanath o Bharate Burjua Juger Udbodhon* (Banlga). Kolkata: Progressive Publishers.

Ghosh, Sachindralal. 1970. *Raja Rammohun Roy: Pathmaker of Modern India*. New Delhi: National Council of Education and Research and Training.

Godrej, Farah. 2011. *Cosmopolitan Political Thought: Method, Practice, Discipline*. New York: Oxford University Press.

Guha, Chinmoy, ed. 2018. *Bridging East & West: Rabindranath Tagore and Roman Rolland Correspondence (1919–1940)*. New Delhi: Oxford University Press.

Guha, Ranajit. 2002. *History at the Limit of World History*. New York: Columbia University Press.

Hatcher, Brian A. 2020. *Idioms of Improvement: Vidyasagar and Cultural Encounter in Bengal*. New Delhi: Primus.

Hatcher, Brian A. 2014. *Vidyasagar: The Life and After-life of an Eminent India*. Oxford: Routledge.

———. 2006. 'Remembering Rammohan: An Essay on the (Re)emerging of Modern Hinduism'. *History of Religion* 46 (1), August.

Hay, Stephen H. 1970. *Asian Ideas of East and West: Tagore and His Critics in Japan*. Cambridge: Harvard University Press.

Hees, Peter. 1997. 'Bengal Religious Nationalism and Communalism'. *International Journal of Hindu Studies* 1 (1), April.

Inden, Ronald. 1990. *Imagining India*. Oxford: Basil Blackwell.

Jones, Kenneth W. 1994. *Socio-religious Reform Movements in British India*. Cambridge: Cambridge University Press.

Kaviraj, Sudipta. 2006. 'Tagore and Transformation in the Ideals of Love'. In *Love in South Asia: A Cultural History*, edited by Francesca Orsini. Cambridge: Cambridge University Press.

Khilnani, Sunil. 1997. *The Idea of India*. London: Hamish Hamilton.

Kopf, David. 1998. *The Brahmo Samaj and the Shaping of the Modern Indian Mind*. New Delhi: Archives Publishers Pvt. Ltd.

Kripalani, Krishna. 2008 (1951). *Rabindranath Tagore: A Biography*. New Delhi: UBS Publishers' Distributors Pvt. Ltd.

———. 1980. *Dwarkanath Tagore: A Forgotten Pioneer*. New Delhi: National Book Trust.

Kumarappa, J.C. 1951. *Gandhian Economic Thought*. Bombay: Vora and C.

Mahalanobis, Prasanta Chandra. 2002. *Rabindranath* (in Bangla). Kolkata: Ananda Publishers.

———. 1985. *Prasange Rabindranath* (in Bangla). Kolkata: Mahalanobis Trust.

Mehta, Uday Singh. 1999. *Liberalism and Empire: India in British Liberal Thought*. New Delhi: Oxford University Press.

Metcalf, Thomas R. 1998. *Ideologies of the Raj*. Cambridge: Cambridge University Press.

Mittra, Kissory Chand. 1962. *Dwarkanath Tagore* (translated from English into Bangla). Kolkata: Sommodhi Publication.

Mukherjee, Kedar Nath. 1982. *Political Philosophy of Rabindranath Tagore*. New Delhi: S. Chand & Company Ltd.

Mukherjee, Subrata. 2020. *The Political Ideas of Rabindranath Tagore: Reflections of a Public Intellectual*. New Delhi: Rupa & Co.

Mukhopadhyay, Amartya. 2010. *Politics, Society and Colonialism: An Alternative Understanding of Tagore's Responses*. Delhi: Foundation Books.

Nandy, Ashis. 2006. 'Nationalism: Genuine and Spurious, Mourning Two Early Post-nationalist Strains'. *Economic and Political Weekly* 41 (38).

———. 1994. *The Illegitimacy of Nationalism: Rabindranath Tagore and the Politics of Self*. New Delhi: Oxford University Press.

———. 1970. 'The Culture of Indian Politics: A Stock-taking'. *The Journal of Asian Studies* 30 (1), November.

Naoroji, Dadabhai. 1901. *Poverty and Un-British Rule in India*. London: S. Sonnenschein.

Nehru, Jawaharlal. 1989 (rpt). *The Discovery of India*. Delhi: Oxford University Press.

———. 1941. *An Autobiography*. London: John Lane the Bodley Head.

Neogy, Ajit K. 1985 (rpt). *Santiniketan and Sriniketan*. New Delhi: National Book Trust.

O'Hanlon, Rosalind. 1985. *Caste, Conflict and Ideology: Mahatma Jotirao Phule and Low Caste Protest in Nineteenth-century Western India*. Cambridge: Cambridge University Press.

Omvedt, Gail. 1994. *Dalits and the Democratic Revolution: Dr Ambedkar and the Dalit Movement in Colonial India*. New Delhi: Sage.

———. 1976. *Cultural Revolt in a Colonial Society: The Non-Brahmin Movement in Western India, 1873–1930*. Bombay: Scientific Socialist Educational Trust.

Palit, Debabrata. 1995. *Dwarkanath Tagore, 1794–1846* (Bangla). Kolkata: Tagore Research Institute.

Parekh, Bhikhu. 2015. *Debating India: Essays on Indian Political Discourse*. New Delhi: Oxford University Press.

Petit, Philip. 1999. *Republicanism: A Theory of Freedom and Government*. Oxford: Oxford University Press.

Philips, Anne. 1995. *The Politics of Presence*. Oxford: Clarendon Press.

Poddar, Arabinda. 2004. *Tagore: The Political Personality*. Kolkata: Indiana.

Ray, Bharati. 2010. 'New Woman in Rabindranath Tagore's Short Stories: An Interrogation of Laboratory'. *Asiatic* 4 (2), December.

Roy, Satyendranath. 1985. *Rabindranather Samajchinta* (in Bangla). Kolkata: Granthalaya.

Rudolph, Lloyd and S.H. Rudolph. 2008. *The Realm of the Public Sphere: Identity and Policy*. New Delhi: Oxford University Press.

Saha, Poulomi. 2013. 'Singing Bengal into a Nation: Tagore the Colonial Cosmopolitan'. *Journal of Modern Literature* 36 (2), Winter.

Sen, Amartya. 2009. *The Idea of Justice*. New York: Allen Lane.

———. 2006. *Identity and Violence: The Illusion of Destiny. London*: Allen Lane.

———. 2005. *The Argumentative Indian: Writings on Indian history, Culture and Identity*. New York: Picador.

———. 1999. *Development as Freedom*. New Delhi: Oxford University Press.

———. 1997. 'Tagore and His India'. *New York Review of Books* 44 (12).

———. 1993. *Hindu Revivalism in Bengal, 1872–1905: Some Essays in Interpretation*. Delhi: Oxford University Press.

Sen, Ashok. 2004. *Rajnitir Pathakrame Rabindranth* (in Bangla). Kolkata: Visva-Bharati Granthan Bhivag.

Sen, Sachin. 1947. *The Political Thought of Tagore*. Calcutta: General Printers and Publishers Ltd.

Sengupta, Kalyan. 2005. *The Philosophy of Rabindranath Tagore*. Burlington: Ashgate.

Seth, Sanjay. 1999. 'Rewriting Histories of Nationalism: The Politics of "Moderate Nationalism" in India, 1870–1905'. *American Historical Review* 104 (1), February.

Sinha, Dikshit. 2019. *A Poet's Experiment in Rebuilding Samaj and Nation: Sriniketan's Rural Reconstruction Work, 1922–1960*. West Bengal: Birupjatio Sahitya Sammiloni.

Stokes, Eric. 1959. *The English Utilitarians and India*. Cambridge: Cambridge University Press.

Thompson, Edward. 1926. *Rabindranath Tagore: Poet and Dramatist*. London: Macmillan.

Thompson, E.P. 1993. *Alien Homage: Edward Thompson and Rabindranath Tagore*. New York: Oxford University Press.

———. 1992. 'Introduction to Rabindranath Tagore's *Nationalism*'. New Delhi: Rupa & Co.

Vajpayi, Ananya. 2012. *Righteous Republic: The Political Foundation of Modern India*. Cambridge: Harvard University Press.

Index

About the Author

Bidyut Chakrabarty is the vice-chancellor of Visva-Bharati, West Bengal, India.